CINEMA EYE, CINEMA EAR

ALSO BY JOHN RUSSELL TAYLOR

ANGER AND AFTER,
a Guide to New British Drama

Cinema Eye, Cinema Ear

SOME KEY FILM-MAKERS
OF THE SIXTIES

John Russell Taylor

London
METHUEN & CO LTD
11 New Fetter Lane EC4

FOR
BRIAN AND WILLIAM

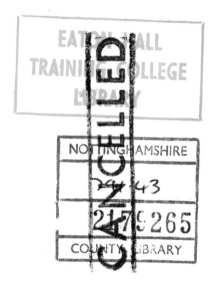
First published in 1964
© *1964 John Russell Taylor*
Printed in Great Britain by
W. & J. Mackay & Co Ltd
Chatham, Kent

Contents

Illustrations

Introduction

IF THE CINEMA IS AN ART, WHO IS THE ARTIST? EVER since people began to consider, very tentatively, the possibility that the cinema might be a new art-form, this has been a favourite topic of discussion among intellectual enthusiasts. Perhaps the question sounds absurdly academic: the important thing, after all, is that the finished result is a good film (whatever that question-begging term may mean); whom one agrees to *call* the artist is, comparatively, a trivial matter of terminology. And yet the question does have some real meaning, and in trying to answer it the great theorists have got as near as perhaps we shall ever get to a precise definition of film art.

We take it for granted that art is the product of an artist, one man who is responsible for at least the overall conception and general effect of any given work of art. Of course, the architect may well require an army of people to realize his design, a painter or a sculptor may employ pupils and assistants to execute the inessentials of his work, the writer, even, may use capable literary craftsmen to rough out portions of a work which he himself polishes and completes. But however many hands may go to the production of any work of art worthy of the name, we accept it as axiomatic that it will be the issue of one brain. But how does the film fit into this pattern? Whose brain does it come from? In the theatre we tend to make a distinction between the 'creative' art of the dramatist and the 'executive' or 'interpretive' arts of the actor and director, in the same way that in music we distinguish between composer and performer. Does this mean, then, that the writer is the real artist of the cinema, and the rest – director, actor, cameraman, editor, etc. – only the executants of his design?

Well, that is one way of looking at it, though not a way which has found much favour with film theorists of late, despite some enthusiastic attempts to reinstate the writer as the creative element of the cinema in a series of arguments which swept the film world around 1950–1. Of course, one can think of films which seem primarily the creation of their writers, just as one can think of theatre productions which seemed to be primarily the creation of their directors (the whole movement of *théâtre totale* made this its logical conclusion). And there have been and no doubt will be again writers who have exerted enormous influence on the cinema as a whole without ever directing a film. In the silent German cinema Carl Mayer was undoubtedly the motive force behind many of the best films, not only writing scripts of such detail that they often amounted to blueprints that the director had only to follow (hence the great superiority of many minor directors' work when scripted by Mayer to their work when scripted by anyone else), but playing a decisive part in casting, choice of technicians and so on. In the French cinema of the 1930s and the war years the poet Jacques Prévert scripted innumerable films, often working merely as a skilled technician capable of covering any bare bones of continuity with literate dialogue, but in a number of films, notably those directed by his most regular collaborator Marcel Carné and his brother Pierre Prévert, creating an unmistakably personal form of cinema, sometimes veering wildly in the direction of off-beat poetic knockabout and sometimes in the direction of heavily symbolical drama; either way, they were Prévert films first and their directors contributed little except technical knowledge. Similarly in America Ben Hecht, among innumerable straight commercial chores, achieved in many of his scripts a highly individual quality which made them at once recognizable, both for the bitter cynicism of his comedy and the lunatic pretentiousness of his drama (though it is notable that these qualities are found in their purest form in the handful of films he directed himself, such as *Crime Without Passion*, *The Scoundrel*, and *Spectre of the Rose*). Even today in the films scripted by Paddy Chayefsky there is no doubt that Chayefsky's rather than his various directors' is the dominant personality.

But in general these are the exceptions. The usual answer to the question of who has primarily creative responsibility for the film is the director; it is the answer sanctioned by theoreticians since the earliest days, and it is that accepted without demur by most of the critics. And ideally there seems little doubt that it is the right answer. But that 'ideally' involves a lot of conditions which are by no means always fulfilled. It assumes, for instance, that the director will, even if he does not actually choose his subject (though preferably he should do that, too), be in on the preparation and scripting from an early stage, choose his cast, work with the writer to see that the script evolves the way he wants it, choose a cameraman whose known talents and characteristics fit in with his require- ments, direct all the film himself, or at least closely supervise any work done when he is not actually behind the camera, and then control the editing, post-synchronization if any, musical score and all the minor matters which go to the making of a finished film. The mere fact of having directed a film to the extent of physically direct- ing the actors and supervising the camera set-ups is not sufficient to make a director the creator of the film, in the sense that the film as shown is essentially the product of his brain. In Europe most of this has been taken for granted for some years, but not in America, where it is still the case that most of the creative functions of film- making belong to the producer, and the director is probably only one more technician on the payroll, hired to direct an already chosen cast in a finished script and dismissed from the studio after the last day's shooting (hence the urge of many directors to become as soon as they can their own producers, in name or in effect). It is failure to understand this basic fact of life which makes European critics, particularly French, so often praise or blame American directors for things which cannot possibly be their responsibility, and to build up into 'auteurs', with a fully-worked-out philosophy of life and cinema, capable technicians who have little or no say in anything but the physical staging of the films they make.

Mention of the word 'auteurs' brings us to the crux of the matter so far as the cinema in the 1950s and 1960s is concerned. The *auteur* in current French critical parlance (defined by a famous article by François Truffaut in *Les Cahiers du Cinéma* on *La Politique des Auteurs*) is our complete film creator, the director with complete control over all aspects of the film he is making. But he is also something more: his work has the urgency of personal crea- tion; he has something to say as well as the freedom to say it. Now, this is easy to describe as an ideal, but not so easy to bring about in practice. It is a fair generalization to say that the simpler the resources of film production, the easier it is for one man to control them. In the early days of the silent screen it was quite simple for one man to make up or choose a film story, pick some actors and just shoot it himself, either as his own cameraman or, if he starred in it himself, with the assistance of a cameraman who would do what he was told. But before very long films got longer and more complicated, and the jobs involved in their production more specialized. Large amounts of money began to be spent on them, and unless the director became his own producer (something which until the last few years happened fairly infrequently in the American cinema) he was likely to find himself more and more restricted by those who controlled the financial side of film-making. Moreover, the cameraman was likely to become more and more the touchy specialist, consulted by the director instead of told what to do, and the editor, even if he did not subscribe to Eisenstein's theories of film as a medium built especially on montage, the meaningful juxtaposition of shots and the rhythm of cutting, probably came to be employed by the producer to shape the raw material provided by the director rather than to carry out the director's specific intentions for his film. The advent of the talkies added a further complication in that someone had to write literate dialogue for them, and another expert with ideas of his own was added to the payroll.

In general, in fact, the cinema became bigger and bigger business, and as is the way with big business, the more responsibility was divided the better the financiers were satisfied. Even if a director was a good enough businessman to control all the aspects of production himself, it did not necessarily mean that he was an *auteur*; in the case of a Hitchcock or a Hawks it might, but nothing could be taken for granted. And anyway to achieve the status of *auteur* the film-maker had to have something besides the right intentions; he had to have something we have not yet considered, the ability to think from the outset in terms of his medium.

Obviously, what exactly this entails is very difficult to define: it is at best largely a matter of subjective judgement – what seems to me totally filmic may well seem to you intolerably stiff and literary, or vice versa. To the very earliest film-makers it was simply enough to stage an interesting happening and then let the camera record it. But almost immediately after Lumière came Méliès, a magician who was interested in the cinema precisely for its ability to show things happening which could not happen in real life. From then on the most 'cinematic' cinema was likely to come mainly from those who arrived in it with no important preconceptions derived from literature, the theatre or elsewhere, so that they were forced to make up their own rules as they went along (witness the best of silent comedy). But this became with the passage of time more and more difficult, as the processes of film-making became more and more complicated and as, inevitably, more and more rules were devised about what was and what was not permissible. As the cinema advanced in sophistication it became increasingly a matter of distinct stages. A story and leading players would be picked – that was the producer's job. Then a script would be fully worked out by an expert scriptwriter. A designer would translate the backgrounds into visual terms, a director would arrange the action within these settings for a cameraman to photograph, and then an editor would put the material together as a film. And though, as mentioned, there would be the occasional director who combined a number of these other functions, the tendency was still for them to be done separately in a series of translations and adaptations rather than as one single, complex process. (René Clair, for example, one of the most individual and accomplished film-makers of the late silent and early sound period, has persistently denied that he is primarily a director; he is a writer who stages his own screen plays.)

With a new medium this is no doubt inevitable to begin with; the creator who approaches it as a new phenomenon is bound to be circumspect, and though some from the start seemed to grasp the essential nature of the film which made it different from any other medium (Dovjenko, Murnau, Sjöström, Keaton, Sternberg, Renoir, to mention half a dozen at random), any overall intuitive understanding of film-making as one indivisible creative process was bound to be delayed until such time as a generation of artists could grow up to whom the film was as natural a means of self-expression, as much part of the habitual furniture of their world, as painting or writing or music or architecture. The arrival of the sound film, overturning much that had previously been accepted without question, put off this advent for a decade or so—Orson Welles is perhaps the first died-in-the-wool film man who could take to the cinema without a moment's question – but since the early 1940s such an approach to the cinema has been perfectly possible in theory and, here and there, where the commercial organization of the film industry permitted it, possible in practice too.

In this book I have set out to analyse the work of six major film-makers of our own day who seem to me to create directly in terms of film, to wield what one French critic, Alexandre Astruc, called the 'caméra stylo', the camera as a fountain-pen. In a famous essay in *L'Écran Français* in 1948 Astruc wrote what might be regarded as the manifesto of the new cinema:

> I call this new age of the cinema that of the *Caméra Stylo*. This image has a very precise sense. It means that the cinema will break away little by little from the tyranny of the visual, of the image for its own sake, of the immediate anecdote, of the concrete, to become a means of writing as supple and as subtle as that of written language. No area must be barred to it. The most austere meditation, attitudes to all human works, psychology, metaphysics, ideas, passions are very precisely its province. Indeed, these ideas and visions of the world are such that today the cinema alone is capable of giving them full realization.

This is true in various ways and to various degrees of Fellini and Antonioni, Buñuel and Bresson, and even Bergman and Hitchcock. They are not only the outstanding creators of the modern cinema, but the dominant influences on the younger generation. There are others, older or more geographically remote, that may claim similar distinction; Wells himself, Cocteau, the ever unpredictable perennial *enfant terrible* of the French cinema whose influence crops up in the most unlikely places (notably all over Godard's films); of such great survivors as Renoir and Dreyer; of the Japanese Mizoguchi and Ozu, of the Indian Satyajit Ray. . . . But the six I have chosen seem to me to constitute a very fair cross-section of the big, unassailably individual talents working in the cinema today. I have added some notes on the French New Wave, and in particular on the two directors I find most interesting in themselves and most solid in their achievement today, Truffaut and Godard, as some indication of the way things are tending. But essentially this is a book about six great individualists, whose main common denominator is their steadfast refusal to fit neatly into any preconceived patterns one may devise. In this, at least, they are representative of cinema in the sixties at its best, and this is my excuse for studying them in detail, and many other in their own ways admirable directors at work today not at all. This is not a history of the cinema now, but an introduction to some of those who have decisively shaped what it is today.

Federico Fellini

FEDERICO FELLINI'S CAREER IS A VERY INTERESTING AND significant example of one important way an all-round film creator may evolve: an established film-scriptwriter, he worked his way up from gag-man to adapter and dialoguist to author of complete original screenplays, and then from there felt the urge to direct. This urge, at this stage in a film-writer's career, may signify all sorts of things, but the two most usual are that he is an all-round film-maker who writes in his head not just scripts but whole films, script and realization inextricably mingled and fused; or that as a literary creator in a dramatic form he craves the respect, and the power over the interpretation of what he has written, which is normal in the theatre, and realizes that the only way he can achieve this within the normal structure of the film industry is to become either his own director or at least his own producer, able to fire any director who tampers too much with what he has written.

Which sort of director any given writer will turn out to be it is virtually impossible to tell in advance, and, of course, in any case the distinction is not so hard and fast as all that: if Mankiewicz is obviously the second sort of writer-director, and René Clair, in his earlier days at least, the first sort, where would one classify, say, Launder and Gilliatt, or for that matter John Huston, who began as a writer, went on to be a writer-director and seems now increasingly inclined to take only a small, supervisory hand in scripting and concentrate all his energies on realization instead?

With Fellini, certainly, it would have been impossible to guess beforehand, though looking back, wise after the event, one can see signs. For a scriptwriter he had already an unusually wide acquaintance with other elements important to the director. Born in Rimini in 1920, his first passion was the theatre, or at least show-business, and when he was only twelve he outraged his solid *bourgeois* parents by running away to join a circus. Before the war he had worked in the theatre, writing and acting with Aldo Fabrizi, and during the war he wrote sketches for radio, *Cico e Pallina*, in the process meeting and marrying the actress Giulietta Masina.

There was also another side to his interests which was later to stand him in good stead: his first job was as an artist on *fumetti*, the illustrated magazines beloved of Italians then and now, and later he made his living as a caricaturist around the Roman restaurants. Hence, as well as the purely literary abilities, he had a marked interest in and talent for the visual expression of his ideas, and to this day his characters more usually start with a quick sketch than with a written description.

His arrival in the cinema was very modest, and caused no sort of stir at all: when his friend and collaborator Aldo Fabrizi was drawn into films Fellini continued to provide stories and ideas for him, and from 1942 to 1945 collaborated on the scripts of some half-dozen forgettable comedies. The turning-point came in 1945, when Fabrizi became involved in a project of Roberto Rossellini, a young director with a handful of conventional patriotic films to his credit, to make a short film on a recent event, the shooting of Don Morosino by the Germans. Fellini, as usual, came along with Fabrizi, and the resultant film grew to be *Roma, Citta Aperta*. It was, still very much Rossellini's film, and so was the one which followed, *Paisa*, on which Fellini was assistant director (in which capacity he was responsible for one or two little scenes, especially in the Florence sequence, and the script, to which he contributed one sketch, that concerning three American padres, Catholic, Protestant, and Jewish, who visit a group of simple Franciscans and leave them mystified but praying enthusiastically for the conversion of Protestant and Jew).

A series of routine jobs followed – collaborations with Pietro Germi (*In nomine della legge, Il cammino della speranza*), Alberto Lattuada (*Il delitto di Giovanni Episcopo, Senza Pieta, Il Mulino del Po*), and others. Then, in 1948, Fellini's first important original screenplay – and what we can see now as the clear emergence of the Fellini subject and the Fellini view of life – in *Il Miracolo*, the longer section of Rossellini's two-part film *Amore*.

In *Il Miracolo* we meet for the first time the characteristic Fellini heroine we have come to think of as the 'Gelsomina figure' (from the character in *La Strada*), usually played by Fellini's wife Giulietta Masina in later days, but on this occasion played (if not overplayed) by Anna Magnani. She is a simple-minded peasant woman who meets a tramp (played, incidentally, by Fellini himself) and takes him for St Joseph. Some months later she finds she is pregnant, and proclaims that it is a miracle. Everyone jeers at her and drives her away, and eventually she goes up on a mountain to give birth to her child, greeting him with the words 'Mio santo filio'.

There is more that is characteristic of the mature Fellini in *Il Miracolo* than the character of the heroine, though. The tramp, St Joseph, is one of a line of almost inevitable counterparts to Fellini's holy simpletons, rough and callous, animal even, but perhaps not finally incapable of pity. And the curiously ambiguous relation to religion in the script is also characteristic: the violent arguments which raged within the Roman Catholic Church between those, like Cardinal Spellman, who found the whole thing blasphemous, and those, mostly Jesuits, who took it all as profoundly religious, have been re-enacted on several subsequent occasions, notably with the pilgrimage scene in *Le Notti di Cabiria* and the supposed vision in *La Dolce Vita*.

This ambiguity was carried almost as far in Fellini's next significant script, *Francesco Giullare di Dio*, derived for Rossellini from *The Little Flowers of St Francis of Assisi*. The title itself is significant, for nothing of the medieval grotesquerie and occasional coarseness inherent in the subject is shirked: these are not sentimental plaster models of saints, but the real thing as they emerge in contemporary documents, gay, naïve, rough, humble; jesters of God indeed, and the most explicitly holy of all Fellini's holy simpletons. But like all the other films Fellini scripted merely, this is still not primarily a Fellini film; it is, for better or for worse, a Rossellini film, even if starting from a Fellini script (Fellini himself believes that it is the best film Rossellini has ever made). However, in the same year, 1950, Fellini was given a chance to direct for himself (with the technical guidance of an old collaborator, Lattuada) and the result was the first unmistakably and completely personal film of his career, *Luci del Varieta*.

In this film we first get the full flavour of what French critics delight to call 'l'univers fellinien'. In what does it consist? Well, basically, in a certain way of regarding human beings and a certain way of regarding places, and a certain attitude towards the relationship between the two. It is the last which is crucial. In parts of *Paisa*, in *Francesco Giullare di Dio* and especially in *Il Miracolo* we encounter Fellini people and Fellini places, but separated from each other, as it were, by the personality of another director, Rossellini (a much later film scripted by Fellini but directed by someone else, *Fortunella*, is also very instructive in this respect). In the Rossellini films the balance is always towards objectivity: if what he seeks is the essence, he seems to start from the assumption that the first step is the meticulous examinations of the externals (I have sometimes wondered if the reverence in which Rossellini is held by many younger French intellectuals is partly due to his unexpected meeting at this point with the aesthetic of the *nouveau roman*). But for Fellini what matters first is not the outward reality but the inner reality; landscapes for him become an objective correlative to the mental and spiritual states of his characters, to be created (if with real locations then by precise choice of viewpoint, weather, time of day and so on to produce exactly the effect required) – he has, in fact, remarked on at least one occasion that what draws him most to the cinema is its quality as a domain in which he can play God, in which everything is, not as it is, but as he thinks it ought to be. Hence the real world around him, from which he selects what he wants, yields finally a world of his own in which nothing is merely what it seems: it is what it seems – to that extent he is still a realist – but it is also something more – and in consequence Fellini is also something more, a 'surrealist', as he himself puts it, in the same sense that Giotto, Botticelli, Bosch, Breughel, and Uccello were surrealists.

Since everything in his films therefore has its validity, on some level or another, as reality observed, it is very difficult to illustrate the difference between Fellini's approach and that of Rossellini in the way that one could at once show the difference between Rossellini's attitude to the film in his adaptation of Cocteau's *La Voix Humaine* and Cocteau's own in *Les Parents Terribles*. At first glance there is nothing to mark them as fundamentally different; only Fellini's evidently greater love of technical polish and his more atmospheric, romantic approach to the reality observed (but then that is a characteristic shared by many others whom nevertheless one would not hesitate to classify as neo-realists). No, rather it is an atmosphere which little by little makes itself felt, something impalpable, beyond mere recurring characters and themes, which links Fellini's works together into a uniquely coherent *oeuvre*.

Most of the elements are present already in *Luci del Varieta*. On the surface it is a little tale, half satiric, half sentimental, of a girl who is infatuated with the idea of the stage, joins a tatty band of poor players, becomes the object of the seedy comedian's infatuation and the centre of his ambitions to found a troupe of his own, and finally moves on – perhaps to some sort of success, who knows? – leaving the troupe much as they were, a little older, a little sadder possibly, and not much wiser. It is not, as a whole, ideally unified; some odd passages of social satire stand out rather sharply from the rest, and may perhaps be attributed to the influence of the capable academic craftsman Lattuada (Fellini himself says that they collaborated very closely from sequence to sequence, and it would be impossible to separate their individual contributions). But nevertheless it remains in all essentials the first real Fellini film.

It is so, obviously, in the subject-matter: the faded underside of show-business, the gaudy, tawdry, improvised world of one-night stands and not knowing where the next meal is coming from. Here Fellini is speaking from his own experience of people he has known. But that, after all, Lattuada could have put on the screen unaided, if not with such exquisite fidelity. What makes it a film which no one but Fellini could have invented (both conceived, that is, and put on the screen) may perhaps best be illustrated not by generalities but by studying two particular sequences: the party at the castle and the wanderings of Kecco, the comedian-manager, after he leaves his new star Liliane one night in the city. Each is developed according to a ravelling and unravelling process which is to become characteristic of the key sequences in Fellini's work: from a simple beginning, through a complex action in which the main characters and their problems become swallowed up, or nearly, and then a gradual disentanglement which leaves them alone at the crisis of their troubles before they and those around them are scattered – to a new and probably joyless day, I nearly said, taking it for granted that all these scenes take place at night, and their aftermath in those bleak, cheerless dawns which punctuate Fellini's films with confirmation of the old despair.

The first, the party in the castle, is, in fact, the first of a long line of party scenes which culminates, for the moment at least, in the final sequence of *La Dolce Vita*. Liliane, incompetent performer as she is, catches the attention of a local landowner one evening, and the whole company gets itself invited up to his castle. The two principal factors behind what happens then are Kecco's hopeless infatuation for Liliane (tolerated by his mild and sensible companion Melina) and Liliane's stupefying *naïveté*. First all is glittering confusion as the ravenous actors ransack the house for food and drink and general *bonhomie* reigns supreme. Then little by little the principal actors in the drama are separated from the rest; Kecco alone with his jealousy, Liliane with the rich man whose precise intentions she discovers too late in the day for tactful evasion. As drink and too much food reduce most of the revellers to sleeping hulks and they fade into the background the principals are brought into relief, and only when their drama has worked itself out does the result make itself felt on the rest, who are roused and bundled unceremoniously out into the cold morning air. In ones and twos they drift down the hill and back to ordinary life: the dream of paradise is over.

Similarly with Kecco's wanderings later in the film. Leaving Liliane, he makes his way to his wife's house and gets no response. But outside it he meets a negro with a trumpet, follows him aimlessly, and soon there gather round them a gipsy who sings and plays the guitar, a policeman, beggars, prostitutes: there is music and dancing, and then with the dawn it all fades away again and Kecco is left alone with his problems as dawn breaks over the deserted streets and squares of Fellini's city of dreadful morning. The night can bring comfort and forgetfulness, but only for the time being: the morning restores clarity of vision and the harsh realities of everyday life.

As might be supposed in a private world so coherent as Fellini's, there are certain backgrounds – and, naturally, the characters and situations they so intimately complement – which recur again and again, and so acquire, beyond their general effectiveness in colouring our vision of what takes place in front of them, the quasi-independent significance of a constant symbol. Once one starts trying to pin them down in this way, though, it is all too tempting to force everything into the pattern, and clearly Fellini's mind does not work that way. The city square at night is one frequent location: it occurs again in Fellini's next film, *Lo Sciecco Bianco*, and thence right through to *La Dolce Vita*, Fellini's episode in *Boccaccio 70* and, in a slightly modified form, in *8½*. It is a place, perhaps, where night-wanderers meet on equal terms, cut off for the time being from their ordinary relationships and responsibilities: this is, after all, a characteristic of 'real-life' city squares on many nights not staged by Fellini, and so the device works without question even on the most functional, realistic level. But is there, beyond this cloud of vague associations, a set significance for all these squares? Are they a sort of filmic shorthand, an emblem which always conveys the same thing to us? We are surely sadly misunderstanding Fellini's temperament and way of working if we persist in thinking so.

The same with the sea, which dominates much of *Lo Sciecco Bianco* and plays a significant part in all his other feature films except *Il Bidone*, where its marked absence is equally significant. In *Lo Sciecco Bianco* it might be taken to symbolize romantic adventure: the young bourgeois bride runs off from her conventional tourist's honeymoon in Rome and encounters her favourite dream, the 'white sheik' who stars in a silly photo-romance she follows, on the sunny sands by a glistening sea. In other films it appears much more gloomily as perhaps the reminder of impossible dreams, unrealized possibilities (the grey uninviting sea of *I Vitelloni*, the bland sea from which the monstrous fish is drawn in *La Dolce Vita*), and Fellini commits himself no further than to say that for him in general the sea is a comforting mystery, conveying the idea of permanence, of eternity, of the primal element. But, he adds, of course it takes colour in any given situation from the character and attitude of those who see it: again the inescapable union of foreground and background, of people and things in Fellini's work, which makes such terms as 'objective' and 'subjective' quite irrelevant to the central phenomenon and totally incapable of indicating its nature. The sea is a real sea; the sea is also a sort of extension of the characters' moods and attitudes, a mirror to which their natures are held up; a stage further, and both characters and location are embodiments, or rather the single unified embodiment, of their creator's moods and attitudes – those of the little God who within his own world can make everything be as he would have it be.

In *Lo Sciecco Bianco*, however, perhaps because the attitude of the heroine is for most of the day one of simple excitement, only towards nightfall tinged with disillusion, whatever symbolic value the sea might be taken to have is not stressed: it is a sunny day on the beach, and the sea forms merely a glittering backdrop for the activities of the company shooting the photo-romance; it is hardly even a menace when the heroine and her fantastically garbed would-be lover drift out to sea so that he can seduce her and he accidentally gets knocked out, since the episode is played entirely on a tone of lightly ironic farce. Rather, it is for its qualities at once of fantasy – the immense beach and the sparkling, limitless, too-good-to-be-true sea – and its nevertheless indubitable reality – this is, after all, a *real* beach and a *real* sea – that the location assumes significance for Fellini here: between the two aspects dance and flutter the flimsy, gaudy inhabitants of the photo-romance's fictional world, weaving in one of Fellini's most brilliant *scènes à faire* an intricate ballet at once matched by the fantasy and shamed by the reality of its surroundings.

Again it is a ravelling and unravelling, a drawing of the solitary central character, Wanda, into a crowded, bustling world of confusion, her involvement and virtual disappearance in it, and then her detachment from it along with the others who will bring her face to face with her own reality – the sheik himself, magisterially played by Alberto Sordi from his sublimely absurd apparition swinging insouciantly high aloft between two trees to his final deflation, and the sheik's wife, who brings this about and with a slap restores the star-struck Wanda to some of her senses. Later on Wanda's husband, too, has his moment of truth, this time more familiarly in the Roman streets at night, when wandering by now aimlessly in search of his vanished bride he falls in with a couple of amiable prostitutes (one played by Giulietta Masina and instantly recognizable as Cabiria *avant la lettre*) and a well-disposed fire-eater before returning alone to his hotel to face what the morning will bring.

What strikes one most forcibly about *Lo Sciecco Bianco* in retrospect, however, is not anything directly to do with the technical procedures or the way scenes are constructed, characteristic as they are, but the Fellini atmosphere they all help to create, and which now, without even the marginal intervention of another director, is at last appreciable at full strength. There is something almost womblike about a Fellini film; Fellini does not so much sympathize with his characters – often he clearly doesn't approve of them at all – as envelop them, and however uncomfortable they may be in the world he has made for them there is always the comfort, for the spectator, of knowing that they are watched over and in some way protected – perhaps because they are fragments of Fellini himself, or of the past which has made him, and so he cannot bear to see them totally lost. It is the consciousness, basically, in Fellini and in us, that by salvaging these fragments and embodying them in works of art that he has saved them, that *temps perdu* has become *temps retrouvé*. The characters of *Lo Sciecco Bianco* may be stupid, petty, even despicable, and certainly incorrigible (the last words of the heroine to her husband, after all she has supposedly learnt, are 'You shall be my white sheik'), but the strength of Fellini's affection for them somehow transfigures them with the unreasoning power of imaginative identification.

All this, of course, even if it conveys a little of the overall effect a Fellini film has, is impossibly vague unless one can explain also to some extent how he does it: it is one thing to say that Fellini *is* all his characters and all his places, quite another to show how this identification is made a reality on film. Perhaps the best place to start doing so is with his next film, and for many still his masterpiece, *I Vitelloni*. 'Vitelloni', it should be explained, are drifters, wastrels, not necessarily bad but aimless, restless and bored. Fellini himself and his two invariable script collaborators from this film on, Ennio Flaiano and Tullio Pinelli, had all shared such a condition in their time, and the film arose from an evening laughing over old times, old escapades, and the melancholy which descended afterwards. So the film is in a vital sense autobiographical: not necessarily that the details of any single incident actually happened to Fellini or Pinelli or Flaiano, but that the depiction of a way of life – a very unsatisfactory way of life as it turns out – is very much from the inside.

But what is Fellini's attitude to his film vitelloni? There has been much argument, and in the abstract, judging solely from the script, a number of solutions are possible. The film might, for instance, be a light social satire about wide boys with a happy ending when the two principals reform and opt respectively for happy fatherhood and a new constructive life somewhere else. It might be a grim picture of a lost generation, cut adrift in the modern world from their roots in a settled faith and a stable social order. It might be a denunciation of the decadent petty *bourgeoisie*. A case, of sorts, could be made out for any of these views from the script, but the film itself rejects them all. To begin with, it is clear at once from the way the actors are directed that though none of the characters is exactly a shining hero, they are certainly not either double-dyed villains, but merely contradictory, likeable, insufficient human beings. Nor can the 'happy ending' of the ringleader, Fausto, with his wife and their child be taken at its face value: his last appearance, playing childishly with his new son under the troubled gaze of his wife, makes it clear that the child is just another new toy, and that nothing has really changed. And as for the view of the film as a moralistic tract for the times, one can set against it scene after scene in which the camera is very much with the characters, involving us willy-nilly on their side, inviting us irresistibly to sympathize with them instead of shake our heads.

The first way that this is done is by a very flexible, subjective attitude to time. The time of the film is the vitelloni's time, not ours. It can expand suddenly for an improvised dance in the street, an impromptu game with the stones or, stretched out beyond endurance, it can crucify its victims in an aching void before the aimless, endless fury of an icy, windswept sea. Equally it can contract as the camera weaves and dodges and turns in an ecstasy of swift motion at the climactic ball sequence which swallows them all and then at length spews them out into the empty, unwelcoming streets. We are with them; this is the way not so much that it was as that it felt. And as the film progresses it becomes heavier, as the characters become heavier with the weight of ills unremedied and chances missed, so that when the elusively idyllic interludes of Moraldo, the quietest and most sensitive of them, with a mysterious boy railway worker (a smiling embodiment of innocence) lead finally to Moraldo's secret departure for the city, the sense of escape brought by the smooth, purposeful acceleration of the train is almost palpable.

Moraldo's crisis, though – the confrontation with the unspoilt boy which finally decides him to break away completely – is only the last of several. Nearly all the vitelloni meet themselves face to face at some point, and all except Moraldo turn back from this crucial encounter. For Fausto it is the marriage he is pushed into and slips out of at the side door, the rules of the job he is finally edged into which require a decision of him that he shirks, and fatherhood, which will soon bore him. Alberto is shattered by the departure of the sister he dearly loves with her lover in the dawn after the ball, but even in his utmost grief continues to act, to pose (significantly, at this juncture he is heavily disguised for the ball in cloche hat and twenties dress); the affectation and the real thing are no longer distinguishable. Leopoldo, a budding poet, is disillusioned when an old actor performing in the town who seems interested in his work proves merely to be sexually interested in him. But though they all have to face some sort of unpalatable truth about themselves and the world they live in, only Moraldo assimilates it and makes use of it to move on: the rest avoid, smother it, and go on as if nothing had happened. They are Peter Pans, eternal boys who will never grow up.

Or, as Geneviève Agel perceptively remarks in *Les Chemins de Fellini*, *I Vitelloni* could be a sort of modern *Grand Meaulnes*: and the comparison suggests precisely the magical tenderness which irradiates Fellini's evocation of this life no longer wholly innocent but yet rejecting the fruits of experience and the adult responsibilities that come with them. It is an intensely romantic view, of course, and the physical appearance of the film is similarly romanticized: the real streets taking on the aspect of deserted baroque stage sets; the delicate, diffused greys of the railway and Moraldo's morning departure; the harshly etched scene on the shore; the almost expressionist lighting of the theatre sequences; the hysterical, nearly indecipherable eddies of movement which rip and swirl over the screen during the showily impressionistic ball scene. Indeed the vitelloni, whose real background one half appreciates to be drab and ordinary, live through Fellini's eyes in a world full of unexpected, inexplicable beauties almost as visionary as Alain-Fournier's own distant land of lost content.

The technical means by which Fellini achieves his effects, here as elsewhere in his work, are in principle very simple, though the application of the simple principles is often extremely complex. Fellini's films are built round a number of long, sustained scenes worked out in the characters' own good time: not only are we encouraged to adjust our time-tense to that of the characters, but we are forcibly compelled to, since there is no escape in constant changes of locale, artful intercutting of separate sequences or anything like that: once we embark on a key sequence we are with it obsessively through to the end. Fellini loves to begin his scene with a long shot establishing at once the place, the number of people involved and their spatial (and generally by implication emotional) relationship with each other and their surroundings. This done (as in the scene on the seashore, or the aftermath of the ball) he can move in to a closer examination of his actors. Faces fascinate him – well, to a certain extent I suppose they must fascinate all directors, but few go so far as Fellini in casting by lining his office walls from top to bottom with photographs and then eliminating day by day until he is left with faces which still have some mystery intact, faces he can live with. He casts, then, with a most meticulous attention to physical type – the face, one sometimes suspects, is for him the ultimate in symbolic landscape, the object which is at once a thing-in-itself and a token of something more.

In *I Vitelloni* the face that everyone remembers is Alberto Sordi's, puffy, melancholy, self-indulgent, and irresistibly comic, and in the scene in which he weeps for his lost sister still terrifyingly all these things and heart-rending as well. It is a combination of qualities which has served many artists well – and for the moment inevitably gets them branded 'Chaplinesque'. This, indeed, was the almost invariable word applied to the character of Gelsomina, the waif in Fellini's next feature film, *La Strada*, played, of course, by his wife Giulietta Masina, possessor of the most memorable face in all Fellini's *oeuvre*. It was the face and the character, a perpetual underdog brutalized by her 'husband', Zampano, ignored by almost everyone else, and yet preserving throughout a Franciscan (the word is Fellini's) cheerfulness and simplicity, which won the world's affections, for all sorts of reasons only marginally filmic; it was the face which first and foremost enabled Fellini to win through to a mass audience. For *La Strada*, made very rapidly on a relatively tiny budget, was an enormous success commercially, and has perhaps subsequently fallen rather into critical disrepute for this very reason.

But there is far more to *La Strada* than a wonderfully expressive face and a sentimentally appealing character – and that far more we are now probably in a better position to appreciate than we were at the time. Again the parallel with *Le Grand Meaulnes* is illuminating: the inspiration of the story we know dates back to the earliest memories of which Fellini has told us: those of childhood holidays spent at his grandmother's in Gambettola, where gipsies still wandered and travelling showmen were the principal diversion of a poor and remote countryside. And where in *I Vitelloni*, which harked back to Fellini's young manhood in Rimini, the material never loses touch with recognizable actuality despite the nostalgic aura which surrounds it, as we move farther back in Fellini's life the link with actuality grows thinner. In *I Vitelloni* the landscapes may represent 'states of soul', but they are also acceptable on the realistic plane; in *La Strada*, though they are still 'real' in the sense that the film was made in real places, not constructed in a studio like Visconti's snowbound Italian town in *Le Notti Bianche*, they are so selected and so photographed that their 'soul-state' aspect predominates and their actuality is minimized (*La Strada*, as a matter of fact, represents Fellini's farthest swing in this direction). Similarly in *La Strada* the characters themselves become even more patently projections of different sides of Fellini's own character, as he himself has explicitly recognized, though defending nevertheless his claims to be a realist ('There are more Zampanos than bicycle thieves in the world').

La Strada, in fact, is, more overtly than any other of Fellini's films, a parable, and for that reason perhaps more liable to provoke violent partisanship or violent hostility. I had better own up, I suppose, to a high regard for the film in spite of the gravest doubts about its premises, and so *La Strada* for me is the key demonstration in Fellini's works of his sovereign quality as a thinker in film, whose script is merely a sketch of the complete film in his mind, as against the scriptwriter who writes first and then sets laboriously about translating a finished article into film terms. I am prepared to believe that any competent director could make something interesting out of the script of *I Vitelloni*, possibly even in a different way something almost as effective; but I doubt whether anyone else, given the script of *La Strada*, could have made it seem anything but tiresome and pretentious. But the script – the story-line and the words said – is only a single strand in the intricate pattern existing in Fellini's mind and now put on the screen: it is story seen in a certain way – a symphony of muted greys, beautifully caught by Martelli's camera; a pattern of sounds and music – and not only the Gelsomina theme by Nino Rota which sold millions of copies round the world; a journey through, conditioning and conditioned by a series of bleak, ghostly winter landscapes which hardly seem to belong to this world at all. Because it is all these things simultaneously and indissolubly, and has the unmistakable feel of springing fully armed from one man's brain, it is a great film whatever one thinks of the ideas behind it; with films, after all, it is not where they start from but where they get to that counts.

The story has been described by G. B. Cavallaro in a famous phrase as 'the fantastic history of a sad honeymoon with a posthumous declaration of love', which is all right as far as it goes. Like *I Vitelloni*, it is built round a series of key sequences which bring characters face to face with the truth, but this time there are only two characters involved, Gelsomina and Zampano, and the crises, not being shunned, bring progressive revelation, first to her and then, after a long evasion, to him. The principal progress in the film is that of Gelsomina from innocence to active goodness, goodness tested by an intuitive encounter with religion during the procession early on; a confrontation with suffering (the sick child at the wedding party); a realization of the woman's role as a wife (at the convent); and a first experience of violent death when Zampano kills Il Matto, the well-disposed, mercurial but to him slightly demonic acrobat who keeps crossing their path. Zampano's realization of himself and his role comes more slowly and with a greater struggle: the crucial moments of his life are the first almost involuntary act of taking on Gelsomina, his decisive abandonment of her after several twists and turns on the hook of his unacknowledged love for her, and his final facing of the truth after she is dead and he is left alone, weeping on the shore of a dark and desolate sea.

The symbolic pattern of the story, it will be seen, is very precisely laid out and schematic: in fairy-tale terms it could be described as the Beast melted and transformed – too late, of course – by his feelings for Beauty; in terms of the novelette it would be the strong bad man touched at the last by the love of a good woman; in religious terms it would be the way of two souls to redemption, one through understanding and sacrifice, the other finally through the effects of that sacrifice. In severely realistic terms, however, what is it? A mildly incredible fantasy about the relations of two people bizarrely atypical in themselves and divorced by their situation and occupation from any recognizable pattern of social behaviour. At best, the neo-realistic purist could take comfort only from the sharply observed peasant wedding (which even then would be rather too formally handled for his comfort) and a few hints of satire at the expense of the clergy. In short, while proclaiming himself a realist and indeed making the film, save for the employment of professional actors, in a way of which even the earliest, most doctrinaire theorists of neo-realism would have to approve, Fellini has produced something which has more genuine validity on practically any level one can think of than that of straightforward realistic observation of things as they are. And in doing so, of course, he has shown up the fallacy of doctrinaire neo-realism very clearly: its failure to accept that film realism is entirely in the eye of the beholder. We may say that Rossellini's early films are more objective – and therefore more 'realistic' – than Fellini's, and mean something by it; but what we mean is that when his camera is turned on a scene it is likely to be recorded with the emphases falling where they would normally fall for most of us, and with the ordinary and typical receiving more attention than the atypical and extraordinary. When Fellini looks at the same scene, though, with equally 'realistic' intentions, it is precisely the extraordinary, unexpected, and unpredictable which catches his eye.

When, for example, at one point in *La Strada* Gelsomina is sitting alone and dejected by the side of the road a solitary, riderless horse suddenly traverses the screen the effect is positively surrealistic: totally arbitrary, yet giving an instant visual reinforcement to the mood of the scene. The lost horse might well be a figment of Gelsomina's imagination, an image of her own state. But it is also a real horse, and its appearance here at this time is not impossible, only mildly peculiar. There may, for all we know, have actually been a stray horse there at the time of shooting which was seized on and pressed into service, in the same way that the three musicians whom elsewhere she falls in behind as they march along playing cheerfully to the empty countryside were, in fact, itinerant musicians who turned up in just this way. But what has struck Fellini about the horse and the musicians is their peculiarity and oddity, their – terrible word to the neo-realist – picturesqueness, their ability to embody the mental states of the protagonist, rather than their value as documents of any sort. All Fellini's films filter and select – and therefore colour and distort – external realities in this way, but the process is so much clearer, so stripped of ambiguity in *La Strada* that it can at once be recognized and accepted for what it is.

Up to *I Vitelloni*, or even *Un' Agenzia Matrimoniale*, Fellini's subsequent contribution to *Amore in Citta*, a portmanteau film of documentary reconstructions (of which more anon), it would have been quite possible, if increasingly odd, to continue regarding Fellini as a realist with a special gift for social satire, but *La Strada* makes it clear (or should have made it clear, though by *La Dolce Vita* many seemed to have forgotten the lesson) that he is nothing of the sort and never has been: his forte, even when his films have nearly all the trappings of external reality in their expected places, is symbolic fantasy of almost baroque elaboration and artificiality (the word, in this context, had no hint of denigration). Looking back from the viewpoint of *La Strada* at the earlier films we have been considering, indeed, we are likely to find that the perspective changes everything, and that brilliant though the touches of observation are (whatever else one may say about Fellini's films, every frame of them is undeniably bursting with life) it is the non-realistic side which now comes uppermost in the mind, so that even the most obviously comic and 'social' in its outlook, *Lo Sciecco Bianco*, comes in retrospect to look like a variation on the plot of *La Strada*, played for laughs and with the male and female roles reversed.

This is all worth spelling out at this juncture – though most of it has been at least implicit in my comments on the other films – because from *La Strada* on the purity and directness of the style, which enable us at once to discern its precise nature in this film (inevitable consequence of its being the farthest stage of Fellini's voyage into his own past?) become overlaid and transformed: the later films, while not deserting Fellini's basic source of inspiration in his own experience, become increasingly complex in their handling of their resources, the interplay between 'real' reality and imaginative reality becomes increasingly involved and elusive. His very next film, in fact, *Il Bidone*, moves us forward in Fellini's life to his early days as a journalist in Rome, and shows an instant increase in artfulness and complication: Fellini himself has remarked that while *La Strada* was made right off, in one breath, *Il Bidone* caused him a lot of care and trouble, and shows much more clearly the hand of the artisan hard at work mastering his craft.

Il Bidone is otherwise in many ways a sort of counterpart to *La Strada*; if *La Strada* is a *Purgatorio*, *Il Bidone* ends in Hell. Again two progressions can be traced in it, or rather the same progression can be traced on two levels, the symbolic and, this time much more fully articulated, the actual. A 'bidone' is a particular type of crook in Italian (that language so curiously well equipped for defining the various grades and shades of roguery): a confidence trickster who thrives particularly on invention, humour, intrigue, and a gift of the gab. The bidoni in Fellini's film might, in fact, be vitelloni who have taken the wrong turning or, if the phrase suggests too decisive a move, have drifted in the wrong direction. Restless and discontented like the vitelloni, but older and perhaps more desperate, they make a living by cheating the poor of their savings; they do it, however, with good grace and not too deep a consideration of what they are doing – until, that is, they are pushed inexorably towards their separate crises, the almost unbearable confrontations with the truth of things which always stand at the centre of Fellini's films.

Of the three principals, indeed, Roberto the uninhibited fantasist might well be Alberto of *I Vitelloni* ten years on (the role was intended originally for Alberto Sordi). Picasso (played by Richard Basehart, Il Matto in *La Strada*) might be Fausto, married, full of good intentions, able quite seriously to think of giving it all up when his wife finds out what he really does for a living, but congenitally weak and vacillating, and destined always to go on taking the easier, the more immediately appealing way out. His wife (Giulietta Masina) has rather the role of Fausto's wife, with more than a dash of Gelsomina's simple goodness and strength as well. Only Augusto (Broderick Crawford), the central figure of the film, has no clear earlier counterpart, despite one or two characteristics in common with Zampano. And it is his descent into Hell in the course of the film that we watch.

It starts, visually and emotionally, in the bare upland world of *La Strada*; even Nino Rota's music takes up again the theme associated with the snow scenes in *La Strada*. The bidoni, disguised as priests, are practising an elaborate confidence trick on some peasants by searching for treasure on their land, near a solitary tree just such as that which brooded over the wedding feast in *La Strada*. After various other tricks played on the credulous and pitiable poor, they go back to the town and there we are at once plunged into the world of *I Vitelloni*, with a festival in progress, a wild party to which they are all invited, the entangling of the principal figures in and then their progressive detachment from this background, and inevitably the moment of truth in the small hours. Picasso might be saved; he would be if he were capable of salvation, but probably he is not, any more than Fausto; he is a spiritual lightweight. But Augusto, touched also by something akin to remorse, only hides it from himself by plunging further into shame. After an extraordinary drunken night scene in which his attitude and Picasso's are contrasted he goes off first to a meeting with his daughter which suggests an attempt at redeeming himself, but leads only to his arrest and imprisonment, and then to his final trick, where he pushes his priestly imposture to sacrilegious extremes with a crippled girl and then double-crosses his associates into the bargain, and so finally to his agony and death.

This whole final sequence, with its ultimate degradation, its bitter accent on physical pain and its ambiguous conclusion, is one of the most remarkable in all Fellini, and deserves closer attention on several counts. To begin with, there are an extraordinary number of overtly symbolic correspondences where they have the most unequivocal effect: in the dialogue. Practically everything in the conversation between Augusto (disguised as a bishop) and the paralysed girl has a direct bearing on what subsequently happens to him; he becomes paralysed as she has been; when she says that suffering has shown her the way to God the implications of her words for the interior action of the last sequence are unmistakable. Then, too, the sequence offers an extreme example of Fellini's use of a real location quite realistically on one level (how many gangsters in American films have not met picturesque ends in rubbish dumps, railway sidings and other wastelands without any real significance being attached to the circumstance?), but with an unashamedly symbolic overall effect. Flung by his infuriated associates down a steep slope of stones at the roadside, Augusto finds that he is paralysed and probably dying, alone and far from help, in a dry hellish waste of infertile rock (water is conspicuous by its absence in *Il Bidone*; there is no seashore scene at all, and when at one point it rains the moisture is made to fall like a benediction on those below). Here he is at last, and this time quite inescapably, brought

1a. *I Vitelloni*. Dir: Federico Fellini

1b. *La Strada* (Giulietta Massina). Dir: Federico Fellini

2a. *La Dolce Vita* (Audrey McDonald, left; Niko Otzak, centre). Dir: Federico Fellini

2b. *8½* (Marcello Mastroianni). Dir: Federico Fellini

face to face with himself: with the falseness of his standards and his total uselessness to everyone in the world, even himself.

And so, at this deep point of self-judgement and self-condemnation, he starts what can only be described as a calvary, an agonizing ascent towards, literally and functionally speaking, the road, but much more prominently towards recovered humanity, redemption, and salvation. As he edges painfully up the slope the village bells are heard in the distance, then, later, when he is too worn out even to call for help, a group of peasants pass, with a little girl singing. And finally, alone to the last, he dies, and the camera, which has clung obsessively to him and his torment of stones up to now, suddenly draws back from him with a short, discreet gesture of abandonment. Has suffering shown him the way to God? We are at liberty to believe so if we wish, and the majority opinion seems to be that he has. One wonders if Fellini himself would feel competent to give a decisive answer, but whatever the verbal reply he would offer to an intellectually formulated question, there is no doubt of the efficacy of the answer the sequence gives in film terms to the questions formulated in film terms by what has gone before. In location, in the direction and duration of Augusto's ascent (again we share the character's time, on this occasion almost unbearably long drawn out), in the grey, stone-obsessed quality of the photography, Fellini offers the perfect resolution of the film's earlier conflicts between light and dark, the worlds of *La Strada* and *I Vitelloni*. The final sequence completes the film's structure with unmistakable authority, and here director's authority: the sequence could hardly have been conceived, let alone successfully realized, by any writer who was not a director to his fingertips, dealing all the time, from the start, essentially in film rather than the words on paper which may eventually go towards making it.

If after this climax some even of Fellini's most enthusiastic admirers felt and expressed disappointment with his next film, *Le Notti di Cabiria*, that may be attributed to various causes, some of which on examination seem to be reasonable, some less so. The most immediate, I think, were Fellini's return, after the clear, single dramatic developments at the centre of *La Strada* and *Il Bidone*, to a loose, episodic form of organization reminiscent of *I Vitelloni*, only if anything less purposeful, since the argument of the film is essentially circular rather than progressive; and the fact

that he used Giulietta Masina again in a way which suggested to
the wary that he was deliberately trying to repeat the success of
La Strada with another lovable Gelsomina figure. This latter
charge is probably unfair: certainly it seems likely that he would
have been moved to make a film like *Cabiria* even without the success of *La Strada*, though after *Cabiria* he seems to have realized
the possibility that too single-minded an obsession with his wife's
personality on film might well prove stultifying for both of them,
and significantly he decided not himself to direct *Fortunella*, a third
film with Giulietta Masina as a character with a family resemblance
to the other two. The first part of the first charge is true, but not
really important: it is the prerogative of the artist to take us by
surprise and disregard our predictions for him, and what seemed at
the time a formal regression may now be seen as a reaching-out,
rather, towards the boldly elliptical, discontinuous form of *La
Dolce Vita*; not a weak reiteration, but the first steps in a new direction.

No, it is the point about the circular movement of the story
which brings us to the most debatable aspect of the film. All
Fellini's other films chart in some way a moral progression, upwards or downwards, and the characters in them are brought by
events to a situation where truths have to be faced and decisions
made. In other words, they are all dynamic, and only *Le Notti di
Cabiria* is essentially static. That statement may provoke disagreement, and certainly at first glance the film does appear to progress
by a series of such encounters with the truth for Cabiria. But, in
fact, what we are shown is a series of trials, each one, if only by
virtue of being one more, that little bit worse than the one before,
and the point of the film is that through them all Cabiria remains
the same, indestructible. She does not really develop; indeed, she
is in many ways hardly a character at all, but a yardstick by which
the turpitude and degradation of the world around her can be
measured. And as such she is, inescapably, a sentimental device;
even her apparently shocking profession – she is a prostitute and
therefore might normally be expected to symbolize the very opposite – fails in its desentimentalizing effect simply because the tart
with a heart, to which breed she unmistakably belongs, is itself one
of the oldest clichés of sentimental fiction. So, right at the film's
conception, there is something wrong; perhaps, as Renzo Renzi

suggests, it is that while setting up a model of perfect Christian charity and humility Fellini cannot himself believe in it as a human possibility, however passionately he is for it as a principle.

But, as ever in Fellini's work, such academic objections are swept aside (or very nearly) by the force and life of the film itself: each episode is so fully, vividly imagined and embodied in visual imagery that we do not as it goes along notice the lack of that inner development which elsewhere gives impetus and direction to Fellini's abounding invention. The first and last sequences are attacks on Cabiria, the first by a lover she has trusted who pushes her in the river and runs off with her money; the second infinitely more brutal and premeditated, a sort of nightmare intensification of the first, in which a mild, quiet-looking man leads her on to believe he loves and will marry her, lets her sell everything she owns, and then takes it all from her and leaves her apparently desperate at last, crying out that she doesn't want to live any more. But the final shots show her surrounded by happy young people who serenade her, and it is clear that from this last trial also she has emerged unscathed, with enough hope and strength to start again.

In between there are three major sequences making this point in various ways: a strange, fantastic episode in which she is taken up by a rich actor after a lovers' quarrel, swept through a fantasmagoric Roman night-life and finally thrown out and disregarded when the girl-friend comes back and the actor's life returns to normal (a classic instance of our old friend the ravelling-unravelling technique); a pilgrimage to the Divino Amore, which seems to hold out some possibility of religious understanding and consolation to Cabiria, and then turns into a prostitutes' picnic; and a scene in which she becomes the victim of a music-hall hypnotist, is induced to act out her most cherished fantasies of love in an idyllic dream world and then rudely returned to reality amid the cruel laughter of the onlookers. There is also quite a bit of squabbling among the prostitutes and one curious, unexplained little sequence (eliminated in many copies of the film) in which Cabiria falls in with a mysterious man with a sack who takes food and help to a group of destitutes living out in caves on a misty upland near Rome – the only other good person she ever meets in a thoughtless, cruel world.

Whatever may be the dramatic weaknesses of *Le Notti di Cabiria* as a whole, there is no denying the remarkable brilliance with which these sequences are handled. The direction, in fact, is more obtrusively artful in effects than ever before – which might also be interpreted as a sign of doubt in the director's mind about the workability of the basic material. Fellini has never previously been so ready to indulge in decorative extravagance as in the various scenes in which the prostitutes squabble in the night streets, or indulged in such spectacular editing as in parts of the Divine Amore sequence. Some of the prostitutes, too – la Bomba Atomica in her cave, full of threats of a big come-back; Matilde in her leopard-skin bolero, screaming insults – are more uninhibitedly grotesque than ever before in his work. Even the style of photography favoured fluctuates considerably from scene to scene: bold chiaroscuro in the night-club scene and the street-scenes; dead grey in the sequence involving the man with the sack; blanching neo-realist daylight for the scenes near Cabiria's house; expressionistically strange and unnatural illumination for the theatre scene (reasonably) and the final disillusionment which springs indirectly from it.

For that matter, even in the script itself the areas of contribution by the various writers can be more clearly marked out than ever before. It is known that within Fellini's overall responsibility for the story and layout of his films, Ennio Flaiano represents the sharply humorous, iconoclastic side of his nature, the sceptical link with the realities, while Tullio Pinelli (himself a religious dramatist of some distinction) represents the mystical, elevated side of Fellini's nature, the love side of his love-hate relationship with Roman Catholic doctrine and the Church. One would guess Flaiano to have had the more important part in scripting *Lo Sciecco Bianco* and *I Vitelloni*, Pinelli to have been the major collaborator on *La Strada* (as was, in fact, the case; Flaiano collaborated only on the final draft), and Flaiano to have been more involved in the mechanics of the crooks' trickery than in their subsequent painful progress towards grace in *Il Bidone*. But with *Cabiria* one could assign their work almost scene by scene just on guesswork: to Flaiano the scenes with the assembled prostitutes, the minor tangles with customers and the whole sequence with the star; to Pinelli the sequence of the Divino Amore and the whole last part of the film. And this is precisely how they worked on it (the ubiquitous Pier Paolo Pasolini was also called in for advice on slum dialogue). The fact that nevertheless the finished film holds together as it does as the unmistakable expression of one man's vision is in the circumstances no small tribute to Fellini as the originator, coordinator and realizer of the enterprise. The film bears his stamp throughout, and if not the outright masterpiece we might have hoped would follow *I Vitelloni*, *La Strada* and *Il Bidone*, a demonstration still that even with a, for him, fundamentally unsatisfactory subject Fellini just could not make a film that was for a moment boring or dead.

Fortunella, the next film he worked on, may be taken, as I remarked earlier, for a sign that Fellini himself recognized the dangers inherent in *Cabiria* and determined not to succumb to them. The script, an original by Fellini and his two usual collaborators about a Masina-waif who is convinced she is the long-lost daughter of a prince, and her various picaresque adventures with wandering actors and a scholar-tramp called 'the Professor,' was therefore handed over to be directed instead by Eduardo de Filippo. The result is extraordinarily revealing in the comparison it offers with the films directed by Fellini himself. Here the story is played quite straight, for comedy or even at times for farce. The time sense is completely different: instead of the fluctuating, subjective time-scale of Fellini's films, forcing the viewer willy-nilly into experiencing things the way the characters experience them, we have a clearly uniform, objective timing, the director's timing imposed from without, which at once suggests that we are required to observe rather than involve ourselves. The poetic side of Fellini's vision also disappears: a deserted square may be a projection of his characters' mood to Fellini, an embodied soul-state, but to De Filippo it is just a picturesque, rather theatrical background to action. And action means action; there is no atmospheric brooding over inaction: if nothing obvious is happening, business is introduced to fill the gap. *Fortunella* is, according to its lights, a thoroughly competent and enjoyable film, if rather evidently put together with scraps left over from *La Strada* and *Cabiria*. But as a piece of creative film-making it simply serves to underline with unusual force and clarity just where competence leaves off and genius begins.

And so to *La Dolce Vita*, Fellini's largest and in many ways his most controversial film to date. First a few words about where it came from. To begin with there was Fellini's eagerly worked-for project *Moraldo in Citta*, which would take up the story of Moraldo where we left him at the end of *I Vitelloni*. Basically *La Dolce Vita* derives from this same impulse, though meanwhile Moraldo has changed character considerably to become the weak-willed, decadent journalist Marcello; however, at least one sequence, that between Marcello and his father, comes straight from *Moraldo in Citta*. Next, there is the episode Fellini directed for Zavattini's collection of documentary reconstructions, *Amore in Citta* – though by the time Fellini has finished with his material there is nothing noticeably documentary about it at all; it is a fully-fledged Fellini film in miniature. The theme is humility and human suffering, as revealed when a journalist inquiring into matrimonial agencies interviews an applicant for the position of wife to a (non-existent) invalid of bizarre and possible violent tendencies. The point of interest here is the ambiguous and ultimately rather heartless figure of the journalist, whose inquiry seems to be entirely in the abstract and whose attitude to the suffering he sees and presumably exacerbates by his interference remains oddly remote and unfeeling. It might almost be a detached sequence from *La Dolce Vita*; its journalist hero certainly has in embryo a number of qualities more fully explored in the character eventually played by Marcello Mastroianni.

And thirdly there is *Viaggia d'Amoro*, the project Fellini was working on immediately before *La Dolce Vita*. In this an intellectual city Italian (possibly an Americanized Italian; at one time Gregory Peck and Sophia Loren were announced for the principal roles) goes back to his provincial home in the company of a simple, motherly mistress with whom, under the influence of renewed contact with his old way of life, he thinks of settling down to lead a simpler, more 'natural' life, thereby escaping from the stultifying surroundings of his last few years. But their ways of life are irremediably separate, and their relationship is doomed to be mutually destructive, so finally nothing comes of it. In the end, Fellini decided not to make the film (though he says the mother-son relationship in it still interests him, and it is briefly touched on in *8½*), and instead incorporated the essentials of the central relationship into that in *La Dolce Vita* between Marcello and his mistress Emma, while the theme of the intellectual seeking escape permeates the whole film.

So already at its inception *La Dolce Vita* had in it the makings of a summary of Fellini so far, a complete statement of his mature views on all the recurrent themes in his work. And so, perhaps too readily, it has been taken to be by many critics, a savage denunciation of the world as he sees it now, bringing his spiritual autobiography on film up to date with a gesture of despair because the visionary gleam of his childhood (which shone most brightly in *La Strada*) has now faded for ever. This seems to me a dangerously partial view of what the film actually says, and an evident distortion of Fellini's interests and intentions in making it. In the first place it is highly doubtful if Fellini ever sets out to make a film of ideas, putting forward a certain interpretation of society and human personality: these may emerge, though invariably defined exclusively in terms of the single, special case (his films are more like novels or fairy-tales than allegories), but embodying them never seems to be the first impulse towards creation. Rather is the first impulse an image or series of images. As Fellini himself puts it:

A film is like an unknown castle. First you glimpse an odd roof or turret from a distance, then you gradually get some vague idea of how the whole thing looks, then suddenly you find yourself approaching the main entrance, you knock and (maybe) are let in. And only when you are inside do you begin to explore the individual corridors and rooms, to see how they are furnished and how they join on to each other. When I catch a first glimpse of a turret, as it were, I start scribbling and sketching. Perhaps it is a character or a costume, perhaps a place, perhaps just some little detail which helps me to define the *ambiente* in my mind. It's really all my excuse for not getting on working, but it's also useful, because it's the way films gradually materialize for me.

So with *La Dolce Vita*:

I just thought of it as a vast fresco—I saw it this shape [carving a Cinemascope screen out of the air with his hands] and then gradually characters and incidents emerged to fill it out, but several sequences, such as the 'miracle' and the orgy, were almost entirely improvised in the course of shooting. I like to keep my mind open as far as possible to the miraculous gifts the world may bring: a face, a building, even a piece of clothing – look, that dress over there [pointing across the room], the green of it, the way it falls in three folds – that might be the germ of a whole sequence, a whole film . . .

These pronouncements are of interest, of course, simply as

reflections of the way the author sees his film, but more than that, while many authors' accounts of their work are conspicuously un-helpful, these seem to me to put us on exactly the right lines best to appreciate the film. To begin with, we should accept the immediate impact of the film on our senses, which is not at all that of a reasoned argument against a way of life and its representatives. Rather, it is as a series of vast decorative compositions on the same basic theme, like, say, Doré's illustrations to Dante's *Inferno*. They trace a sort of intellectual rake's progress downwards in seven giant steps, represented by seven confused, dreamlike nights and seven terrible dawns stripping away whatever illusions the nights have left. One of the compositions, that involving the mistress of Marcello, the central character, and his curious philosopher friend Steiner, is fragmented to provide a sort of continuity, but when put together the pieces of this fit into the same pattern as all the rest, which is precisely the scene structure which we have noticed as the basic shape throughout Fellini's work, the principals starting alone, being drawn into a more and more intricate pattern of action as the night draws on, and then unwound, left alone to face their own personal problems, and scattered as day breaks.

First, a brief prologue: the famous sequence in which an enor-mous statue of Christ is carried high over Rome suspended from a helicopter – an image which defies any single, neat interpretation, but sets, with its rich ambiguity, the tone of all that is to come. Then the first major sequence in which Marcello (Marcello Mas-troianni) meets at a crowded night-club a bored young heiress of his acquaintance, they pick up a prostitute, and then spend the night together in her bed for kicks while she waits on the stairs, before paying her and leaving in the morning; on his return home Marcello finds that his mistress Emma has attempted to commit suicide, but gets her to the hospital in time to save her. The second big sequence begins in broad daylight with the arrival of the American sex-symbol film star Sylvia, and follows Marcello's pur-suit of her through a day of sight-seeing and a night of parties to a dawn which finds them paddling euphorically in the fountain of Trevi and restores them to cold common sense; if Maddalena, the heiress of the first sequence, represents for Marcello the refine-ments of sexual pleasure, Sylvia represents for him rather the wholly physical life of the beautiful, mindless body, but just because she is mindless all real contact, even purely physical, is impossible for them.

Next, in daylight again, Marcello meets Steiner in a modern church, and listens to him playing Bach on the organ; they talk about Marcello's writing and he expresses his doubts about being able to write seriously at all. Then the third major sequence, that in which Marcello and Emma go to the site of a supposed vision of the Virgin, which has been taken over by the television cameras and built up to a pitch of hysteria which precipitates a near riot and complete disillusionment as the rain starts to pour down; when the morning comes there are only a few subdued figures around the body of one who came in hopes of a miracle and merely died in the crush: recourse to religion, too, it seems, has failed. After this the Steiner sequence is continued in an extended scene of an intellectual party to which Marcello and Emma are invited by Steiner. Steiner seems ideally happy with his wife and two children, his music, his books, his civilized friends, but this ivory-tower life of the mind is also doomed to offer no recourse; later on in the film, just before the final sequence, we see Marcello and Emma quarrelling bitterly on the road at night and making up in the morning just as news comes to Marcello that Steiner has killed himself and his two children – the sleep of reason, presumably, has also brought forth monsters.

At this half-way mark in the film, however, just after Steiner's party, there comes a strange interlude, belonging to none of the principal segments of the film, in which for a few minutes the darkness retreats, the hectic contrasts between the dreamlike nights and the harsh light of high noon with which they are usually alternated dissolve, and we are given instead an idyllic scene in the pearly morning light where Marcello, trying vaguely to work in a small open-air restaurant by the sea, meets an innocent young girl whose unaffected gaiety seems totally untouched by the world from which he comes. The respite is only temporary, though. Next it is night again, and Marcello's father turns up unexpectedly; Marcello takes him out on the town and he goes back with an attractive night-club dancer, but then he has a mild heart attack and sets off home again in the morning, shamed, ailing, and no closer to his son than before – the recourse to the persisting, settled values of family life does not work either.

Then the pace quickens – a wild, fantastic party is given in a castle near Rome, at which the rich and aristocratic disport themselves without much appearance of enjoying it; Marcello, moved to declare his love for Maddalena, asks her to marry him, suggesting that together they may overcome each other's despair, but she, after seeming sympathetic, only abandons herself at once to another man. Marriage to Maddalena is no answer and neither, we gather in the next short sequence, the overnight quarrel with Emma, would marriage to her be. Fast on that comes the suicide of Steiner, and then the final orgy, in which Marcello, by now no longer a writer but merely publicist for a stupid, bumptious star, gradually assumes the role of an impresario for the entertainments, offering bitterly to devise enough perversions and outrages to keep them amused for a week. But nothing can make this party go, and in the morning the participants wander out across the sands to – what? A new monster fished out of the sea, which interests them for a moment and then away they drift, leaving Marcello gazing wanly across a small stream at the girl from the seaside café. She smiles and beckons him; he shakes his head and is drawn away, back to whatever further hell may be in store for him. The film closes on her, looking after him – the lost innocence and freshness of childhood to which, even if he wanted to, he could never return.

And so Fellini's *Inferno* leaves us looking sadly across the stream at Paradise; a paradise of sorts is assumed to exist, somewhere else, back in time or removed in space, but whichever it is, and whatever the precise nature of this paradise may be we are not told. However, the very fact of its existence, and the way that its existence it expressed, serves to discountenance the view that *La Dolce Vita* is a complete picture of Fellini's imaginative world at the present stage in his career. It is, rather, an exhaustive exploration of one side of that world: the dark side which we have previously encountered with some admixture, particularly in *I Vitelloni* and *Il Bidone*. Admittedly the world of *La Dolce Vita* is more unrelievedly dark than either of these: it is a city of dreadful night, experience of which forcefully conveys

> *The sense that every struggle brings defeat*
> *Because Fate holds no prize to crown success;*
> *That all the oracles are dumb or cheat*
> *Because they have no secret to express;*

That none can pierce the vast black veil uncertain
Because there is no light beyond the curtain;
That all is vanity and nothingness.

or would convey this if it were not for the two small glimpses we are
allowed behind the curtain, beyond which we see the clear air and
the children playing on the shore. Fellini's habitual selection of
reality could hardly go further: here all is monstrous, misshapen,
overgrown, the settings, the clothes of the characters, the faces,
startlingly beautiful or shockingly grotesque, but never ordinary.
All these elements are found in life, everything that appears in the
film may well have been seen somewhere in the streets or clubs of
Rome, but this unremitting concentration on the peculiar, the
exceptional, the larger-than-life gives the film, within its superficially realistic coating, a feverish, expressionistic quality which
takes it in effect farther away from reality than anything Fellini had
previously done, even *La Strada*. 'This town is not Rome – it is *my*
Rome,' says Fellini, 'a town which has its external appearance in
common with Rome because that is the place I live in and know
best, but is really a creation of my own imagination'; and, of course,
this is not merely a craven evasion, as determined social-realists
would have it, but simply a fact. Fellini's Rome corresponds no
more and no less to the world we normally live in than his time –
the long, hectic nights, the almost non-existent day – corresponds
with ours; that is to say, it has imaginative validity as a nightmare
image of modern life, but hardly any literal validity as documentary
picture of things as they prosaically are.

I must apologize for labouring this point, which ought to be
obvious, but the film has been so much misunderstood as a piece of
savage social criticism, an inside picture of Roman high life by a
man who knows (and praised or blamed according to the critic's
assessment of its efficacy in these fields) that I can only suppose it is
not so obvious after all. The very look of the film, surely, ought to
put such commentators on their guard: the bizarre locations; the
intricately baroque chiaroscuro effects of light and shade in the
night scenes, often not even vaguely explained in realistic terms;
the highly artificial composition of many of the shots, the complete
antithesis of unvarnished actuality; the bold use of symbolic trappings like the deceptive echo-chamber from which Marcello makes
his proposal to Maddalena; the occasional excursions into complete

unreality like the instantaneous and in this instance overtly subjective dawn over the fountain of Trevi. And yet, and yet. . .

La Dolce Vita, then, remains a monument, and a very imposing one, to Fellini's doubts and fears. Life here is hell, and no one escapes from it, like Moraldo, or learns from it, even in extremes, like Zampano and Augusto, or even manages somehow to pass through it unscathed, like Cabiria. Relentlessly the film gathers force, as one after another every escape route Marcello might consider is closed in his face, and instance piles on instance; it works not by logical argument, but sheer agglomeration of circumstances, each one weighing the protagonist down further. But there is always one character, the girl on the beach, free from all this, living in a different world, and it is towards this world, with its clear, pearly grey light (visually very much the world of *La Strada*), that our attention is turned in the closing sequence. What does it stand for, the brightness beyond this dark side of the moon? Intimations of immortality from recollections of early childhood? Perhaps: we cannot but remember that Fellini's other major embodiment of innocent goodness, Gelsomina, also grew out of the landscape of Fellini's earliest childhood recollections. For whatever more there was to it, what *Paradiso* was to provide the counterpart to this *Inferno* (if any), Fellini directed our attention to his next film *8½*, saying of it, cryptically, that 'it will probably seem even more arbitrary and disorganized than *La Dolce Vita* and will try to explain and demonstrate the mysterious message the girl on the beach signals to Marcello, and which he cannot or will not act on'.

Before starting work on *8½*, however, Fellini contributed an episode called *Le Tentazioni del Dottor Antonio* to *Boccaccio 70*, a vast omnibus film supposedly intended to re-create the spirit of Boccaccio in modern terms. In it Peppino de Filippo is a puritan outraged by a sensual poster of Anita Ekberg (the Sylvia of *La Dolce Vita*) advertising milk, and is chastised for his pains in a fantastic dream sequence which returns us to the nightmare world of *La Dolce Vita*, but this time with its horrors played firmly (if not very lightly) for comedy. The result is strange and not very successful, though admittedly the fact that the version of the episode finally shown is half an hour shorter than the original version as edited by Fellini makes certain judgement difficult. It is chiefly interesting for the bold and imaginative use of colour (Fellini's first), which is exploited with some skill for the further possibilities of telling incongruities and unexpected effects it offers: there is, in particular, a memorable scene in an ultra-modern white-painted church scattered with conventionally black-suited men and grotesque old crones, looking as though they have just been set down on another planet.

But the film's most significant aspect in the perspective of $8\frac{1}{2}$ is its overall style, which makes its effects in terms of much broader, coarser burlesque than anything Fellini has attempted before. Here it does not quite come off, and the whole thing turns out rather heavy, but at the same time one can see what Fellini is getting at; the very exaggeration of the playing and the extravagant visual style make even the relatively straightforward 'real life' scenes seem somehow hectic and nightmarish, while the nightmare itself unrolls with great ease and naturalness. If the style is not quite under control in *Boccaccio 70*, the experiment nevertheless proves to have paid off when we get to $8\frac{1}{2}$, another film about dreams and fantasies in which, too, a gargantuan maternal image of womanhood figures prominently; in many sections there the broad burlesque is integrated with perfect ease and finesse into the more familiar pattern of Fellini's style, giving it greater range and suppleness than ever before.

$8\frac{1}{2}$ (why '$8\frac{1}{2}$'? Because Fellini had up to then made seven features and two episodes, adding up roughly to a half) really does seem to be the ultimate summary and personal confession that *La Dolce Vita* was rather prematurely taken to be. Though, of course, this statement, too, may prove to be premature, at the moment Fellini himself seems to believe it, and has said that he regards it as his final working of autobiography out of his system. But then his pronouncements on what he will or will not do next are notoriously unreliable; a true intuitive, he never seems to know quite what he is doing until after he has done it (he cheerfully admits that he prefers working 'blind' and as far as possible avoids seeing his own rushes while directing), and this seems to have been more than usually the case with $8\frac{1}{2}$. When Fellini announced that his next film after *La Dolce Vita* would explore the message and world of the girl on the shore he was evidently voicing a genuine intention, but one which when he came to the point he was just not able to carry out. But if a film-maker finds himself unable to do justice to a subject which he has much at heart, what is his obvious, almost his necessary, next move? But of course; to make a film in which he works out why he could not make the film he originally intended. And this, under a great cloak of secrecy and, one suspects, with much less idea of where he was going than he let on even to his closest collaborators, is exactly what Fellini did.

The hero of his film (played by Marcello Matroianni, his perfect cinematic *alter ego*) is a film director with all the means of making a film at his disposal and no film to make. Or at least, he has a lot of ideas for a film, but they will not crystallize into a coherent script; essentially because, though he does not at first realize it, he is trying through the film to work out the problems of his own life, and so cannot make sense of the film's pattern until he has made sense of his own life as well. The action of the film takes place at a weird and dreamlike Edwardian spa (one occasionally suspects parody of *L' Année Dernière à Marienbad* lurking at the back of Fellini's mind) where Guido, the director, is taking a cure, scouting locations, and generally trying to sort things out while a gargantuan set of a rocket-base rises inexorably on a near-by lot and the whole machinery of a mammoth production little by little engulfs him. Throughout the film we, and he, flit backwards and forwards between dream and reality, sometimes seeing bits of the film he means to make as they form in his mind, sometimes the dreams which come to him while he sleeps, and sometimes the discussions with his producer, his unhelpful script collaborator and others in which ideas are considered, modified, or rejected. Indeed the film, finally, proves to have a structure rather like Gide's *Les Faux Monnayeurs*, being at once a film about making a film, and the film which in the process is made, and containing in addition a complete auto-critique, in that the harshest things which can be said against it – that it is pretentious, empty; that Fellini has nothing to say and does not alter that fact simply by openly admitting it to be true – are already said, by the director himself or by the critical intellectual he works with.

The film starts with a straightforward dream sequence, in which Guido finds himself shut in a car in the middle of a traffic jam, suffocating under the accusing eyes of those around. It is the image of his emotional situation, as we soon learn when we return to waking reality. The emotional constants of his life are his cool, unsensual wife (Anouk Aimée, Maddalena in *La Dolce Vita*, but corresponding more closely to Emma), whom he loves and needs, but who cannot reconcile herself to his constant infidelities, and his plump, stupid, maternal mistress, who represents comforting femininity uncomplicated by brains. These at least are real, though we see them variously transformed in Guido's fantasies as well. But there is a third figure who is almost entirely fantasy; the girl played by Claudia Cardinale, who flits through Guido's dreams and plans as an embodiment of innocence, a beautiful messenger from a lost and inaccessible paradise. In her we encounter again the girl on the beach in *La Dolce Vita*, and we do learn more clearly what her ambiguous message might be: not an invitation to a world without sex, but an invitation to a world without shame.

This, in fact, is what Guido dreams of again and again in one form or another. It is behind the two episodes from Fellini's own childhood (as he has elsewhere told us): that in the farmhouse at the time of the wine-making, which is filled with a warm glow of uncomplicated maternal feeling, and that in which the young Guido sneaks away from his religious school to watch a mountainous mad prostitute, La Saraghina (obviously the original of La Bomba Atomica in *Le Notti di Cabiria*, incidentally) dancing on the shore, a sexual experience without shame which his clerical mentors subsequently do their best to spoil by drumming into him that La Saraghina is the devil. It is also at the root of Guido's adult sexual fantasies, such as the brief scene in which he imagines his wife and mistress, in fact grimly separated at opposite ends of an open-air restaurant, embracing and weaving gaily in and out of the tables in an impromptu dance, and the much longer and more involved scene in which he imagines himself as the master of a harem (located, significantly, in the farmhouse of his childhood) where women of all types to suit all his moods and whims live happily together, contented only to serve him for as long as he wants and be dismissed when he wants to dismiss them (one remembers that back in the days of *Il Bidone* Fellini was toying with the idea of a man who keeps fifteen separate families and eventually unites them all under one roof in a sort of patriarchal community; clearly it is a long-standing fantasy of his own). And it is certainly the principal factor in all his dealings with Claudia, though when at long last a real Claudia turns up to star in his film he is forced to the bitter conclusion (in one of Fellini's favourite scenes of self-confrontation in a deserted square at night) that his hero (and he) will never accept what she offers, because he is too cowardly, too involved ever really to believe in the possibility of a simple truth; once one has entered the domain of Experience, one can never, however much one may want to, find one's way back to Innocence again.

There are other threads running through the film; it is not only on his emotional-cum-sexual problems that Guido continually interrogates himself, consciously or unconsciously. Like *La Dolce Vita*, *8½* is a series of attempts by a disorientated intellectual to find his way, to find a truth, about himself and the world around him, by which he can live. Back-to-the-womb, a contracting-out of the complexities and discomforts of adult life, is only one way of dealing with his problems, and evidently right from the start one which is not practicable: even in his childhood the seeds of shame are sown, and in his ideal harem the image of his wife, a contemplative housewife straight out of Vermeer, and her clear-eyed, disenchanted friend, suggest their own judgement on the possibility of his dreams. Religion, too, is tried: Guido considers bringing his hero into contact with a cardinal by chance at the baths, and when assured that this is impossible does so nevertheless in his imagination. But the real cardinal speaks of nothing more relevant to his dilemma than the song of a bird, and the encounter with the dream cardinal produces only the oracular assurance that nothing is possible with the Church.

Recourse to masculine friendship is also denied Guido; the only old friend of his that we encounter, Mezzabotta, is himself hopelessly involved in a middle-aged infatuation with an unscrupulous, slightly demonic pseudo-intellectual, and quite incapable of helping. Guido's parents are dead, or seem to be: his father (Annibale Ninchi, Marcello's father in *La Dolce Vita*) is certainly dead, and is seen in one of the dream sequences complaining about the form of his tomb; his mother figures only as a vaguely accusing ghost flitting through Guido's fantasies, a judging woman whose role has been taken over effectively by his wife (in the scene at the father's tomb the mother actually changes into the wife in Guido's arms). In any case, there is clearly no escape into the happy haven of settled family life. The occult, represented in *8½* by a cabaret act involving an old woman who claims to be able to read thoughts and

3*a*. Michelangelo Antonioni directs an episode of *I Vinti* on Wimbledon Common
3*b*. *Le Amiche* (Anna Maria Pancani, above; Valentina Cortese, centre; Yvonne Furneaux, right). Dir: Michelangelo Antonioni

4a. *L'Avventura* (Monica Vitti; Lea Massari). Dir: Michelangelo Antonioni

4b. *L'Eclisse* (Alain Delon; Monica Vitta). Dir: Michelangelo Antonioni

sometimes actually can, does not offer much comfort either; if she has any real powers they enable her only to give back to people what they already know they possess. Even the purely physical escape from the world with which Guido means to end his film is dismissed when the set of the launching-pad from which his characters are to be shot into outer space is abandoned along with the film Guido has finally decided he will never make.

In fact, there is no escape, only acceptance: Guido has in the end to face the fact that even suicide, of which he dreams as the climax to a disastrous press conference, is not possible for him, and that he must just settle down to live with his own contradictions; not to seek the one, 'true', uncomplicated him, but to accept instead that all the different aspects of his character are necessarily and inescapably part of him for the rest of his life. His only answer is the classic artist's answer: to try again to make sense in his art of what in his life remains ever unsatisfactory and elusive. In his life he may be hopelessly incapable of coming to terms with the world around him, but in his own world of cinema, where he is a little god, he can order things as he thinks they should be; there life is a circus, and he the ringmaster cracking the whip, which is exactly what, in the last scene of the film, he turns out to be. As the adult Guido acts as master of ceremonies, the characters of the film, real and fantasy, alive and dead, the most disreputable and the most respectable, all join together in a happy band to take their bows, among them the young Guido, who is the last to leave, pursued by a spotlight into the gathering dark.

The material of *8½* evidently, and deliberately, recalls at many points that of Fellini's earlier films. Favourite images recur: the sea, suggesting freedom and infinity, the empty square at night as a setting for self-examination. So do Fellini's two principal types of women, the thin, angular, exacting wife and the plump, warm, complacent mistress, as well as the unseizable, mysterious innocent who passes momentarily across the scene, like the boy in *I Vitelloni* and the girl on the beach in *La Dolce Vita*. The seamy underside of show-business, which has fascinated him ever since *Luci del Varieta*, is to be recognized again in the person of the ageing French refugee from the follies who is unkindly banished to the attic of Guido's harem when he has grown tired of her. The mind-reader of the night-club scene in *8½* recalls the hypnotist in *Le*

Notti di Cabiria, while the setting in which she performs suggests unmistakably the Baths of Caracalla in *La Dolce Vita.* Three of the principal actors in *La Dolce Vita* recur, two of them, Marcello Mastroianni and Annibale Ninchi, in the same relationship in both films. The musicians in the last scene of *8½* at once bring to mind the wandering musicians in *La Strada;* La Saraghina, La Bomba Atomica in *Le Notti di Cabiria;* the love-hate relationship with the Church that previously suggested in *Cabiria, Il Bidone, La Dolce Vita* and elsewhere. . . . The list could be continued almost indefinitely; *8½* is rather like a poet's notebook, which can only exert its full fascination for someone already well acquainted with the author's previous work and his whole imaginative world.

But that is only one aspect of the film. It remains part of the film, to the extent that it perhaps never quite achieves total independence as a self-sufficient work of art (one wonders what someone who had never seen a Fellini film before would make of it). But is the comparison with a poet's notebook suggests that the film is unpolished, unfinished, a succession of parts which never add up to a whole, this is quite unfair. In construction the film is Fellini's most intricate and in some ways his most masterly; the pieces, apparently so different and incompatible one with another, ultimately fall into place with fantastic precision and inevitability. Above all, it is a triumph of style; a new, fuller, wider-ranging Fellini style which finally leaves realism, in any sense that a neorealist would recognize, far, far behind. Working for the first time (apart from the insignificant *Agenzia Matrimoniale* episode) with Antonioni's favourite cameraman Gianni Di Venanzo, Fellini has evolved an ornate, extravagant visual style to match the fantasy of his plot. Not only do the dream sequences veer towards the expressionistic in their nightmarish exaggeration – never have we been drawn more deeply by the camera into the centre of Fellini's world; never have we been forced more ruthlessly to live by the characters' time rather than our own – but the 'real' scenes are often equally dreamlike, as in *Le Tentazioni del Dottor Antonio,* so that the edges of dream and reality are constantly blurring for us, as they are for Guido. When we start with a blanched, ghostly panorama of the springs themselves, with dozens of mysterious figures in black standing out in hallucinatory relief, many of them extremely strange and grotesque, are we in a dream or in life? In life, as it turns out, but by the time we can be really sure the significance of the distinction is liable to escape us. In *8½* Fellini clearly shows himself to be what we have always at least half suspected him of being, a baroque fantasist whose private world has nothing more than a few accidents of apparent time and place in common with any 'real' world which we may obstinately persist in supposing we know and can recognize.

Can *8½* really be Fellini's farewell to autobiography and private myth? Though he insists that it is, it seems unlikely that anyone will believe him until he proves as good as his word. But whatever his detractors have said of him he has never been content to stand still and repeat himself: technically and emotionally each of his films has gone on from the one before to conquer new ground, and, autobiographical or not, his next film seems unlikely to be an exception. As a film-writer, as a creator of plots and characters, Fellini is remarkably gifted, but by no means unique: where his real greatness lies is the complete certainty with which he builds up his films not by a series of careful translations and transformations from a purely verbal origin, but by a process of co-ordination, bringing together and into focus sights and sounds, the character he sketches on a menu-card and the place he knew as a child, the hut on the Via Veneto and the face on the Spanish Steps, the fold of a dress and the manner of speech of a tawdry vaudevillian or a sleek aristocrat, into one complex, coherent, indivisible film. If any creator expresses himself in film first, last and always, it is Fellini; his films may sometimes appall the nicer sensibilities with their unashamed sentimentality, their occasional self-indulgence, their complete lack of inhibition, but these, if faults they are, are the necessary faults of his virtues. Above all with his films, even the most complex, one has the feeling of instantaneous creation, an undivided and joyful process from first conception to finished result. If that is not the mark of a great film-creator I don't know what is.

Michelangelo Antonioni

ONE COULD HARDLY IMAGINE TWO MORE UNLIKELY
people to emerge at the same time from the same movement as
Federico Fellini and Michelangelo Antonioni. Especially if the
movement happened to be neo-realism. But, in fact, the Italian
cinema, dominated as it was in the post-war years by the realistic
film-making of Rossellini and de Sica, and all that they stood for at
that epoch – working-class drama, non-professional actors, a deliberate disregard of style, or at least an attempt to achieve a 'styleless
style' of grainy untampered-with actuality – did manage to throw
up in 1950 these two new feature-directors as different in temperament from each other as they were different in their respective
approaches to the cinema from the current orthodoxy of the Italian
film at that time.

Antonioni's temperament and interests could be described to a
considerable extent simply by reversing everything I have said
about Fellini. Fellini is one of the cinema's great extroverts; a
generous, prolific imagination and an almost exhibitionistic flair for
putting himself, his own emotions and experiences directly on the
screen go with a passion for the bizarre and the extravagant to make
a cinema of baroque boldness and opulence, grandly unconcerned
with niceties of taste. Antonioni, on the other hand, is the complete
introvert, meticulously self-disciplined and working ever towards a
more rigorous examination of his materials, a severer exclusion of
himself from his work. His is, superficially at any rate, a cool,
hermetic sort of cinema, a minority taste which has managed to
reach a majority, it seems to me, mainly by the lucky chance of his
having hit on a star, Monica Vitti, whose personality and physical
beauty, while corresponding exactly to the feminine ideal of his
films, could at the same time convey a human warmth sufficient to
attract filmgoers who would otherwise find his films cold and impersonal.

This – the combination of director and star in an ideal cinematic
relationship – did not come about until 1960, though, when they
made together *L'Avventura*, and up to then Antonioni, though

making from the start distinguished films which won prizes at festivals and the approval of highbrow critics, had never won through to public approval in the way that Fellini did quite early in his career. Antonioni was indeed an unusually late starter: he did not make his first feature until he was 42, and did not enter films at all until he was 30. He was born in Ferrara in 1912, of a prosperous middle-class family, and his favourite hobbies as a child were painting and designing and building architectural models (he still sometime paints) – which may go some way to explain his preoccupation in his mature works with architecture and décor. He studied at Bologna University, within easy commuting distance of his home, and began a classics course before changing to the technical institute (because, he recalls, he had fallen in love with a girl studying there) and going on to study political economy. While still at university he became interested in the theatre, writing a number of comedies himself and founding with other students an amateur theatrical group for which he directed a number of plays, his own and other writers'. At the same time he wrote short stories and film criticisms for the local newspaper, *Il Corriere Padano* (the latter so severe that he got into trouble with the authorities on several occasions for his attacks on the official Italian cinema of the day), and experimented with amateur film-making, his first effort being an abortive documentary about a lunatic asylum.

At the end of 1939 Antonioni finally decided to make the cinema his life, and set off to Rome to do so, meanwhile taking a job in the preparation of the Universal Exhibition planned for 1942 and, of course, never actually staged. He wrote articles for *Cinema*, the official Fascist film magazine directed by Mussolini's son Vittorio and therefore, paradoxically, in a privileged position which allowed its contributors considerably greater latitude politically than they could enjoy anywhere else, but finally he was dismissed over a political disagreement. Eventually he entered the Centre Sperimentale at Rome to take their course in film technique, but stayed for only three months, at the end of which he made a short film which gained him a first-class diploma: it was made, apparently, in one long take, and concerned one woman coming to reclaim some compromising letters from another after paying blackmail money on them; the two roles were, in fact, played by the same actress and the film was actually in two takes, so cunningly joined when the camera panned from one to the other that no one could tell exactly where.

Equipped with his diploma Antonioni was ready, at the relatively ripe age of 30, to begin working professionally in the cinema. First he wrote a script which was for various reasons not produced, then worked with Rossellini, Ugo Betti, and three other writers on the script of Rossellini's *Un Pilota Ritorna* (1942), and the same year worked on the script of the costume drama *I Due Foscari* and was assistant to Enrico Fulchignoni in its direction. Contacts he made during the shooting of *I Due Foscari* brought him a contract to go to France and assist Carné on *Les Visiteurs du Soir*, a Franco-Italian co-production in which he was to represent the Italian production company (actually, his contract named him as co-director, but, he says, he never dared reveal this to Carné). After this, called back to Italy for his military service, he managed to persuade the Luce Institute to finance a short documentary on the life of the fishermen of the Po River, *Gente del Po*. In this he depicted with ruthless objectivity the miserable lives of the poor, as well as evoking vividly the flat, mournful countryside of the area near his native Ferrara, to which he would later return in his feature *Il Grido*. The film had a slight thread of narrative, following the progress of a barge downstream, and was intended to run about twenty-five minutes. But unfortunately the Italian campaign intervened before Antonioni could edit the material he had shot, and when he was able finally to gain access to it at the end of the war about half of it proved to have been irrevocably damaged by damp, so that the film as finally edited and shown in 1947 represents only a fragment of the work originally intended.

The Allied invasion of Italy and its aftermath put a virtual end to cinematic activity there for some time, and Antonioni made his living instead by translating from the French books such as Gide's *La Porte Étroite* and Chateaubriand's *Atala*. He also wrote regularly on films in *L'Italia Libera, Film Rivista, Film d'Oggi*, and *Cinema*, and took up his career as a screen-writer again with two scripts commissioned by Visconti – *Furore*, about an all-women orchestra which goes to play at the front, and *The Trial of Maria Tarnowska*, based on a *cause célèbre* which took place in Venice in 1911. Neither ever reached the screen, unlike de Santis's *Caccia Tragica*, on the script of which he collaborated in 1947. In 1948, after editing what was left of *Gente de Po*, Antonioni was able to begin directing again on his own account, still on documentaries, and made six more shorts in the next two years. One of them, *La Funivia del Faloria*, a commissioned film about a cable-car which connects Cortina d'Ampezzo and Mount Faloria, he regarded entirely as a diversion, though even here there is something quite personal about the way Antonioni turns it into a highly subjective evocation of his own feelings of vertigo on the roof of the car. Two of the others, *Sette Canne un Vestito* (1949) and *La Villa dei Mostri* (1950), are straight documentaries, the latter about the fantastic sculptures in the gardens of a villa at Bomarzo, near Viterbo, and the former about the manufacture of rayon, notable mainly as a piece of virtuoso editing far removed from Antonioni's usual style.

But the other three shorts of this period are far more representative of Antonioni's interests and his personal point of view. The first of them, *N.U.* (*Nettezza Urbana*) is an evocation of a day in the life of those who keep the city clean, following them and their work through from dawn to dusk, when the last street-cleaners make their way home. The second, *L'Amorosa Menzogna*, is about the shabby lives of the 'stars' of *fumetti*, those photo-romances beloved of the less-educated Italian reader and most familiar to foreigners from Fellini's *Lo Sciecco Bianco*, which Antonioni helped to write in 1952 (at about the same time that he was himself directing *La Signora Senza Camelie*, which also concerns the seamy underside of the entertainment industry). And the third, *Superstizione*, takes as its subject the survivals of witchcraft and necromancy in the Roman Marshes. In each of these films the accent is, far more than in most documentaries, placed fairly and squarely on the people: the street-sweeper, the hopefuls on the fringes of show-business, the camera-shy old men and women of Camarino weaving their spells (camera-shy with some reason, since their practices are still illegal in modern Italy). And the thing which all these people have in common, as pictured by Antonioni, is their solitude: the sorcerers are as alone in the modern world as the forgotten fisherman of the Po: the 'performers' in the photo-romances are pathetic in their hopeless ambitions and set apart by the tawdry glamour which surrounds them in the eyes of their equally foolish and pathetic readers; even with the street-cleaners, who do a job of work just like anyone else and no doubt lead perfectly ordinary family lives, the emphasis is placed rather on their aspect as 'forgotten men', moving unnoticed about the city streets, doing the most squalid work for a populace which asks only to remain unconscious of their existence. To match this view of life the style of photography adopted is correspondingly bare and unadorned, avoiding strong contrasts and concentrating on the middle range of greys to evoke the misty banks of the Po, the cheerless Marshes, the empty streets of Rome at dawn and nightfall. Already, without being more than a little wise after the event, we can see the hand of the mature Antonioni at work in these small but very characteristic works.

After completing *La Villa dei Mostri* in 1950 Antonioni was able at last, at the age of 38, to begin work on his first feature film, having, according to his own account, found a Turin businessman to finance it less because he liked the subject himself than because he was impressed by Antonioni's passionate determination to make it. And so *Cronaca di un Amore* went into production, in the proper neo-realist manner, in the streets of Milan. But that is about all of neo-realism it had in it; otherwise, right from the first, Antonioni showed his independence of the style then dominant in the Italian cinema, and in which as a documentarist he had been nurtured. Most obviously, he forsook the working-class milieux which were almost a *sine qua non* of the neo-realist film, and turned his attention instead to the prosperous middle classes which had been more or less taboo as a subject of serious film-making in Italy since the dominance of the much-despised 'white telephone' school of the 1930s. They were, however, the class that Antonioni knew best, and in a way the film could be regarded as a logical extension of neo-realist principles to hitherto more or less unexplored territory. But in other respects the film deviated markedly from the neo-realist norm. It used professional actors, for one thing; its social criticism, if there at all, was present only very indirectly, by implication, the story concentrating with almost Racinian intensity and single-mindedness on the relationships of the three central characters, whose social situation is only a small, relatively insignificant element in the plot; and above all the film is made in a highly conscious, rigorously disciplined style about as far distant as can be imagined from neo-realism's preoccupation at the time with making feature films look as much as possible like newsreels. Even in this first full-length film it was clear at once that a major new talent had arrived, already mature and highly personal in his means of self-expression.

The most remarkable element of originality in the film's making can perhaps be indicated in Antonioni's own words (in a radio interview published by *La Table Ronde*):

> My habit of directing in long shots was born the first day I began work on *Cronaca di un Amore*. The camera rooted to its stand at once upset me: I felt paralysed, as though I was forcibly prevented from following closely the only thing that interested me in the film, the characters. The next day I had a dolly [a small platform on wheels] brought in and set about following my characters round, until I felt the need to pass to another shot. This was to me the best way of achieving truth, reality: to get right inside the scene just as in real life. I have never been able to put together a scene except with the camera under my hand, any more than I have been able to make my actors speak according to a scene which was already completely worked out in advance. Right from the first I felt the need to see the characters, even to their simplest gestures, after everything had been said, after all the answers had been given and there was nothing left but the consequences of what had happened in each one's soul. . . .

The type of cinema which resulted from all this has been labelled 'anti-cinema', on the model of the 'anti-play' and the 'anti-novel'. And in a sense this is true; Antonioni's approach to film-making contradicts a lot which at the time of his appearance was taken as axiomatic. It is against the neo-realistic concept of cinema, certainly, but it is also against, for example, Eisenstein's earlier concept of a cinema built on dynamic montage (to which, despite a general unwillingness to practise it, cinema intellectuals continue to pay a sort of lip-service) and equally against his later concept based on histrionic performance. It is against, too, the concept of the cinema as a bag of tricks, most influentially put about by the cinema's arch-magician Orson Welles and seldom without powerful advocates, from Ingmar Bergman to Akira Kurosawa. Instead, what we are given is a quietist, interior cinema such as few have attempted in the past – most notably Carl Dreyer and Robert Bresson: it is a concept of cinema very similar to the concept of theatre put forward by Maeterlinck, who like Antonioni was not interested in external action but only in soul-states.

However, all this is rather to anticipate. In *Cronaca di un Amore* the procedures of Antonioni's later films are just hinted at, though clearly and unmistakably. The scenario is original, like those of all Antonioni's films with the debatable exception of *Le Amiche* ('freely inspired by' a Pavese novella), and already in many respects characteristic. It concerns a prosperous Milan industrialist who, worried about the fidelity of his wife, Paola, after seven years of marriage, hires a detective to look into her past. The inquiry reveals that she was previously involved with a young man called Guido, whose fiancée was killed at that time in a lift accident, in circumstances which attached some suspicion to the couple. Finding out that the inquiry is going on, Guido comes to Milan, seeks out Paola, whom he has not seen since her marriage, and despite the present difference in their situations the affair begins again. Paola wants to dispose of her husband, and persuades Guido; they plan a murder, but on his way to the scene of the intended crime the husband dies in a car accident, perhaps deliberately. His death, apparently just what they wanted, ends by separating the lovers for ever, since now they feel guilty of the deaths of two innocent bystanders and in their guilt come near to hating each other.

The plot, it will be seen, has elements of melodrama – a sort of *bourgeois Postman Always Rings Twice* – but at each crucial moment turns aside from it. Though the husband hires detectives to spy on his wife, there is nothing for them to find until, paradoxically, the fact of the inquiry brings her and Guido together again. Although the thought that it would be convenient if Guido's fiancée were dead may have crossed Paola's mind in the past, and now she and Guido deliberately plot her husband's death, in fact they are directly responsible for the death of neither. They feel responsible, though, and that is enough if we are concerned not with external action but with states of the soul: what matters is not what actually happens, but what is felt to have happened; the plot is the barest framework for an entirely internal psychological drama. To achieve this Antonioni already makes extensive use in this film of settings and props to convey states of mind. The characters are rarely if ever seen in large close-up, isolated from their context, and the contexts are never merely neutral backgrounds (or, to be more precise, neutral only if their neutrality itself serves some dramatic function, as when Paolo and Guido meet in the open country as a neutral ground between the two very different worlds to which they now belong). The casual luxury of Paola's present home, the furs, the jewels, the chandeliers, contrast strongly with Guido's gloomy, sordid room, which is still all he can afford. Occasionally there are moments of overt symbolism – the scene, for instance, where Paola and Guido plot her husband's murder, standing on a bridge while behind them men can be seen raking mud from the drained canal. But such obvious effects are not usually to Antonioni's taste. The colour is as a rule more delicately applied: in the washed-out greys of the rain-soaked urban streets and the sodden countryside, in all the paraphernalia of modern living, which are not there to make any specific point (his obsession with cars, for instance, has no precise analysable significance), not even to say 'life is like this, take it or leave it', but simply to shadow forth the mental world of the characters.

The revolutionary nature of *Cronaca di un Amore* passed at the time more or less unnoticed, even though Pierre Billard has subsequently called it 'L'a.b.c. du jeune cinéma moderne'. Certainly its originality is not of the showy kind, and though many critics (many, that is, of the few who got to see it, since it has never yet been publicly shown in this country, and received only a rather desultory distribution in France) recognized at once in Antonioni a new stylist of unusual finesse and distinction, few recognized in precisely what way. The film was generally taken, understandably if not altogether forgivably, as an elegant variation on a familiar triangle theme, and pious hopes were expressed for what this clearly talented director might do next.

These hopes were not immediately realized. For one thing, though the critic could hardly be expected to guess this from the evidence of *Cronaca di un Amore* alone, Antonioni's method of dealing with his subject-matter needs room: it is never the story which interests him, but the attitudes of his characters towards what is happening to them, and for this a slow pace and a fair amount of elbow-room are essential. But two of the works which followed were in short-story form: *I Vinti* (*The Vanquished*), which is made up of three short stories about youth in France, Italy, and Britain respectively, and *Tentato Suicidio*, a sketch in an episodic film based on an idea by Zavattini, *Amore in Citta*. *Tentato Suicidio* stands in any case outside Antonioni's main line of development. It is an essay in pure neo-realism (the only episode in *Amore in Citta* to put Zavattini's ideals literally into practice), reconstructing three unsuccessful suicide attempts by talking to the would-be victims and those involved in each attempt and its prevention, and getting them to re-enact the parts they played in real life. The result as it stands in the finished film is obviously truncated and unsatisfactory (for example, two of the characters to whom we are introduced at the beginning do not reappear to tell their stories as promised); accounts vary as to whether this was because the sketch was originally too long for its place in the whole film, or simply that the two who were dropped were just too bad to be used. Why ever it was, however, we need not waste any time on the film except to remark that the inquiry (suggested by the film's producers) seems to have stirred Antonioni's interest in and clarified his ideas on suicide, which had already appeared (possible or attempted) in *Cronaca di un Amore* and *La Signora senza camelie* and was to play an even more important role in *Le Amiche*, *Il Grido* and (putatively) *L'Avventura*.

I Vinti, which Antonioni made immediately after *Cronaca di un Amore*, is altogether more interesting, in the way that major failures of major artists often are. It demonstrates clearly that he has no aptitude whatever for telling simple action stories without psychological profundity, and moreover that he has precious little aptitude either for direct social criticism in the neo-realist tradition. The three stories are all apparently meant to demonstrate something about 'modern youth' (the version intended for England, though never shown publicly, is improbably entitled *Youth and Perversion* and begins with a lengthy 'commercial' about the 'lost generation' of modern youth, accompanied by a montage of newspaper clippings; how far if at all this reflects Antonioni's original intentions I have not been able to discover). But the main thing they demonstrate in fact is that the generation is not so much lost as merely stupid. In the first sketch some (very mature-looking) teenagers, gullible beyond belief, accept the tall stories of a schoolboy who claims to be the leader of an international gang, lure him on to a country picnic and murder him for his money, only to find out that he hasn't got any and be arrested before they can even hide the weapon. In the original script of the second episode set in Italy, a young post-war Fascist's plots misfire and he is dismissed from the party, only to kill himself in such a way that he appears to have been a martyr to the cause. When this was rejected by the Government department responsible for film finance another script was cooked up at the last minute, involving a young murderer who panics and goes through a sort of half-hour parody of *Odd Man Out* before dying of his wounds just in front of a police car advancing on him. The third episode is that set in England: it concerns a young and unknown writer who commits a murder (of an elderly prostitute, on a common) to make himself known as the discoverer of the body and write his own story in the papers; when the interest from this dies down he confesses and again finds some of the limelight he craves.

Of the three episodes the British is, rather surprisingly, the best. It is well acted (by Peter Reynolds and Fay Compton, of all people) and apart from touches of unconscious humour in the rather bizarre English dialogue it has a genuine element of *comédie noire* which is rather appealing and up to now virtually unique in Antonioni's work. The Italian episode is, perhaps expectedly in the circumstances, a dead loss, wholly pointless and doing badly the sort of thing dozens of hacks could without difficulty do quite well. The French episode again suffers from the sheer pointlessness and patent improbability of its story as a story, though it does have one or two flashes of imagination. But for the most part, lacking any possibility of psychological subtlety in the scripts, Antonioni falls back in desperation on making the backgrounds for these unlikely events as exquisitely evocative as possible. The French countryside is lovingly observed with the sharp eye of a well-trained outsider, and there is great pleasure to be derived from seeing the grimy London suburbs of the last episode, which are shown with something of the excitement of new discovery that distinguished René Clément's *Knave of Hearts* a few years earlier. But that, finally, is not much to get from an Antonioni film, and *I Vinti* must be regretfully written off as his only really bad mistake.

Much, much better is his next feature film, *La Signora senza camelie*. At about the same time that he made it he was working also on the script of Fellini's *Lo Sciecco Bianco*, which takes up the subject of the *fumetti* and their stars first broached cinematically in Antonioni's earlier documentary *L'Amorosa Menzogna*, and *La Signora senza camelie* reflects a similar interest in the unglamorous realities of that show-business which is to most outsiders a glamorous dream-world. It is the story of the rise and fall of a star, though again told almost entirely in psychological terms: she does not rise very high, she does not (to anyone but herself) fall very low, but her progression within the film is complete and soul-destroying. When we first see her she is waiting anxiously for the end of a sneak preview of the film in which she has her first featured role. It is a success, and meanwhile she goes on starring in a cheap cloak-and-dagger epic, with lots of sex and violence. But the producer who discovered her has fallen in love with her, rushes her into marriage (with the assistance of her parents), and then decides that she must not finish the film she is making or make any others like it; she must become a good actress in quality films. So the ex-shop-girl finds herself playing St Joan. The film is a disaster, and her producer-husband is nearly bankrupt as a result. Rejecting for the moment the eager advances of a diplomat out for what he can get, Clara determines to do what she can to save the situation, and after succumbing to the diplomat while her husband is unsuccessfully trying to commit suicide, she decides to complete the film her husband did not want her to finish. The film is a success, but Clara breaks with her husband and then, realization of his true character at last dawning, with the diplomat. She is persuaded to ask her husband for the star part in his new film, but he cruelly rejects her as unsuitable, and at the end we see her going back to star in another tatty sex-and-violence piece, and then presumably another and another, as long as youth and sex-appeal last, because that's all she knows how to do.

The film has weaknesses – one of them is the casting of Lucia Bose, the heroine of *Cronaca di un Amore*, as Clara, since she is evidently too classy and intelligent (the part was first destined for Gina Lollobrigida, and then for Sophia Loren, but neither was available at the time) – but it is still well worth collecting. The interesting thing about it, as about *Cronaca di un Amore*, is the way Antonioni takes a story which might easily become novelettish, and makes something much more out of it. First of all he more or less drains it of obvious external action: practically all the principal happenings are on the fringes of the story, or right off-screen. Clara's success in the first film, her disastrous failure as Joan of Arc, and her new success in *La Donna senza destino* (significant title!) are all barely suggested, though each marks a turning-point of sorts in her external career: the first is left as we see a timid Clara joining the other film-people in a darkened cinema and a radiant Clara up there on the screen singing, not very well, a jolly popular song; the second goes no further than one or two ribald comments from the audience before Clara leaves; the third is retailed at a distance by her mother on the telephone. Always what most other directors would play as big scenes are here consistently played down. Similarly Clara's change of heart over Naldo, the diplomat, takes place off-screen; after repulsing him until he is ready to give up she suddenly turns up on his doorstep, saying simply: 'Don't ask me any questions.' And her husband's suicide attempt also takes place off-screen; we just find out about it afterwards, as a *fait accompli*.

Instead, all the significant action is internal: it is the progress of Clara towards a clear realization of how impossible her situation is. She comes gradually to know how little she does know, to see how she can never really be anything but the little shop-girl she started out as. She will never be an actress, never a really important star, and her career depends entirely on her looks, which won't last for ever. She has no resources within herself: when first married to a rich man she does not know what to do, and the only thing she enjoys is buying materials for the house, since at least materials are something she knows about from her days behind the counter. After she has broken with both husband and lover she has nothing and no one to fall back on; like Blanche Du Bois she is always dependent on the kindness of strangers – on the co-star who tells her to work on her acting, as that is all that can help her when youth vanishes; on the sympathetic director who gives her practical if not very cheering advice. And when at last she determines on what she must do, it amounts to a spiritual suicide just as complete and effective as a physical one; with her eyes open she throws her life away, or at least she would if she had ever really had one in the first place.

To mirror this internal action Antonioni brilliantly evokes the most depressing side of the cinema industry as a background. Even Clara's successes are made tawdry, from the run-down try-out cinema in the suburbs where her first film is shown, to the opening of *La Donna senza destino*, the foyer spattered with vast, hopefully provocative pictures of Clara for her mother to look on with simple pride. Moreover, all the resources of the pathetic fallacy are called in for the final sequences: the drive to *Cinecitta* is accomplished in gloomiest mid-winter; the studio itself is a quagmire; and the film for which Clara finally signs is represented by a group of bedraggled Arabian Nights extras huddling thankfully round a small stove amid the sagging tents of an overworked desert set. Even at its best film-making is shown as a dreary job of work, and at its worst as almost unbearably depressing. By comparison with *Cronaca di un Amore* and even more with the films which come after, *La Signora senza camelie* is a slight, fairly superficial piece, but the image it creates of a film man's disenchantment with the film industry stays, even when the rest has begun to fade, powerfully present in the mind.

La Signora senza camelie did not have much commercial success in Italy (it was hardly shown anywhere else) and for a couple of years, until 1955, Antonioni was relatively idle, directing only the episode of *L'Amore in Citta* and producing a documentary for an international organization on overpopulation and migration in Italy, *Uomini in Piu*. In 1955 he finally managed to get backing for another feature, and though his troubles were by no means over (at one point money gave out and shooting was suspended for some months) the film was actually completed with little or no sign of its vicissitudes. This was *Le Amiche*, by far Antonioni's most mature and accomplished work up to that time, fulfilling the promise of *Cronaca di un Amore* and establishing him as an important figure in international cinema even before *L'Avventura* made his name a household word with intelligent (and merely modish) filmgoers the world over. As has already been remarked, it is the only one of Antonioni's films which has a literary origin – a short novel by Cesare Pavese, *Tra donne sole*. But, as Pierre Leprohon acutely remarks in his book on Antonioni, by a curious paradox it is in many ways the least Pavesian of Antonioni's films. The parallel between Pavese and Antonioni has often been insisted on: perhaps too far, in that though there are many important resemblances between them (it has justly been remarked that Pavese's statement 'The whole problem of life is this: how to break out of one's own solitude and communicate with others' could equally well be the motto of all Antonioni's films) there are also many important divergences. Antonioni's remark 'Pavese committed suicide; I'm still alive' points to only one of them, but far more important, considering Antonioni's work in general and *Le Amiche* in particular, is the difference in their attitude towards women.

In practically all of Pavese's writing, and certainly in *Tra donne sole*, there is evidence of a profound distrust of women amounting at times almost to misogyny; in all Antonioni's films, and most significantly in *Le Amiche*, where on the whole women are shown at their worst, we find a profound sympathy and devotion. In fact, like Racine, Antonioni builds nearly all his dramas round the female character, and seems least certain when called on to make a detailed study of a man. So in *Le Amiche* it turns out that in the course of making his free adaptation (with the help of two woman writers, Suso Cecchi D'Amico and Alba De Cespedes) Antonioni has taken a group of characters from Pavese and fitted them into an articulated plot of which there are only hints in the original, and in the process has tended to make man the villain and blame man and his treatment of woman for most of the faults in his female characters. For they do, it must be insisted, have faults: Antonioni may be on their side, but he is not a naïve apologist.

The 'friends' are a mixed bunch, ranging from the almost wholly sympathetic Nene to the almost wholly unsympathetic Momina. Somewhere in between is the central character, Clelia, through whose eyes in effect we see them. Arriving in Turin to manage a new dress-shop, she becomes involved in an abortive suicide attempt on the part of Rosetta, a rich and idle young woman, and through that gets to know a group of Rosetta's aimless friends. Most influential among them is Momina, married, separated from her husband and living on a generous allowance which gives her power to pursue her own pleasures and regulate the little intrigues of her circle. Then there are Nene, a potter, and her painter lover, Lorenzo, with whom Rosetta proceeds to have a hopeless, impossible affair – hopeless because Nene is really the centre of his life, and when she threatens to leave him he at once brutally rejects Rosetta, driving her to another suicide attempt, this time successful. Among the other characters involved are another girl, Mariella, perhaps the most empty-headed of them all, and two men, Cesare, the architect of Clelia's shop, with whom Momina is having a casual affair, and Carlo, Cesare's struggling assistant,

C.E.–E

between whom and Clelia an attraction springs up, though it is fated, like that of Paola and Guido in *Cronaca di un Amore*, by the present difference in their social status. Finally the three parallel stories work themselves out together when Lorenzo returns to Nene, who sacrifices her career for him, and Clelia puts her job in jeopardy by denouncing Momina in public for her part in Rosetta's death, only to seize on the chance of taking up her career again when offered, even if it means rejecting love in the shape of Carlo.

To tell like this the plot (if one can properly use the term at all) sounds impossible, complicated, and confused – and even so I have left out several twists and turns. But as Antonioni handles it it is a model of clarity and compression. His art can be seen to particular advantage in the three big scenes at the film's centre: the trip to the seaside, Momina's tea party, and the dinner party Clelia throws for her intimates, and from which Rosetta rushes off to her death. The most elaborate of these is the first, which gathers together nine characters (all those mentioned except Carlo, and with Mariella's current boy-friend Franco and her brother Vincenzo added for good measure) on a disastrous outing to the grey, wind-swept sea-shore; it is, indeed, one of the most remarkable 'set-pieces' in all Antonioni, and the more so for not at once obtruding itself as such. While one is watching it it seems quite casual, carrying on the manœuvres of the plot and throwing light on the state of mind of the characters naturally, making full but not too extravagant use of an atmospheric location and so on; it is only when one comes to consider it afterwards, and see the film several times, that the brilliance of its organization becomes fully apparent. The sequence has been exhaustively analysed by Ian Cameron in his monograph on Antonioni, and there is little that can be said about it without repeating what he says there. Not only is the whole scene so meticulously organized that the exact placing of any character as they move constantly in and out of frame, group, scatter and re-group could be pin-pointed at almost any given moment but, much more importantly, the character who is to be at the centre of our interest from moment to moment infallibly is, and the relations between the characters, particularly the isolation of Rosetta and the semi-detachment of Clelia (the only one who really wants to help her) and Lorenzo (who is interested in her for his own disreputable reasons), are graphically indicated by compositions and camera-movements which appear perfectly uncalculated, even unthinking, and yet prove on closer examination to have as well a precise quasi-symbolic significance.

The main criticism which has been urged against *Le Amiche*, certainly in terms of construction, exact matching of visual style to content, direction of actors and the rest one of Antonioni's most completely successful films, is that in it he has sentimentalized Pavese. Little as this would matter – even if it were true – to our judgement of the film as such, the suggestion is perhaps worth looking at more closely, since it has a lot to do with how one takes all Antonioni's works. He is, as has been said, not only inclined to make women the protagonists of his films, but also passionately on the side of women, and this naturally suggests to a predominantly male-orientated criticism that at bottom his subjects are women's-magaziny. Also, it may be remarked, in *Le Amiche* he for the first time allows in a ray of hope; Clelia's potential happiness with Carlo may be impossible, because even if she did once come from the same background as him she now belongs to a different world, but Nene is willing to sacrifice the artistic success offered to her and not to Lorenzo in order that they shall stay together and have at least a chance of happiness. In general a writer, dramatist or film-maker who centres his creation on woman can maintain a reputation for seriousness only if his view of life is unequivocally tragic, but without even this refuge, where is Antonioni then?

I personally (for what little that may be worth) can see no reason why a major artist should not be optimistic and find women as fruitful a subject of contemplation as men. However, if one feels otherwise there will be from now on less and less to hold on to in Antonioni's work. The plot-framework, slight but still existent in *Cronaca di un Amore* and *La Signora senza camelie*, is dissolved by the time we get to *Le Amiche* to a web of fine lines of which we are permitted to see a portion bounded, pretty arbitrarily, by Clelia's arrival in Turin at the beginning and her departure at the end. In every way what happens between Rosetta's two suicide attempts is an irrelevance, and almost nothing is changed at the end by her few more weeks of life. Nothing changes Momina, Clelia is back where she started, and so are Nene and Lorenzo except perhaps with a little more hope for the future. In the films which come after *Le Amiche* Antonioni progressively cuts down plot in the normal sense of the term to the absolute minimum represented by *L'Eclisse*, and as he does so the critic, deprived of any possible assistance from the films' literary values, is thrown back increasingly and (for most critics it seems) disconcertingly on his response to the films as cinema and his intuitive sympathy with Antonioni's approach and subject-matter.

I am not saying that this sort of sympathy is a *sine qua non* for appreciating Antonioni's later work (though there is no denying that with him as with any artist it helps), but simply that when the subject-matter is left, literarily speaking, so naked it becomes very easy for the viewer insensitive or hostile to Antonioni's strictly cinematic art to isolate the necessarily very thin plot-content (thin, again, in its purely literary aspect, what can be put down on paper) and then say: 'If that's all he's using this great battery of cinematic know-how to say, is it really worth the trouble?' The answer to that is that, if the solid literary values of a traditional 'well-written script' are what you are looking for in the cinema it is probably not worth the trouble: Antonioni's films (any of them, but particularly from *Le Amiche* on) are not for you. By the time we come to *Le Amiche* there is no doubt that Antonioni has passed decisively beyond the stage at which a writer-director's work can be compart-mentalized: this much is scripting, and then the director sets out to realize on the screen what the writer has put on paper. Indeed, he had passed this stage already with *Cronaca di un Amore*, but in *Le Amiche* the fact that he has done so becomes inescapable. From here on the scripts come to have virtually no meaning in themselves: though they have all been published it would be impossible to gain any adequate idea of the films from them; they are at best the scant *aide-mémoire* of someone who already has something very like the finished film complete in his mind before he starts work.

This development gets well under way in Antonioni's next film after *Le Amiche*, *Il Grido* (1957). This is perhaps the most con-troversial of all Antonioni's films, opinion ranging from those (I am one of them) who consider it, in spite of its many refinements, a relative failure, and those who share Pierre Leprohon's view that it is Antonioni's masterpiece. The story is episodic and repetitive. Aldo, a simple, unthinking workman, has been living for some years with Irma, whom he cannot marry because she already has a husband, though he long ago deserted her and went to Australia.

At the news of the husband's death Aldo expects her to marry him, but she won't; she no longer loves him and wants to marry another man. He beats her in public and leaves the village, suddenly lost and disorientated, taking with him Rosina, his and Irma's small daughter. On his travels he makes three major attempts to rebuild his life with another woman, and many attempts to find a new job to replace the responsible skilled job in a sugar refinery which he has left. But nothing he can do is any good; he cannot forget Irma and he cannot put down new roots. First on his wanderings he looks up Elvira, an old flame, and stays for a while with her and her sister, but Elvira knows he has come back to her only because Irma has left him, and her sister complicates things further by making drunken advances to him, so he moves on. Next he falls in with Virginia, who owns a petrol station. He soon becomes her lover and fits in quite well, but Virginia regards Rosina and her own senile father as nuisances and when she has got the old father shut up in a home makes Aldo send Rosina back to Irma after Rosina has come upon Aldo and herself making love. When Rosina leaves without speaking to him, Aldo promptly leaves Virginia and gets a job on a dredger. From this he gets involved with Andreina, who works in the rice-fields when there is work going and otherwise gets by with a bit of part-time prostitution. With her he finds some sort of happiness, but it is fated: when the waters rise their home on the mudbank will be submerged, they are both out of work, and though violently jealous Aldo is in no position to dictate to Andreina when she gets a meal by going to bed with the local restaurant-owner. So again, he sets off, this time back the way he came, and after seeing Virginia briefly on the way he arrives back at Goviano, the town he came from, in the middle of a riot over a projected American air-base. Catching sight of Rosina he follows her home and looking through the window sees Irma happy with a new baby. He goes to the refinery and climbs the tower where he used to work; from this, before the eyes of Irma, he falls, or jumps (exactly which is left unclear), and is killed.

It is easy to feel that there is something wrong with *Il Grido* (in fact, I find it difficult to understand exactly why its admirers admire it), but much more difficult to say what is wrong with it. Superficially it has most of the qualities which help to make Antonioni's other work so distinguished: the sensitive response to

landscape and weather, the unobtrusive reinforcements of points
made in dialogue and action about the relations between the characters by composition and camera-movement. But still something is
missing, something which makes this, the only Antonioni film to be
centred on a male character, the one which comes nearest to justifying the criticism of him as a purveyor of elevated woman's-
magazine stuff. Perhaps the basic reason for this is that, unlike any
other Antonioni film, *Il Grido* does not convey any really close
involvement on the director's part. It strikes one much more as a
film he decided to make than a film he had to make. For one thing,
it takes him outside his usual milieu – that of the urban upper
middle class – for a story of working-class life in the country. It all
has rather the air of a demonstration that he could do something
different – a feeling perhaps borne out by the amount of pre-
liminary research on life in the Po valley we are told he did.
Research or no research, these workers and peasants do not carry
the same sort of conviction as, say, the rich idlers of *Le Amiche*.

The effect is compounded by some spectacularly improbable
casting, with three of the leading roles played by non-Italians and a
fourth by Alida Valli, an excellent actress, but hardly anybody's
idea of the girl next door. Actually one of the foreigners, the English
Lynn Shaw, fits in very well as Andreina, perhaps because she is
not an actress but a stripteaser, and was therefore all the more
likely to take Antonioni's curious mode of direction, which requires
actors for the most part not to act in the ordinary sense of the term,
but simply to do what they are told without understanding why.
The fact that the other three principals, Steve Cochran, Betsy
Blair, and Alida Valli, were not used to this treatment and did not
take kindly to it may well be one of the reasons why their performances are less satisfactory than those in most Antonioni films, but
even if they had been more amenable to this discipline it is difficult
to imagine that they could have been convincing as simple working
men and women, especially Italian. Antonioni himself recognizes
that the acting in *Il Grido* is not really satisfactory; otherwise he
has not committed himself to any view of it in public. It is quite
possible that personally he is attached to the film, and that it corresponds to some need in him at the time he made it. If so, however,
this has all been lost in the finished film, and all that really remains
is some remarkably beautiful photography of the Po landscape in

winter and a number of extraordinary moments, such as that when Aldo and Rosina come upon a group of lunatics quietly exercising in a field.

So though *Il Grido* marks a decisive stage in Antonioni's rejection of plot – which is replaced by a string of incidents all reinforcing the same point: that Aldo cannot forget Irma and cannot start again – the results are not immediately very happy. Nor, presumably, was Antonioni happy with his work in 1958 on *Tempest*, a spectacle based on Pushkin, and the rubbishy *Sign of the Gladiator*, since his name is not on the credits of either. In his next film, *L'Avventura* (1960), though, he solved his problems, both artistic and commercial, with spectacular success. Oddly enough, for a film which was to make its director one of the biggest names in international cinema more or less overnight, it was his most unconventional and uncompromising film so far: long, slow and with virtually no story at all – indeed, not only cutting plot to a minimum but also wilfully refusing to complete the story it apparently set out to tell. Everything, in fact, calculated to infuriate the average audience, and at Cannes, where it nearly caused a riot, this appeared to be exactly what it was going to do. And yet it became a big commercial as well as critical success all over the world. Why? Partly, of course, because it was, with *Le Amiche*, Antonioni's most achieved film to date. But I think it owed its really phenomenal popular success to the one obvious thing it had that *Le Amiche* lacked: Monica Vitti.

With Monica Vitti, Antonioni was lucky enough to chance on the ideal mediator between the difficult creator and his public: a great star. She may well be an actress, too – she has appeared successfully on the Italian stage in a variety of roles, among them Sally Bowles in *I am a Camera*, and is particularly noted as a comedienne – but the way Antonioni directs her she might as well not be. She appears to follow his instruction precisely, but brings to her appearances that extra indefinable something ('An Italian Garbo!' cry the popular papers in unison) which forces an audience to watch with fascinated absorption whenever she is on the screen. This enables her to form a bridge between Antonioni and his audience by giving emotional immediacy to something which otherwise might seem – and has seemed, even to fairly sympathetic observers – intellectually fascinating but emotionally arid.

But, the question now arises, was what Antonioni was trying to do in *L'Avventura* all that obscure anyway? The fact that to us, at only a few years' remove from the film, it does not seem particularly obscure is largely a measure of the influence Antonioni has been exerting on us meanwhile. Let us look again at the film's 'story'. A group of rich, restless, discontented people go on a boat trip to a rocky islet off the Italian coast, among them Anna, an heiress in the middle of an unsatisfactory affair with a weak and dissolute architect, Sandro; Claudia, Anna's best friend; and Sandro himself. In the course of the day Anna disappears. An accident? Suicide? Has she perhaps just run away? The rest of the party search every inch of the islet, much concerned, and then drift away; the only ones to pursue the search on the mainland, following up various clues and rumours, are Sandro and Claudia, but they never find out any more, and we never know what happened to Anna. The story of the quest gradually becomes a study of the impossibility of remembering: the attraction between Sandro and Claudia, already hinted at before Anna disappeared, becomes the dominant subject, and as they continue to search for Anna, more and more just as a matter of form, we follow the development of the affair between them along to Sandro's first betrayal of Claudia with someone else and Claudia's forgiveness of him in the cold dawn, Anna now at last wholly forgotten.

There are other strands of plot, or at least other recurrent characters, notably an older married couple who are on the yacht to begin with and whose bitter relationship, strewn with insults and infidelities, provides a warning ironical counterpoint to the awakening passion of Claudia and Sandro for each other. But all this taken into consideration, it does not add up to a plot as the term would normally have been understood in the cinema in 1960. For the first half-hour or so Anna is a central character and we are led to believe that this is going to be the story of her relationship with Sandro, presumably with Claudia as the third side of the triangle. But if this is, in fact, the subject of the film, it is so in the last way we would expect: Anna remains a presence throughout the developing affair of Sandro and Claudia, a point of reference, an excuse, a reproach; while the search for her is gradually dropped on a physical level, and slips from the consciousness of the other characters, it continues indefinitely in their minds, and to that sort of search there can be no end, which is why it is unthinkable that the film's 'story' should be tied up neatly at the end with definite news of Anna's fate.

All this is perhaps obvious after the event, but by no means so evident at the time, to the film's first spectators. And yet it was successful in a way and to a degree that none of Antonioni's earlier, easier films had ever achieved. The reasons for this are involved and controversial, but I think some can be discerned at once. As I have said, I think the most important single factor in the film's success with a wide public is the presence of Monica Vitti in the role of Claudia. What everyone carries away unforgettably from the film is the image of Vitti, her finely boned face, her tangle of honey-blonde hair, lovingly photographed in lingering close-up registering the dawn of love, the misery of loss, the wildest *joie de vivre* or the uttermost desolation. Whether, in fact, *she* registers these emotions, or whether she is used by the director as a beautiful object placed in certain relationships, certain juxtapositions, in order that the complex whole conveys them, is a point which can be argued long and fruitlessly. In any case it does not really matter: if she is being used as a non-actor, at least she has that irreducible, indefinable necessity of an effective non-actor, screen presence. The non-actor cannot be an empty vessel; he must contribute, even if it is a purely passive contribution, something positive of himself to the film, or there will just be a hole where a presence should be: even Bresson, arch-hater of actors in the cinema, discovered this to his cost in *Pickpocket*. And Monica Vitti is undeniably one of those people who glow on the screen, who have, inexplicably but inescapably, the power to rivet attention merely by existing in front of the camera.

She, then, is one of the principal reasons why the film got over to a wider audience than Antonioni's earlier films: it does not, to put it at its lowest, require any particular intelligence to appreciate her contribution to the film. On the other hand, it must equally be said that *L'Avventura* shows more complete control of means and ends on the director's part than any of Antonioni's previous films except perhaps *Le Amiche*, and beside that masterpiece of classical concision and concentration it is a far more expansive, romantic, emotional work. All the qualities we have previously recognized and admired in Antonioni's work are evident here in full flower.

His remarkable feeling for the expressive qualities of landscape, for instance: *L'Avventura* has been slightingly dubbed 'the cinema's greatest travelogue', and in a sense one would accept the description; it is a landscape with figures in which the landscape is almost as important as the figures and certainly, as in objective correlative (to use the intellectually respectable term, rather than getting involved in the ambiguities of the pathetic fallacy), contributes enormously to our understanding of the figures placed in it.

This is true both of the indoor and of the outdoor settings. The elegant, almost too chic and contemporary flat in which Sandro lives at the beginning, the comfortable, traditional hotel room of Sandro's and Claudia's first, happiest time together, the styleless, impersonal bedroom in the more modern hotel of the last sequence, all colour significantly our view of the inhabitants and their emotional situation. But even more telling are the outdoor scenes: the departure of Anna from her father's country villa outside Rome, now caught up in the inexorable advance of blocks of modern flats striding across the countryside; the harsh volcanic landscape of the Lipari Islands where Anna disappears; the bleak hillside by the railway where Claudia and Sandro first make love; the deserted clump of boxlike, lifeless modern villas, like some mysterious shattered necropolis through which they pass on their search; the elegant, self-sufficient Baroque of Noto; the bare, remote landscape of Taoromina in which their final reconciliation is effected – all these are flawlessly chosen to give precisely the right emotional colouring to the scenes they provide the stage for.

Antonioni's ability to waste nothing, to make everything in the picture contribute positively towards the total effect, works even further in *L'Avventura*, down to the smallest details: the photographs on the wall of the rough hut on the island where the searchers take refuge for the night; Claudia considering her nose in a mirror; the bottle of ink Sandro wilfully upsets over the drawing of a young architect at Noto who reminds him of his own inadequacy; the strange paintings of the boy the wife from the older couple seduces at a villa where they are staying; the fitting-on of wigs by Claudia and the Principessa; even the sounds assembled in the intricate sea-symphony of the opening reels or the train passing in the first scene of passion between Sandro and Claudia. The film is built up with loving care from thousands of such details,

like a pointilliste painting, and yet as in a good pointilliste painting
the overall structure is never allowed to slip from mind: when one
steps back each individual dot of colour proves to have its place in
the whole composition. For though we tend to forget it in delight
over individual details, the whole composition of *L'Avventura* is
eminently satisfactory: developing with the freedom of a musical
rhapsody, it yet achieves a rare degree of emotional completeness;
we are never left for a moment doubting that Antonioni knows
where he is taking us, even if it is seldom precisely where we
expected to be taken, and the wonderful last scene, where the bare-
ness and severity of the images, the slow succession of stripped,
grey-toned long shots give a classic restraint and grandeur to something which, simply read about, might well appear sentimental and
banal, concludes the film with unassailable rightness and finality.

As well as representing the consistent achievement of various
things Antonioni had been striving for and only intermittently
managed in his other films, however, *L'Avventura* inaugurated a
new phase in his career and shows some significant departures from
his earlier technical practice; departures which become even more
significant in the light of his subsequent work. The most immediately apparent change is the considerable reduction in the role of
the travelling camera. Not that it is banished altogether: there are
still many beautiful and memorable instances, like the camera's
slow, almost furtive progress through the sinister, shuttered village,
or Claudia's walk past the silent, watching men at Noto. But in
comparison with *Le Amiche* and *Il Grido*, with their virtuoso use of
camera movement to express relationship, *L'Avventura* shows great
restraint, and a new willingness to build up effects by editing
instead of letting the action evolve unbroken in long single takes.
Only a tendency at this stage, the new technique in Antonioni's
work becomes more marked in his next film, *La Notte*, and by the
time we reach *L'Eclisse* it has become dominant.

La Notte (1961) indeed, proves in retrospect to be a transitional
work, and many of the misgivings even Antonioni's most fervent
admirers felt about it on its first appearance become clearer as they
fall into perspective. Lacking the free lyrical development of
L'Avventura, it does not achieve either the close-knit quality of
Le Amiche, though its action is rather self-consciously limited to
twenty-four hours; the result is jerky and episodic, but without the

consistency in rejecting normal narrative devices that Antonioni reaches in *L'Eclisse*. Moreover, Antonioni has not been so happy in his choice of stars as in either of the flanking films: Monica Vitti plays a supporting role, disguised in a black wig, and the two chief characters, a husband and wife whose marriage has gone stale on them, are played by Jeanne Moreau and Marcello Mastroianni, both excellent actors, but neither, it seems, able to stop acting and merely be manipulated by their director. Mastroianni, admittedly, has the additional disadvantage of carrying half the film himself, when as we have seen Antonioni is really at ease only when concentrating fairly and squarely on his female characters. On the other hand, the misfortune of casting an actor who cannot help acting is more immediately noticeable in the parts of the film devoted to the wife; almost throughout there is a feeling of weakening duplication as Jeanne Moreau acts away, very effectively, to express things which the film as a whole – the lighting, composition, the texture of the photography, the outside events which impinge on the character – does perfectly well and sufficiently for her.

It is difficult, consequently, to know how far the film would have worked with other stars – Monica Vitti and Gabriele Ferzetti, perhaps – who had already proved their receptivity to Antonioni's manner of directing. I suspect the reservation about the prominence given to the character of the husband would still stand (though again, if he had been played by a lesser star than Mastroianni perhaps he would not have had to be so prominent), but it is quite conceivable that the events on the wife's solitary walk on the outskirts of the city would not seem so arbitrary and confected if the wife herself were a more passive observer. But, for me at least, doubts remain about the whole basic premise of the film; as a demonstration of emptiness and sterility in modern life it seems altogether too rigged and contrived, and as the night wears on the director's designs on us become inartistically obvious.

Even from the beginning there are false notes. The relationship between Giovanni and Lidia, husband and wife, and the dying friend they go to visit (the husband's friend and apparently at one time the wife's lover) is clearly observed, but the husband's spectacular entanglement with a nymphomaniac in the same hospital makes little sense in relation to the rest of his character, and seems there only to make a specific point about his weakness and insecurity, which in any case he has to explain in so many words afterwards. He has just written a novel and they are on their way to a publisher's party for him; slipping away from it Lidia wanders round the edges of the city, witnessing among other things a vicious brawl on some waste-ground and a bout of heavily symbolic rocket-firing. At last she calls Giovanni, and he comes to collect her in a place where they were once happy; later that evening they go out together to a night-club which bores them both, and then on to a party given by a rich industrialist who wants to lure Giovanni into a well-paid job as a superior P.R. man. There Giovanni drifts into a brief encounter with Valentina, the industrialist's daughter, who is a curious, disenchanted creature given to brooding over her lot and recording her own literary compositions on a tape-recorder. Meanwhile Lidia is picked up by a stranger and taken off in his car as rain lashes the party-ground, but finally refuses his advances and returns to collect Giovanni. In the cold dawn they wander out and away, talking about old times, Tommaso, the dying friend (who Lidia has been told in the course of the evening is now dead), and their earlier need for and love of each other. Finally they seek refuge in physical contact, making love on the grass as the camera slowly moves away from them, because, presumably, no other sort of contact is possible between them any more.

The trouble with all this as a piece of plotting is that the effects are gained too easily. The nymphomaniac, the fight on the waste-ground, the rockets, the rainstorm at the party, are all too palpably author's devices, and not very subtle devices at that. Even in the last scene there is at least one evident falsity, when Lidia reads to Giovanni a long and impassioned letter and then when he does not remember it, tells him that he wrote it himself some years earlier; apart from any other considerations, it is so unbelievable that he would not remember such a letter at all that our belief is shattered at a vital moment and the scene irrevocably damaged.

If *La Notte* is a misfire, though, it is a very beautiful misfire. Just to look at, it is often stunning, and Antonioni marshals the elements of his imaginative world with extraordinary mastery and precision. It is a bare, cool world where clear geometrical forms, from the ultra-modern hospital where Tommaso is dying, through the chic, rather characterless flat where Giovanni and Lidia live, to the beautiful Bietti house occupied by the millionaire, are contrasted with the more conventionally romantic, natural images of Lidia's walk, especially the overgrown track and the shattered gateway where Giovanni picks her up, representing past happiness soon to be swept completely away. It would be a mistake, I think, to assume as some critics have so readily done that Antonioni must therefore be 'against' modern architecture and 'for' picturesque decay (though the film's ambiguity on this point suggests a further weakness); the backgrounds here may be clinical and impersonal because the people who live in them lead empty, sterile lives, but they are modern for purely practical, realistic reasons – because such people would live in such houses – and at least one of the buildings concerned, the millionaire's house, is in itself very beautiful, if only because he can afford what everyone is agreed to be the best.

It is worth taking up this particular point because it becomes even more important in consideration of *L'Eclisse* (1962). *L'Eclisse* I believe to be Antonioni's most striking and personal film yet. Less sensuously appealing than *L'Avventura*, less rigorously plotted than *Le Amiche*, it yet manages to fuse the romantic intensity of the one with the slightly gnomic laconicism of the other. The décors play a vital part in the film and our understanding of it, since plot is reduced to an absolute minimum and is replaced by a study of mental states performed almost entirely by the use of objective correlatives, and for these to work properly it is necessary for us to be clear about what emotional colouring they should have for us. The plot can, in fact, be disposed of in one sentence: Vittoria, a beautiful young Roman who makes her living by translation, breaks off an affair with Riccardo and shortly afterwards drifts, at first unwillingly, into another affair with Piero, her mother's energetic young stockbroker. That is all there is to it. Externally the drama is virtually non-existent; *L'Eclisse* makes *L'Avventura* seem packed with action and *La Notte* look positively melodramatic. Maeterlinck would surely have recognized in *L'Eclisse* the logical development of his dramatic theories: underneath the verbiage he is talking about the same sort of approach to drama when he writes of 'people in a room talking of the rain and the fine weather; but under this poor stuff their souls are holding such converse as no human wisdom could touch save at its peril; and this is why they have a kind of mysterious joy of their *ennui*, without knowing that which within them is aware of the laws of life, of death and of love that pass like incorruptible floods about the house'. Far from being the gloomy and depressing picture of emotional and spiritual aridity that a number of critics have chosen to regard it, *L'Eclisse* is a full-length portrait of someone vibrantly alive, with a soul more than half awakened to the full potentialities of her situation; it is the portrait of Vittoria.

This is achieved in two ways: by the remarkable performance Antonioni has extracted from Monica Vitti, and by his elaborate use of setting, climate and so on to mirror the emotions he wishes the film to express. As for Monica Vitti, it is difficult to know whether one can properly speak of a 'performance' at all; one can quite conceive that directed by anyone else but Antonioni she might seem quite unremarkable, just as Anna Karina has seemed when directed by anyone but Godard. Certainly in this film even more than in *L'Avventura* and *La Notte* Monica Vitti is used as a non-actress, an exquisite presence whose personality is used in ways of which one suspects she herself is largely unaware. But given that she has the necessary inner quality in the first place, Antonioni has reinforced it here with extraordinary skill and subtlety. His choice of settings is unerring; the bare, deserted corner by the building under construction, with its water-butt beneath the tree; the weird 1984-ish landscape of the opening sequence, with its mysterious mushroom tower outside Riccardo's house, and an affair coming painfully to its end inside; above all, the décors in which the characters live.

This is where the misapprehensions about what Antonioni is trying to do come in. If one finds his world of stark, geometrical modern architecture, of white walls scattered with photographs and abstract art, of desks and shelves littered with books and *objets trouvés*, clinical and depressing in itself, one is likely to come to all sorts of conclusions about the 'meaning' of the film (the impossibility of meaningful life in this sterile world, and all that) which do not seem to be part of Antonioni's intention at all. With each film it becomes clearer that if Antonioni is trying to make any general statement it is not about 'modern life' but about life *per se*. The world which his characters inhabit is an extension of their personalities, just as they no doubt are so many extensions of his; each lives in surroundings of his or her own choosing (there is one beautiful moment when we witness Vittoria's secret, conspiratorial joy as she unwraps a new acquisition and lovingly finds a place for it in her flat), and these surroundings play an unusually active part in the film, elucidating character, creating mood, and giving us insight into past history almost without our being aware of it. But basically, I am sure, Antonioni approves of most of his characters' taste; it is his reasons for finding them interesting which are reflected in their homes, not his reasons for finding them sterile and pitiable, though obviously the effect can work both ways, the qualities the surroundings imply can, as in *La Notte*, be negative as well as positive, just as 'modern' architecture and decoration can be good or bad.

L'Eclisse escapes the strictures I have made on *Il Grido* and *La Notte* by concentrating almost exclusively on the central female role, Vittoria, and perhaps because it does this so single-mindedly the only sequence where she is absent from the screen for some time, and when present not central – the virtuoso picture of a slump in the stock market – seems, though done with great gusto and aplomb, to go on rather too long for something which is strictly speaking irrelevant (unless, that is, we accept the contention of Alberto Moravia and one or two other left-wing Italian critics that the film is really about money as the alienating agent in modern life, which seems unlikely). Otherwise the film is entirely about Vittoria and her state of mind: the dry desolation of the opening sequence; the wild *joie de vivre* of the scene in which an acquaintance's talk and pictures of Africa bring out the primitive in her; her naïve, uncomplicated pleasure in the flight to Verona with friends; the sympathetic absorption with which she follows an old man who has lost a fortune on the exchange; the moments of hesitation in the enclosed, musty old flat of Piero's parents; the meetings by the water-butt; and above all, perhaps, in the long final sequence in which she is not seen at all, when a series of, originally, fifty-eight shots (in the released versions the sequence is slightly shortened) shows, according to Antonioni, that 'the town, material life, has devoured the living things', and reflects Vittoria's state of mind at the point where she has decided to continue her affair with Piero for whatever it may be worth to her.

This famous last sequence has been said to mean nothing, or to mean all manner of different things, and clearly lends itself to all sorts of speculation, but its basic tone, one of slightly sinister melancholy, is unmistakable, like its relevance to Vittoria's situation. It is also the most daring innovation yet in Antonioni's work, carrying his taste for abstraction to an extreme previously unmatched in any of his films. It is difficult to imagine where he can go next, since in many ways this looks very much like a *ne plus ultra*. There have been persistent rumours of his desire to turn to comedy, but for the moment this intention – if indeed he genuinely has it – has been deferred yet again in favour of a new drama, *Deserto Rosso*, which is said to be about a woman (Monica Vitti) going mad. In many ways Antonioni still remains one of the least predictable of the great figures in the modern cinema: a great innovator, not so much in the details of technique (bare compositions with solitary figures lost in great vistas of modern architecture and scenes between two characters who talk mainly with their backs to each other, to 'express alienation', were a fad of 1961–2, but that has little to do with real technical advances and their assimilation) as in his whole approach to story-continuity in the cinema, Antonioni has pursued a consistent and fairly solitary road. And yet the achievement of his films has been by no means consistent: he could not now, certainly, make a film as crude as the French and Italian episodes of *I Vinti*, but the peaks of *Le Amiche*, *L'Avventura* and *L'Eclisse* have alternated with the relative failures of *Il Grido* and *La Notte*. The distinction between triumph and disaster in his work seems to be more finely drawn than in the work of any other director of comparable stature, and every film he makes is liable to elicit in advance almost as much dread as eagerness from even his most fervent admirers – a feeling intensified by the knowledge that his years as the height of fashion are bound to be paid for in the not too distant future by a violent reaction against his work. Will *Deserto Rosso*, his first film in colour, mark the beginning of a new Antonioni? And if it does, shall we like him as much as the old? That, alas, only time can tell.

Luis Buñuel

I THINK FEW WOULD BE MOVED TO QUESTION AT ONCE
Luis Buñuel's right to inclusion in any gallery of the cinema's great
original creators. And yet, on reflection, why not? A man who says
himself, quite happily, 'Except for my three surrealist films, made
between 1928 and 1932, I have never proposed a subject to a producer. I have made only films I was given to make, turning down
those I thought too bad and trying to make something of those I
accepted. Even films like *El* and *Robinson Crusoe* were films I was
hired for.' That sounds, on the face of it, like the credo of a competent technician, acceptable enough in its way, but hardly what
we would expect to hear from a great artist. Moreover, even within
the commercial framework he has so cheerfully adapted himself to,
Buñuel has rarely been employed as a writer-director in one sense
we usually consider important: as inventor of his own subjects – in
fact, only for *Los Olvidados*, *El Bruto* and *Viridiana* has he provided
the plots himself. And, to complete the catalogue, he is and always
has been a specialist in 'invisible *mise en scène*': the hand of the
director obtrusively being 'creative' rarely if ever appears in his
films; there is nothing there for other directors to imitate; it is all
clear, just, simple, and inescapably right.

And yet still, when all this is said, the fact remains that Buñuel is
and is generally recognized to be one of the cinema's few great,
irreplaceable originals, that his films, even when they are not very
good, are unmistakably his, and that more than any other film-
maker (with the possible exception of Fellini) he manages to get on
to the screen miraculously entire his own private world, his own
individual way of looking at things, as though there were no more
obstacles to the film-maker's doing this on film than there are for
the painter alone with his canvas or the writer alone with his typewriter. How, precisely? The immediate answer is simple enough,
and Buñuel has given it himself: 'I put into my films what I want
to put in them.' And beyond that, perhaps, there lies the story of a
successful anarchist who has discovered that the greatest freedom
to practise and spread his ideas may, in fact, be found right at the

heart of the system which on principle would most vigorously oppose him: by making his Mexican films for the most part very quickly, very cheaply, on subjects given to him and corresponding roughly with those of the run-of-the-mill product – jealousy drama (*El*), rustic comedy (*Subida al Cielo*), colour adventure story (*Robinson Crusoe*), great literary love story (*Abismos de Pasion*) – he has achieved more real independence and control over his work than the majority of film-makers who fight a whole lifetime to achieve a nominally independent status, and then only find them- selves more dependent on pleasing everybody all the time than they were before.

It would be an exaggeration to say that Buñuel in his later films need please nobody but himself; in the three French co-productions he has directed, especially, he has had to make concessions which have left only one of them significantly a 'Buñuel film' at all, and that rather mutedly. But in general, considering the speed and the economy with which he films, no one expects each individual film to be a big box-office success; made as to all appearances normal contributions to the endless stream of commercial Mexican films, they can take their chance along with the rest. Recently Buñuel's enormous international reputation has also helped, offering as it does the prospect of considerable financial returns outside Mexico: it has also meant that Buñuel's last two films at time of writing, *Viridiana* and *El Angel Exterminador*, have been relatively large, expensive productions, though whether this development will ulti- mately bring more or less practical independence to Buñuel remains to be seen.

So, within the commercial system Buñuel has taken subjects which film businessmen thought commercial, and has made them his own – to such an extent that at least one producer rebelled in advance: Freddie Buache in his booklet on Buñuel quotes an enraged businessman telling him: 'We asked Buñuel for an adapta- tion of *Therèse Étienne*. Well, what he brought us wasn't *Therèse Étienne* any more; it was Buñuel!' That producer at once assigned the film to another director: fortunately Buñuel's Mexican pro- ducers have not been so fussy, or have even preferred the end result to be more Buñuel than anything else. To find out just how Buñuel has gone about turning Defoe or Emily Brontë or whatever minor writers provided the pretexts for *El* and *La Vida Criminal de*

Archibaldo de la Cruz into pure Buñuel, however, we have to go back a number of years: to Buñuel's background, education, and first sensational steps in the cinema.

Luis Buñuel was born in the Spanish village of Calanda in 1900, into a prosperous family of landowners. He was, it appears, a quiet, well-behaved child – though, a French biographer observes blandly, it is quite true that he did eat and make his sisters eat ants on occasion, it was not by any means a regular practice, – studious and very pious. A period in a Jesuit college seems at once to have equipped him with a subtlety in argument which often leaves his critics confounded and to have induced in him a strong and permanent reaction against the religion of his youth. Just afterwards a period of studies in Madrid brought him to the 'Residencia de Estudiantes' at its most famous and stimulating period, and he soon became one of a group of friends which included Salvador Dali, José Ortega y Gasset, Federico Garcia Lorca, Ramon Gomez de la Sernas, and Rafael Alberti. At this time, too, he did some acting, directed the first performance of Falla's puppet opera *El Retablo de Maese Pedro* and, most importantly, founded one of the first European film clubs, at the university in 1920. The cinema was, in fact, already his dominant interest, and after taking a good degree in philosophy and letters he moved to Paris, where he soon got a job as assistant to Jean Epstein on his films *Mauprat* and *La Chute de la Maison Usher*. He also assisted Malpas and Étiévant on one of their elaborate 'films d'art', *La Sirène des Tropiques*, but drew the line at working with Gance and quarrelled with Epstein as a result. Temporarily at a loose end, he toyed with the idea of an impressionist-realist scenario by Gomez de la Serna, went back to Spain and was given enough money by his mother to make it, came back to Paris, dropped the idea and spent most of the money, and finally, after a bout of surrealist verse-writing, wrote while on holiday with his friend Dali the scenario of what was to become *Un Chien Andalou*.

The story of the first showing of *Un Chien Andalou* to the assembled surrealists, their instant enthusiasm and reception of Buñuel and Dali into their ranks, has often been told, and the film has been for some thirty years one of the old war-horses of the film clubs. In its time it was obviously both important to its makers and symptomatic of new ideas at work in the cinema. But it must be said, I think, that it does not wear well. It is less boring to watch than, say, *La Coquille et le Clergyman* (directed by Germaine Dulac from an interesting script by Antonin Artaud) simply because Buñuel had, even then, a clear idea of how to put a film together and Germaine Dulac hadn't. But there is an evident wilfulness about its use of free-association technique, a quality of deliberate 'naughtiness' almost, which today makes it seem rather tiresome and juvenile. This quality I think it is fair to attribute to the hand of Dali in the film's devising (Buñuel directed the film alone from the outline he and Dali had concocted, Dali being present only on the last day of shooting). Dali had developed, even in those early days, something of his talent for shocking the *bourgeois*, but not too much, just sufficiently to make himself (profitably) the man they loved to hate, and this ambiguity of approach is strongly present in the film. What should be a blow in the audience's face, and promises in the first scene, in which we see a girl's eye cut open with a razor in close-up, to be just that, turns far too early into a series of fantasticated effects, like the notorious dead donkey in the grand piano, which amuse or startle according to temperament, but work ultimately only on the level of scandal.

Buñuel himself became early aware of this, and writes resentfully in his introduction to the published text (*La Révolution surréaliste*, No. 12, 1929) of 'that crowd of imbeciles who found "beautiful" or "poetic" what is, fundamentally, only a despairing, passionate call to murder'. But in a sense he had only himself to blame, or rather, he had only his subservience to Dali in this instance to blame, for the film seems to have had precisely the sort of success Dali hoped for. And in the last analysis it is far more helpful to regard *Un Chien Andalou* as a Dali conception adroitly realized by Buñuel with one or two characteristic touches of his own (notably in the extraordinary scene in which a man and woman make passionate love just after witnessing a road accident from an upstairs window) than as part of the Buñuel canon.

With his next film, *L'Age d'Or*, however, although Dali's name still appears on the credits, there is no doubt possible of who was in control, even without the testimony of both parties that they diverged after only a couple of days working on the script, and only one of Dali's gags (the man walking with a large stone on his head) survives into the film as made. *L'Age d'Or*, in fact, is not only

Buñuel's first characteristic film, his first masterpiece and probably the only film of lasting value to be thrown up by the surrealist movement in its heyday, but it is also Buñuel's credo, the comprehensive statement of all his principal themes and ideas; in it is to be found the key to the whole of his later work.

L'Age d'Or, unlike *Un Chien Andalou*, is a sound film, and uses the medium with fantastic fluency and control – and this in 1930, when most directors were still very much feeling their way. On the sound track alone practically every device known to the modern cinema – interior monologue, overlapping and distorted sound, recurrent aural leitmotifs, appropriate music intensifying what is happening on the screen and deliberately inappropriate music producing dissociation from it – is to be found, and used so rightly and unobtrusively that for many years apparently it never even occurred to anyone to think the film very revolutionary in this respect at all. But perhaps this is understandable considering the startling nature of the film's material, its devastating effectiveness in putting this material over, and the scandalous reputation which pursued it when it became for some years almost impossible to see. It is one of the oddities of French commentators on *L'Age d'Or* and its background that they praise it enthusiastically (and quite rightly) for its iconoclastic fervour, its complete ruthlessness in attacking all that the religious, the conservative hold most dear, and yet at the same time they firmly maintain that the demonstrations against it by Young Catholics, pseudo-Fascist organizations, and conservative chauvinists must have been engineered in advance: I should have thought that they were in general perfectly explicable as genuine reactions to the film, and indeed that it would probably be a sign that the film was missing its target if they or something very like them did not occur. This film at least was not going to be misunderstood in the *salons* as 'beautiful' and 'poetic'.

L'Age d'Or begins like a straight, academic documentary about scorpions (Buñuel had always been an enthusiastic amateur entomologist), all irreproachably factual and objective. This tone once set, we go on without the slightest hesitation or change in the tone of voice to a scene of bishops celebrating mass among the rocks, as though this were a perfectly everyday occurrence placed before the camera in much the same spirit as the scorpions had been. Nearby the decrepit inhabitants of the country set out to oppose the enemy, the mysterious Majorcans of whom the bishops are presumably the advance guard. But they are too feeble to do anything and the Majorcans (all dressed formally, as for some sort of big civic function) process through the rocks (the bishops being by now no more than mitred skeletons) to the spot where they intend to lay the foundations of the New Rome. The ceremony is interrupted, however, by the cries of two lovers rolling in the mud, passionately embraced: this is *amour fou*, a completely single-minded, unquestioning passion which disregards circumstances, annihilates time and place, and is for Buñuel the strongest, most explosive force in the world, or at least can be if it is accepted without question or doubt or hesitation or qualification. The lovers (Gaston Modot and Lya Lys) are separated like animals and Rome is built on their separation (the Church, that is, is the great perverter of humanity, the great frustrating agent in human life). But the lovers cannot be kept apart; in the next sequence Modot is escorted down a street by two policemen while Lya Lys walks her room, distractedly turning a cow out of her bed the whiles, and then the sound of the cow's bell carries over to Modot mingled with the sounds about him, giving the cue for a joining of the lovers in an imaginative union as real and intense as any mere physical meeting could be.

When Modot manages to get free of the police and sets off in pursuit of his beloved we arrive at a society reception in which scrupulous disregard for anything going on around is the order of the day. A tumbril passed through the room, full of peasants drinking wine, and no one takes any notice. A fire breaks out in the kitchens and maids collapse into the flames as the polite conversation continues uninterrupted. The act of the gamekeeper in shooting his son causes a little stir, but his explanation that it was because the son disobeyed him in some trifle is accepted without question. In this setting the lovers can at last meet undisturbed, and they begin to embrace eagerly in the garden, to the strains of *Tristan and Isolde* played by an attendant orchestra. But this time their own inhibitions come into play: they are awkward and maladroit, and some curious taboo seems to prevent them from getting up from their respective chairs to make love efficiently. Eventually Modot is called away to speak to the Minister on the telephone and tells him to drop dead, at which he promptly kills himself.

Back in the garden the lovers at last seem to be about to reach the consummation so eagerly awaited, to the triumphant reiteration of 'Mon amour . . . mon amour . . . mon amour' on the sound-track, but this time the bearded leader of the orchestra intervenes, to be passionately kissed in his turn by Lya Lys. Modot, infuriated, goes in and starts throwing things out of the window – a wheel-barrow, a burning tree, a giraffe, a bishop – all the symbols, it would appear, of his slavery, with some more thrown in for arbi-trary good measure. Finally, the film breaks off to take us to the Castle of Selligny, where de Sade's survivors from *Les 120 Journées de Sodome* are staggering out, tattered and exhausted, and disguised as various characters, with the Count de Blangis as Christ. One more survivor appears, the last of their victims, and the Christ figure goes back to kill her; the last shot is of a crucifix in the snow, as a jolly *pasa doble* plays on the sound-track.

Clearly, the ideas at the root of the film are consistently anar-chistic: the ideal is complete lack of inhibition in the full expression of emotions and desires, and everything which would tend to prevent this by the application of external prohibitions or the inculcation of ideas the acceptance of which would inhibit such expression is seen as wrong and ruthlessly condemned. The Church and the State both clearly come into this category, and so, more specifically, does the whole social organization of society. The Roman Catholic Church, represented by the Majorcans who come to build a new Eternal City, is savagely pilloried, while the final shots, in which a Christ figure is shown as an embodiment of evil, does not even leave room for us to suppose that Buñuel's feelings are merely that safe and almost conventional anti-clericalism often found in otherwise perfectly devout continental Catholics: it is not merely the form of Rome, but the whole Christian religion and way of life which are being attacked. In the foundation-stone sequence, moreover, the State is seen as intimately linked with the Church, and the policemen who arrest Modot and obstruct the course of the lovers' affair are its minions, like the Minister who later phones him at a crucial moment.

As for the members of high society at the reception, we should perhaps see them as victims rather than villains; their whole system of values has been so perverted by the codes of 'civilized life' that their view of acceptable behaviour is hopelessly lop-sided (they accept with complete equanimity the fathers' right to kill his son for a trifling offence, but are outraged when Modot knocks down an obstructive old woman to get to Lya Lys during the reception) and they are so inured to pretending indifference to what goes on about them that perhaps they even really are indifferent or oblivious when the servants are consumed by fire or a tumbril trundles through the ballroom. And not only they: even Modot and Lya Lys, who seem at the beginning to represent natural man, unaffected by the fallen, enslaved world about them, prove at last to be nearly as enslaved as the rest. When they are alone together in the garden their love-making is inhibited by the whole atmosphere of the place and the constraints placed upon passion by society: where once they rolled joyously in the mud together, now they seemed dominated by the ludicrous necessity to make love while remaining demurely balanced on two separate chairs.

The exact significance of the final sequence has been much debated; too much, no doubt, for in this sort of surrealist fantasy it is futile to look for exact correspondences as though one is dealing with an allegorical conundrum to which there is a single cast-iron key. The main lines are plain enough: the bitter satire on religion is unmistakable, and so is the intention of an explicit homage to de Sade, one of Buñuel's great devotions (he has never ceased to proclaim himself a sadist – in the philosophical rather than the popular-psychoanalytical sense, of course). Possibly the implication is that only through a sort of purgation such as the revellers at the Castle of Selligny achieve by sheer satiety can a complete freedom from inhibition be achieved; the 'Christ' here appears paradoxically as an anti-Christ, the messiah of a new religion of liberation from the ties of conventional morality.

Never since L'Age d'Or has Buñuel's expression of his beliefs been so intense and concentrated, not even in Viridiana, the most complete later expression, since then there is a fully articulated plot to be dealt with and the film is more than twice as long. But one L'Age d'Or is enough; no man, not even Buñuel, would need to make two in one lifetime. It offers such riches all at one go that it leaves dozens of fragments of raw material just begging to be taken up again and reworked, as well as numerous ideas to be applied to an infinite number of new situations. The later films, after some twenty years' gap, set out to do precisely this; to build on the firm foundations offered by L'Age d'Or.

Buñuel's next film, *Los Hurdes* (1932) also known as *Land Without Bread*, is a perfect illustration. At first sight it would seem the direct opposite of *L'Age d'Or*, a straightforward social documentary about a depressed area in the mountains of Spain marking, one might suppose, a complete break with surrealist fantasy. And yet it is not like that at all. The first thing we noticed about *L'Age d'Or* was its ruthlessly objective tone, set by the documentary introduction about scorpions: it achieves much of its obsessive power precisely by its 'documentary' quality, its meticulously cool and scientific reporting of the extraordinary things that go on in front of the camera (insect life or human life, passionate love or violent death) without recourse to exhibitionistic cinema 'magic' or even the usual range of atmospheric effects (Epstein's *Chute de la Maison Usher*, on which Buñuel worked as assistant, is a useful stalking horse here). *Los Hurdes* simply offers the reverse of the medal: Buñuel's objective camera-eye applied to the extraordinary gives it the air (all the more disturbing of course) of complete normality; applied to straight actuality, on the other hand, it somehow heightens our awareness to the point where what he sees takes on the colouring of wild surrealist fantasy. The tension in each case between, as it were, the tone of voice and what the voice is saying is exactly the same, and the ultimate effect is astonishingly consistent; not for nothing does Buñuel class *Los Hurdes*, without explanation, or, apparently, a second thought, among 'my surrealist films'.

The Hurdanos, the subject of *Los Hurdes*, are the poverty-stricken peasant inhabitants of a group of isolated mountain villages, living on the verge of starvation (one of their staple foods is unripe wild cherries) in the most primitive conditions, and inbreeding for many generations. Consequently the deformed and the imbecile abound, illness is constant, and practially every effort they make to improve their lot (constructing small artificial fields, occasionally scraping up enough money to buy a domestic animal) are doomed to frustration from ignorance or lack of resources or both. Buñuel presents their situation with deceptive directness and simplicity, accompanied by a flat factual commentary and tinkling popular-classical music like the 'Fingal's Cave' overture. Occasionally a sharp ironical insight is overtly present, as when we see one of the scrawny, underfed children solemnly writing upon the blackboard, and presumably being urged to take to heart, 'Respect the possessions of others', or when the commentator remarks dryly that in this miserable land 'the only luxurious building we came across were the churches'. But usually Buñuel's methods are not so plain. As Ado Kyrou has very acutely remarked in his book on Buñuel, the architecture of the film is based on the single phrase 'Oui, mais . . .': Buñuel shows us something unbearable, offers some hope of amelioration, and then systematically destroys that hope. The Hurdanos are often bitten by the vipers which infest the area, but the bites are not fatal, but the medicines they use to counteract them are. Bread is unknown, but the teacher sometimes gives the children pieces of bread, but the parents, distrusting what they don't know, make the children throw them away. The Hurdanos have no naturally cultivable land, but with great effort they construct tiny fields near the river, but the soil bears almost nothing because they have no fertilizer. In May they would starve, but at that time the wild cherries are fruiting, but the cherries are still unripe and give all those who eat them dysentry. And so on and on, with relentless logic, to the point at which the film becomes, like *Un Chien Andalou* in theory, and *L'Age d'Or* in fact, 'un désesperé, un passionné appel au meutre'.

Los Hurdes was, in effect, the last film Buñuel was to make for twenty years; a script based on *Wuthering Heights* which he wrote at this time remained unproduced, and until 1951 he was almost forgotten, the continuing fame of *Un Chien Andalou* and *L'Age d'Or* being attached, inevitably, to the constantly publicized figure of Dali, and the real nature of *Los Hurdes* mistaken or ignored, as it was unthinkingly bracketed with the works of Joris Ivens, Paul Rotha and others as 'social realist documentary'. Buñuel decided, for reasons now obscure, to give up directing altogether, and worked instead on the dubbing of American films, first for Paramount in Paris, then for Warner Brothers in Spain. While in Spain he also produced four films which no one seems to have seen and which he himself maintains were entirely commercial and of no interest. One of them, however, *Don Quintin el Amargao*, he later remade in Mexico as *La Hija del Engaño*, and another, *Centinela Alerta!* he completed himself after the director, Jean Grémillon, abandoned it. He also made a newsreel-compilation film, *Madrid 36*, for the series *España Leal en Armas*, and when the Republican Government finally collapsed he thought it wisest to go to America.

Here he had a curious career. Employed first at the Museum of Modern Art, he was dismissed when his association with *L'Age d'Or* was discovered by the authorities (ten years earlier, ironically, he had been briefly imported by M-G-M on the strength of the same film); during his time at the Museum he edited an anti-Nazi compilation based mainly on *Baptism of Fire* and Leni Riefenstahl's *The Triumph of the Wall*, which sounds fascinating but has apparently never been shown. Later came another period supervising dubbing in Hollywood; also some work preparing *The Beast with Five Fingers*, which was finally directed by Robert Florey.

Finally in 1947 there was an offer from Mexico for Buñuel to return to direction, with an adaptation of Lorca's *La Casa de Bernarda Alba*, but this fell through and he was engaged instead by Oscar Dancigers to make an inexpensive commercial musical, *Gran Casino*, which had, according to Buñuel, 'one love-scene in the mud, really filmed in the mud', and was a box-office failure. After two years of inactivity he was given another chance with *El Gran Cavalera*, a comedy based on a stage play (adapted by Luis Alcoriza, who was to become Buñuel's favourite script collaborator) and made in a fortnight. It was a success and so Dancigers was emboldened to give Buñuel his head with *Los Olvidados* (1950), which marked his decisive return to the film scene, won a lot of prizes and made a lot of money. Also, and most importantly, it was the first unmistakably 'Buñuel' film since *Los Hurdes*, fully characteristic of his mature vision and showing a quite extraordinary consistency of style and inspiration with the works of his early surrealist heyday.

At one stage, indeed, this was to have been even more evident, since Buñuel intended to include in the film moments of surrealist commentary on the principal story of juvenile delinquents in the slums of Mexico City: the camera, travelling reflectively over a wasteland, would pick out a symphony orchestra playing away in the skeleton of an unfinished building, and then return without lingering to the principal characters, and so on. But ultimately this idea was abandoned, and instead we are given what appears to be a straightforward realistic film, its fantasy carefully limited to a symbolic dream sequence. Appearances, however, are deceptive, as they were with *Los Hurdes*: what Buñuel is really about is the exploration of his private world, under the guise of realism. In *Los*

Olvidados, in fact, he has hit at once on precisely the sort of ambivalence which has enabled him subsequently to make his own films
quite happily within the commercial system. At one level the film
works quite acceptably on the level of an humane social document
(*Pitié pour eux*, it was called in France) and that is the level on
which it has appealed to a vast public. On another level, though,
one can see it as not realistic at all, any more than *Los Hurdes* was
realistic; and if this time the effect stops short of an empassioned
call to murder, nevertheless the nightmarish, hallucinatory quality
of the film is uniquely disturbing.

This result is achieved – though perhaps Buñuel would resent
intensely one's saying it – by Buñuel's power to invest the most
unexpected things with poetry. Not, of course, poetry in the sense
that the appearance of Gabriel Figueroa, Mexico's foremost expert
in lush atmospherics, as the film's cameraman might lead one to
expect; the photography is throughout bare and stripped of extraneous effects, even in the dream sequence. Rather is it the sort of
imagist poetry which comes from an intense heightening of individual sense impressions, so that certain selected objects take on the
quality of a fetish, an instrument of ritual significance in the re-
enactment of some private myth. So in *Los Olvidados* it is with the
cockerels which infest the action, heralding doom; with the dove
whose soft body caresses the back of an invalid; the raw meat which
sets the tone of the dream sequence; the terrible old blind man's
stick; the milk which the girl Meche pours over herself to make her
skin beautiful. Nothing is ever allowed to be completely and merely
what it appears, any more than is the film as a whole.

Through this web of images and symbols runs a thread of story
concerning a group of children and particularly two, the vicious
Jaibo and his victim Pedro, to whom he is bound initially by
Pedro's having witnessed a brutal murder he committed, and
whose only chance of escape from the harsh world they inhabit
(moderately pleasant work; a humane reformatory) he systematically cuts off before finally killing Pedro and himself being killed.
Though Buñuel has been taken to task here and there for allowing
some virtue to the reformatory and to Pedro's employer, his intentions seem clear enough: a similar dialectic is employed here as in
Los Hurdes, with these conceivable goods only as a middle term
between two evils – an unbearable situation is created, hope is held

out, and then taken away again, leaving the situation even worse than before; casual, piecemeal humanitarianism (a slice of bread from the teacher, a nice reformatory for the good bad boy) does not help at all, and in the long run probably makes things worse. And as in *Los Hurdes*, too, the happenings are observed with every appearance of ruthless objectivity; the children and their situation are not sentimentalized in the slightest (the image of black-and-white distinctions, facile apportioning of blame and ready-made solutions summoned up in the American cinema by the very term 'juvenile delinquent' could hardly be further removed, while Buñuel clearly has no time for the idea of youthful innocence, dear especially to the British film). Instead, they are simply presented as a fact; a fact which provokes certain reactions and from which certain conclusions can be drawn.

But as with *Los Hurdes* the apparent ruthless objectivity is only a matter of tone of voice; what is said in this tone of voice is selected with the utmost precision and phrased in such a way as to produce exactly the effect intended by the speaker and no other. Buñuel shines such a hard, unflinching light on external reality that it begins little by little to give itself over to him, to reveal its secrets from the darker, hidden world of instinctive needs or impulses. We look at the reality Buñuel has selected for us so closely and fixedly through his eyes that we begin to lose consciousness of any other criteria: reality takes on something of the feverish intensity of a dream; dreams, when they come, something of the cool matter-of-factness of reality; distinctions begin to blur and dissolve, leaving dream and waking reality alike as projections of Buñuel's own ideas on human life. All is stunted and twisted at the root by society and religion, which organize and limit man in such a way that love without inhibition is impossible, and when the instincts are trammelled in this way they can find expression only in misery, perversion, crime, and death.

As well as being Buñuel's first consistent and successful attempt to accommodate his anarchic, surrealist ideals to the commercial cinema, *Los Olvidados* offers a very fair example of his mature film technique. It is, as far as the use of the camera is concerned, remarkable only in its complete unremarkability. There are no startling 'effects', no beautiful photography, if beauty in photography is conceived only in terms of the arty and artificial, no virtuoso camera movements, no *tours-de-force* of editing. It sounds, therefore, rather as though it must be a dull, conventional film, but not at all. The angle of each shot is chosen and it is framed with an absolutely unerring instinct for conveying the precise nuance intended with the minimum of trouble; the editing style is smooth and free, without any commerce with conventional notions of montage – Buñuel simply cuts from one thing he wants to show to another, with no nonsense about covering and matching or what is and is not academically permissible; if it works he does it, and at least by the time the film is shown it always does. It is the completely confident way of proceeding of a man who knows his technique inside out, and does not have to convince anybody, even himself. Buñuel writes with film much as an easy writer writes with a pen or a typewriter, thinking only of what he has to say and taking his ability to say it more or less for granted. Perhaps significantly, he always films very quickly, and few of his best films have taken longer than two or three weeks in front of the cameras; style is for him the best and most economical way of saying a thing, not an elaboration applied with slow, laborious care.

How far Buñuel found anything worth saying in his next three films is largely a matter of conjecture in Europe. Buñuel himself does not like any of them, which is usually a fair guide; two, *La Hija del Engaño* (a remake of *Don Quintin el Amargao*) and *Un Mujer sin Amor* (a free version of Maupassant's *Pierre et Jean*) seem not to have been shown outside Mexico, and the third, *Susana*, which turned up in France a few years back provocatively retitled *Susana la perverse*, I have not seen. Most French critics seem to regard it as a sort of sketch for *El*; Ado Kyrou quotes Buñuel as saying that it is quite his worst film, and then enthuses – the plot, which concerns a young baggage shaking up a conventional *bourgeois* family, admittedly sounds to have possibilities. And no doubt, despite Buñuel's denials, there are points of interest in all these films and the two others he made in similar circumstances in 1953–4, neither shown in Europe, *La Ilusion viaja in tranvia* and *El rio y la muerte* (of which latter Buñuel remarks gleefully: 'It is very Mexican: seven deaths, four burials, and I don't know how many wakes'). It is certainly the case with the one of his 'commercial' films from this period which has been shown here, *El Bruto* (1952), a characteristic-sounding story of a vicious, impotent

landlord, his brutish henchman who works in a slaughter-house, and
two women, the lustful, unscrupulous wife of the landlord and the
innocent daughter of one of the henchman's victims; Buñuel himself regards it as a workable story spoilt for lack of time, and the
finished film, despite Buñuelian details (the cockerels, the statue of
the Virgin protecting the slaughter-house, the old grandfather who
steals sweets at night), has an air of hurry and non-involvement.
Perhaps the last and best word on the subject of Buñuel's commercial chores has been spoken by Buñuel himself in a Mexican interview:

> I have always been true to my surrealist principles: 'The need to eat
> never excuses prostituting one's art.' In nineteen or twenty films I have
> made three or four which are frankly bad, but in no case have I infringed
> my moral code. To have a code at all is childish to many people, but not
> to me. I am against conventional morality, traditional sacred cows, sen-
> timentality and all that moral filth of society which comes into it.
> Obviously, I have made bad films, but always morally acceptable to me.

In other words, Buñuel, like Ford and many other long-term
survivors in the commercial cinema, recognizes that from time to
time, for whatever reason, the director will have to make films
which do not involve him, which call only on his technical know-
how, and accepts this state of affairs, determining merely that the
work he does just to eat, or to maintain his position to the more
distant end of being able to make films he really wants to, shall not
compromise or contradict his own standards and beliefs.

So, disregarding these films, which have served their purpose
not dishonourably, let us continue our examination of the films
they made possible: the five highly personal works he succeeded in
making entirely within the framework of the Mexican commercial
cinema up to 1955, when he returned briefly to France to make a
film and entered a more confused (and confusing) phase of international co-productions. The first of them, *Subida al Cielo* (1951)
turned out, surprisingly enough at first glance, to be a light-hearted
peasant comedy, written by the poet Manuel Altolaguirre, about a
bus journey in which a young innocent learns something of life.
But there is, finally, no reason why we should be surprised at the
old surrealist Buñuel turning to this sort of material, for what
emerges is not at all the sort of *Bread, Love and . . .* piece it might
have been in other hands, but a picaresque tale full of fantastic

5a. *L' Age d'Or* (Lya Lys). Dir: Luis Buñuel

5b. *Los Olvidados* (Alfonso Mejia). Dir: Luis Buñuel

6a. *El* (Arturo de Cordova; Delia Gracias). Dir: Luis Buñuel

6b. Luis Buñuel directs *Viridiana*

invention, revelling in the unexpected, the gleeful reversal of an
audience's expectations which characterized surrealism even at its
most serious, and mixing dream and reality in the bland, unself-
conscious way which only Buñuel has achieved in the cinema (by
comparison Cocteau seems positively heavy-handed). In this context even the outrageously cardboard rocks through which a very
evidently model bus is sometimes seen travelling become quite
acceptable and even (though this surely cannot have been part of
the original intention) curiously apt to the fantastic world the film
creates.

The purpose of the journey for the film's hero, Oliverio, is to
bring back a lawyer from a town the other side of the mountains to
draw up a new will for his mother which will disinherit his no-good
layabout brothers. Called from his own wedding celebrations to
carry out his mother's dying wish, he sets out in the local bus with a
motley collection of passengers, while his brothers merrily carouse
with the Mayor ('Well,' says one of them, 'you only have one
mother, and she only dies once'). On the bus is a glamorous blonde
in an off-the-shoulder blouse who sends Oliverio off immediately
into an erotic fantasy in which they make love in a bus overgrown
with exotic jungle vegetation. On the way to the town the bus-
driver makes a detour to visit his old mother on her birthday and
all the passengers are welcomed to the celebration; a woman passenger has a baby; Oliverio, driving on apparently by himself from
the party to complete his errand, finds the blonde hiding in the bus
and they make love there, immobilized in a thunderstorm on
'Subida al Cielo', a high pass in the mountains the bus has to
traverse. The lawyer, when Oliverio arrives, refuses to come back
with him, but sends the necessary papers, which will need only the
mother's fingerprint. On the way back a group of peasants get on
with a dead child in a coffin, bitten by a viper (accidental or deliberate reference to *Los Hurdes*?). The passengers join in the funeral
with as good a will as on the outward journey they joined in the
celebration. On his arrival back Oliverio finds his mother already
dead, but appends her fingerprint to the papers so that her wishes
will be carried out, and then, at long last, a wiser but hardly a
sadder man, returns to his waiting bride.

The tone of the film throughout is joyously pagan, full of fresh,
physical delights and unashamed acceptance of the way human

C.E.–G

beings are (Oliverio's infidelity with the girl on the bus is coolly accepted as a perfectly natural occurrence of no particular importance, and no one shows any sign of guilt over it). Birth, marriage and death, celebration and mourning, all just happen because that's the way things are, as natural events on the journey, and even Buñuel's habitual side-swipes at the Church and organized religion (Oliverio seems to be a happy, natural man largely because he comes from a village without a church, and it can hardly be accidental that his infidelity on his wedding night takes place in a location called 'The Ascent to Heaven') are light and jovial. *Subida al Cielo*, in fact, gives the impression of being a film made for sheer delight in film-making: Buñuel's technique has never been more simple or unobtrusive; it is almost negligent except that the simplicity is inspired, and the rough edges (evident model-shots and so on) come precisely at the places where they do not matter. When there is something that has to be very precisely managed – you can't, after all, be careless with jokes – it is handled properly: the whole sequence in which the bus gets stuck in the river mud and is finally drawn out by two oxen led by a tiny girl with a piece of string, leaving a passenger with a wooden leg firmly stuck in his turn in the mud, is staged and shot with the exact comic timing of a born humorist – a quality to be usefully in evidence in more than one of Buñuel's subsequent works.

After *Subida al Cielo*, with the evident affinity of its story to an eighteenth-century picaresque novel, there seems a curious rightness in Buñuel's turning to the real thing for the subject of his next major work. Or there would be if the novel selected, Defoe's *Robinson Crusoe*, did not clearly represent at once, neatly combined, a collection of attitudes as violently antipathetic to all Buñuel's ideas as one could off-hand conceive. For Crusoe is, according to his lights and his period, the completely conventional man: Christian, moralistic even, the captive of reason, convinced of the superior mission of 'civilization'. His whole aim on his desert island is to rebuild his European prison for himself, to reproduce in little the whole system from which his abandonment there has apparently rescued him. Whatever could appeal to Buñuel in this? How, even, given that he did not choose the subject, could he make a straightforward commercial chore of it without compromising the principles he himself had put forward?

The answer, though hardly anyone seems to have noticed it at the time (perhaps because *Robinson Crusoe* is the sort of book most people vaguely know about rather than actually read) is that in filming it Buñuel neatly reverses practically all the points made in the book. Preserving carefully enough the outline of events, Buñuel has turned their significance inside out, and instead of Defoe's triumphant picture of reason ordering hostile nature he gives us instead a penetrating study of solitude breaking down a 'reasonable' man as he tries desperately to bolster his own progressively more shaky beliefs by a hopeless and largely absurd adherence to the external forms of a way of life which has no relevant to his present situation. To do this Buñuel has to add various things to the original narrative, most importantly a sexual element almost entirely lacking – a defect hopefully supplied a few years back with a mildly porno-graphic Traveller's Companion volume called *The Sexual Life of Robinson Crusoe*. The film might also be called *The Sexual Life of Robinson Crusoe*, for though it is not exclusively devoted to that the theme runs through, colouring everything: Crusoe's dreams, his reactions to Friday's innocent dressing-up in women's clothes, and especially the marvellous scene in which a dress used to shade Crusoe from the sun becomes transfigured in his eyes into some-thing living and desirable. Also, in Buñuel's transformation of Defoe much which appears to be taken over almost literally from the book becomes unexpectedly modified by its context: the irony of Crusoe's attempts to civilize Friday (his first action being to chain him) is unmistakably brought out, and the values attributed to religion in the book are so altered that instead of its being one of the main things to keep Crusoe sane in his trials we appreciate rather that its failure to help him even though he clings desperately to its forms is one of the main factors in driving him mad (or nearly): the words of the psalm, when he shouts them in the valley of the echoes, are not of comfort in themselves, but just meaning-less sounds whose echoes from the hills around reassure him that at least he still exists.

Robinson Crusoe being (perhaps fortunately) totally misunder-stood as a film, it gained wide success and even at one stage pre-sented British filmgoers with the surprising spectacle of a Buñuel film showing at the local Rank circuit cinema in a double bill with a new de Sica (*Indiscretion*). But meanwhile Buñuel went on making

Mexican films designed, initially and primarily, to satisfy Mexican audiences. And the very next, *El*, proved one of his strangest and most personal works, as well as one of his most popular in Mexico, where it was taken by most people as a conventional melodrama about jealousy. *El* has been described as a realistic remake of *L'Age d'Or*, and the description, though exaggerated, has enough truth in it to be worth investigating more closely. The film is a story of jealousy, based loosely on a popular and apparently fairly conventional novel by Mercedes Pinto. But just as *Robinson Crusoe* took a given story-line and carried it further, explored deeper into things hardly hinted at in the book, so *El* turns little by little into a scathing indictment of Christianity and the social order for turning aside natural passions from their natural course, by perverting them in the cause of conventional morality. The central character, Francisco, is an obedient son of the Church, a man of the highest moral character. All this is succinctly established in the opening scene, where he is shown assisting in an elaborate and curious church ceremony in which a priest washes and then kisses the feet of a dozen youths; from their feet Francisco's glance travels to a pair of shapely feet in the congregation, then up the legs to take in the face and figure of a beautiful young woman. He is at once obsessed with her, follows her but obtains no response, and takes to haunting the church in the hope of seeing her again. Thus in the space of a few shots Buñuel manages to convey with superb economy Francisco's character and situation as well as the ambiguity of his religious interests: the sensuality of the penetential ritual, with its strong sado-masochistic eroticism, is carefully stressed, and the transition to the overt eroticism of Francisco's sudden interest in the girl is so casually done that its full implications only occur to one later. And ambiguity rapidly becomes direct hypocrisy when Francisco, the perfect churchgoer, begins without apparent qualm to go to church only in hope of making an assignation.

Not that it is as simple as that; Francisco is over forty, and still completely celibate – if the girl who obsesses him so much is to be anything to him she must be his wife. Finding that she is the fiancée of a friend, he carries her off and marries her without a second thought, but passions so long dammed up cannot just flow clear and free. Francisco is too deeply indoctrinated: he does not, like Modot in *L'Age d'Or*, require physical intervention from outside to pre-

vent the proper realization of his desires, since all that is needed is
already deeply ingrained in him. Consequently he invents the
intervention. He is chronically, insanely jealous. He torments his
wife with questions on their wedding night, suspects an innocent
bystander, a slight acquaintance of his wife, whom they meet on
their honeymoon, of spying on them (he jabs knitting-needles
through the keyhole at one point, quite expecting to find an eye
impaled on the other end) and of being a past lover of his Gloria.
When they get back he throws her into the arms of a lawyer handling a case for him, with instructions that she is to be specially nice
to him, and then accuses her of making him her lover. When she
complains, Gloria's mother and the Church both send her back to
her husband with elevating but useless instructions. Francisco's
behaviour grows madder and madder: sometimes he covers Gloria
with passionate affection, at others he threatens to throw her from a
high tower, weeps on his valet's shoulder, roams the house at night
beating a tattoo with a stair-rod on the bannisters, menaces Gloria
with a needle and thread (a direct reference to an episode in Le
Sade's *La Philosophie dans le boudoir*) and finally suffers a complete
mental breakdown in a church to which he has pursued a couple he
wrongly believes to be Gloria and her former fiancé. Imagining
that the congregation, the choir and the priest are obscenely mocking him (an extraordinary piece of objective-subjective intercutting on Buñuel's part) he tries to strangle the priest, and is carried
off to be cared for by the Church. Years later we see him, as Gloria,
her new husband and her children come to ask after him; he is
supposed to be quite cured, but as he walks away he is still walking
in zigzags, as he did at the height of his delusions.

El is one of the most bitter, and the most frenziedly intense, of
all Buñuel's films. His denunciation of Christianity, both directly
and indirectly, through the portrait of the 'good Christian' Francisco, has never been so uncompromising, and the transposition of
the message of *L'Age d'Or* to a superficially realistic setting if anything increases its power. Incidentally, Buñuel, though he claims to
be largely unconscious of what he has put into his films until they
are made, would seem to have been aware of the correspondence,
since there are things in *El* – the clouds of dust from the neighbour-
ing room during the dinner party at which Francisco entraps
Gloria; the party later on, ripe for the tumbrils to grind their way

through it – which can hardly be anything but deliberate reminiscences. *El* is also, perhaps necessarily, Buñuel's most elaborate film technically: the overheated mind of Francisco, his inextricable mingling of fantasy and reality, is allowed to work on the spectator in a number of scenes through the use of technical devices usually confined by Buñuel to dream sequences; especially in the church sequence near the end, where we are shown in rapid alternation the priest, choir and congregation as they are and as they appear to Francisco, grimacing and mocking him. But Buñuel's talent for the extremely simple, unobtrusively right has not deserted him either; the sequences of the knitting-needles and the midnight sewing are all the more nightmarish and terrifying for being recorded quite calmly and straightforwardly, even remotely, with something of the documentary quality we noticed in *Los Hurdes*.

The last film of this Mexican period, *La Vida Criminal de Archibaldo de la Cruz* (or *Ensayo de un Crimen*, as it is sometimes called), is a sort of comic counterpart to *El*, and one of the most delectable of all Buñuel's films. Of course, it would be possible to see even *El* as a *comédie noire*; there are, in any case, at least moments of ghastly humour in it. But *Archibaldo de la Cruz* is unmistakably a comedy all through, though like *El* it is a study of obsession, and on the face of it an even more sinister one than Francisco's. As the result of a childhood experience Archibaldo finds desire and death indissolubly linked in his life. Told as a little boy that a musical box he has been given can bring death to anyone he wishes dead, he experiments on his governess, who is promptly killed by a stray bullet from a revolution going on in the street (there is an extraordinary image of the child watching the blood run down under her skirts). When by chance he comes across the musical box again – he is now grown up and a famous potter – the link becomes explicit in his consciousness, and the film follows a succession of disastrous attempts on his part to realize his desires by killing their immediate object, without the slightest success, since somehow his plans are always anticipated or frustrated and the police will not accept his confession. First his unsubtle attempt on a nursing sister terrifies her so much she promptly falls down a lift-shaft. Then he marries a girl of good family knowing her to have had a lover and imagining in lushly sadistic detail their wedding-night confrontation and his *crime passionel*, but alas her former lover kills her first. Finally his plot to kill another girl and incinerate her body in his potter's kiln is frustrated when a group of tourists arrive to look round his workroom, and he is reduced to burning a wax mannequin in her place. Realizing at last that it is the spell of the past, represented by the musical box, which is rendering him impotent, he throws it into the river and is cured; about to crush an insect in the park with his cane (a characteristic touch), he refrains, and goes off happily with the girl of the last sequence; for him at least the obsession is disposed of, and after the bad dreams are over he can wake to normal life.

In Archibaldo's case the obsession is seen as a personal matter, the results of an accidental juxtaposition of events in childhood, rather than, as in Francisco's case, as the result of a whole training, a way of life in a particular religion and a particular social set-up. Hence the relative lightness of the tone; *La Vida Criminal de Archibaldo de la Cruz* is quite sunny, the humour residing largely in the classic device (an example offering a number of parallels which may have influenced Buñuel is to be found in Preston Sturges's *Unfaithfully Yours*) of showing first of all the way the plotter thinks things will go and then deflating this ideal picture with the unforeseeable actuality, in which, of course, everything goes wrong for all sorts of tiresome, trivial reasons. Buñuel's gifts of fantastic invention have seldom been so happily (in both senses of the term) employed as in some sequences here, notably the child-hood reminiscence, with the boy dressing up in his mother's clothes, the wedding reception, and the group of chattering tourists who break into his best-laid scheme.

With *Archibaldo de la Cruz* Buñuel broke the sequence of his Mexican films, but before it he made one more film which deserves brief comment, a version of *Wuthering Heights* variously called *Cumbres Borrascosas* or *Abismos de Pasion* (1953). Buñuel himself tends to reject this as an anachronism, which in a sense it was, being virtually a literal realization of the script prepared as long before as 1932 in collaboration with Georges Sadoul and Pierre Unik (with Katharine Hepburn in mind!). Nevertheless it is remarkable on several counts. For one thing it is, despite the changes of name and location, a brilliantly clear-headed and faithful piece of adaptation, far superior to Ben Hecht's and Charles Mac-arthur's much-praised script for the Wyler version: it starts with

Heathcliff's return and sweeps the spectator straight into the central conflict in Cathy's soul. But apart from this it has a number of striking ideas – like Edgar's butterfly collecting – and several remarkable sequences, notably Heathcliff's brutal wooing of Isabella before Cathy's eyes on the bare mountainside and the fantastic finale of *amour fou* (the adaptors' principal liberty with their text) whereby Heathcliff breaks into Cathy's grave in the family vault and is shot dead embracing her lifeless body. *Wuthering Heights* was always a favourite work of the surrealists, and here an old surrealist has paid a surprising but remarkably effective tribute to it.

During the next phase of his career, from 1955 to 1961, Buñuel's films become much more resistant to the sort of neat compartmentation into major works and commercial chores which was possible with his purely Mexican films. For during this time he became involved in a series of co-productions, particularly with French companies; the films were mostly more expensive than his Mexican films had been, and consequently the amount of outside interference became greater and more difficult to assess precisely. One of the films from this time, *La Mort en ce Jardin*, for instance, shows signs of having begun as a genuine Buñuel work, and it still has odd scenes with the true flavour, such as that in which the heterogenous band of fugitives escaping through the forest come upon a wrecked plane and dress up in incongruous fragments of miscellaneous finery from the luggage, but in the main the original conception, whatever it may have been, seems to have been fairly thoroughly compromised in the execution. The same is true of *La Fièvre monte à El Pao*, a basically interesting study of the way idealism can prove the most destructive and equivocal element in a revolutionary situation, of which as the script finally emerged Buñuel could say no more than that neither he nor the star, Gérard Philipe, took it seriously for a moment, but they had fun making it. To this period, too, belong a number of projects which came to nothing, among them some which might have been exciting: Pierre Louys's *La Femme et le Pantin*, Evelyn Waugh's *The Loved One* with Alec Guinness, Matthew Lewis's *The Monk* translated by Antonin Artaud, with Gérard Philipe as Ambrosio . . .

However, from this phase also two major films emerged, *Cela s'appelle l'aurore* and *Nazarin*, as well as a fetching minor work,

The Young One. The most underestimated of these is the first, though not by Buñuel himself, who counts it among his favourites, along with *Un Chien Andalou, Los Olvidados* and *Nazarin* (that was in 1959). Based on a novel by Emmanuel Roblès, adapted by Buñuel and the French poet and critic Jean Ferry, it tells of life on an island virtually run by a rich, respectable industrialist – an industrialist, that is, who, as well as being an influential supporter of law, order and the Church and a model husband and father, is perfectly ready, with the blessing of the authorities, to evict tenants who do not come up to his standard of efficiency, keep safety precautions at his factory to a minimum, dismiss anyone he wants to, and have any of the girls in the factory who happen to catch his eye. A number of apparently unconnected incidents establish the brutality just below the surface of life: the children playing at executions; the old man who attacks a little girl, is shut up in a chicken-run by the family and brutally battered in his turn by the police commissioner, who in his spare time has a taste for Claudel (it would, of course, be a Catholic author *par excellence*). Among the brutalities is the eviction of the workman Sandro, who appeals for aid to his friend and former comrade-in-arms Valerio, the local doctor. When as a result of the move Sandro's sick wife dies, Sandro decides to take revenge, and in one of Buñuel's most stunning scenes walks into the middle of a reception at the industrialist's house (another ripe for the tumbrils of *L'Age d'Or*) and shoots the industrialist dead at point-blank range. Meanwhile Valerio, torn between his love for a glamorous stranger and his duty towards his bored, fretful wife, decides to throw in his hand irrevocably with Sandro and the forces of rebellion, to have no more to do with the degradation of the society about him. After Sandro has committed suicide Valerio refuses to shake hands with the police commissioner, and walks away towards the sea with his mistress and three of Sandro's comrades; in rejecting the false values of religion and organized society he has gained love and friendship, to which in Buñuel's world all else must bow. *Cela s'appelle l'aurore* is not a constructive work; it is not the business of Buñuel the anarchist-surrealist to construct, but to tear down, to throw aside, to show the way of rejection, to call to revolution, and that is precisely what the film does. It has been accused of a certain stiffness and formalism, but I do not feel this myself; its realization is of the utmost clarity and simplicity, with no divagations into dream and vision, but all the same it bears Buñuel's stamp, both in being a subject which no director except him would be likely to tackle in the first place, and in the innumerable little personal touches like the rapist in the chicken-run and the head of Christ disfigured by electric cable fittings. And the sequence of the reception and the murder, with its ruthless logic, would have to be included in any Buñuel anthology.

The film Buñuel made in Mexico in 1958, in the middle of this period, *Nazarin*, has been one of the most controversial of all his films, if only for the ambiguity of its 'message'. Based on a novel by the nineteenth-century Spanish writer Perez Galdos, it concerns the life of a saintly priest, and has been seized upon by a number of commentators as evidence that Buñuel, the arch-atheist, returned in his sixties to the religion in which he was brought up, that all his fury against it was just the struggle of a fish irrevocably hooked. But though the film is profoundly ambiguous it somehow just does not come over like that: it seems, if anything, to be Buñuel's most completely non-Catholic film, in that, as Ado Kyrou nicely puts it, 'Buñuel is no longer anti-clerical, he is atheist, he has found calm . . .' Consequently, the central character of the priest is not, as one might have expected earlier, castigated simply for being a priest; instead he is accepted as sincere, saintly even, and a truly heroic character. But because of this the gradual revelation of the impossibility of his position and his gradual disillusion with it become all the more damaging.

Nazarin's only mistake is to try to live quite literally by the teachings of Christ in this world, and as Buñuel has remarked else-where in this connexion, 'One can be *relatively* Christian, but the absolutely pure being, the innocent, is condemned to defeat. He is beaten in advance.' In trying to live a Christian life in the most literal sense Nazarin is misunderstood and rejected by all, becomes an outcast from his own church and people, is followed into the wilderness by a band of devoted women whose motives, he comes to realize, are not of the purest, and finally, completely disillusioned, is saved from despair and brought to new hope (as a Christian, the apologists would say; as a human being with a free soul, as others, including surely Buñuel, see it) by a disinterested act of kindness, the gift of a piece of fruit to a solitary man on a hot and lonely road. The film moves relentlessly forward, but in the picaresque style beloved of Buñuel, with each episode centring on Nazarin and each marking a further stage in his mental evolution, like an elevated Rake's Progress. Indeed, the film progresses almost in a series of Brechtian tableaux, but with endistancement (the quasi-documentary objectivity we have noted so often in Buñuel's work) carried so far that the equivocal nature of the demonstration (it might, after all, be regarded as a series of Job-like trials to which God subjects His servant) is only modified somewhat at the end, where though the meaning of the last sequence seems just as elusive as the rest the accompaniment of drums, those same drums that right through from *L'Age d'Or* symbolize rebellion, links it with Buñuel's pronouncement that 'the "Christian" in his pure, absolute form . . . has no other way but that of rebellion, on this so badly made earth'.

This demonstration is taken up again, even more clearly and forcefully, in *Viridiana*, made in Spain three years later and arguably the greatest of all Buñuel's films. But meanwhile there was an interlude in the shape of a genuine but minor Buñuel film, *The Young One*, finally released in Britain as *Island of Shame*. This English-language film, made in Buñuel's freest and easiest style, is a precise and witty examination of a variety of prejudices, particularly racial. The three principal characters are an anti-negro game warden, a nymphet whom the death of her father places in his charge, and a runaway negro accused – in all likelihood unjustly – of rape. The action takes place on a sunny island off the coast of the United States, and echoes of *Robinson Crusoe* (in the relation of white to black, in the attitude of the girl to Christianity, which parallels Friday's) abound. Indeed, the lesson that the warden Miller learns is very much that learnt by Buñuel's Crusoe from Friday; having himself statutorily raped a minor – the girl Evvie – he suddenly finds himself as much on the wrong side of the law and society as the negro he so despises; the interfering attentions of a hypocritical clergyman (one who professes to have no colour prejudice, but still insists that a mattress slept on by a negro the night before must be turned before he can sleep on it) and a brutal boatman drive the two men finally into an uneasy alliance from which, perhaps, both learn something. But though the point being made is deeply serious, *The Young One* is first and foremost a light film, a comedy for much of the time, in Buñuel's sunniest manner, with many charming touches of character-observation, particularly where the girl Evvie is concerned: one wonders gleefully after seeing it what Buñuel could not have done with *Lolita*, given the chance. Evvie, like Oliverio in *Subida al Cielo*, is Buñuel's conception of a real innocent; that is to say, in the slightly old-fashioned phrase, a child of nature, untouched (and so unperverted) by Christianity and the social conventions. Younger in years but older far in experience than Viridiana, she offers a fascinating contrast with the eponymous heroine of Buñuel's next major film, and perhaps it is significant that Buñuel's two most successful full-length portraits of feminine characters should be thus juxtaposed, and should also be the diametrical opposites of one another in background and temperament.

Viridiana (1961) has been accepted by most critics as *the* Buñuel masterpiece, the director's final summary of what he has to say, and with that (except the 'final') it is easy enough to agree. *Viridiana* has about it a balance, a mellowness almost – if one dare use the word in connexion with Buñuel – which signals it out as the natural successor to *Nazarin* and *The Young One*: Buñuel can still shock, and in certain respects *Viridiana* is one of his most shocking films, but there is no longer the aggressive frenzy with which formerly he attacked the Roman Catholic Church, its priests and its works. Buñuel the atheist, calm and confirmed in his views, has taken over completely from Buñuel the anti-clerical, as *Viridiana* is a work of the most devastating amiability, sweetness and light; if it cuts to the roots of conventional religion, it does so with an understanding, almost a pitying, smile.

The film was actually made in Spain – Buñuel's first film in Spain, supervision apart, since *Los Hurdes* in 1932 – and though it is difficult to imagine how the script, in however rudimentary form, could have been found acceptable to the Spanish authorities, presumably it was; Buñuel, who had completed a draft of the script for filming in Mexico, accepted the invitation of a Spanish producer to make it in Spain, submitted his draft to the censors, and speaks only of certain modifications required, some of which, particularly in the final scene, actually improved the film by making it more subtle and indirect. On completion the film was shown at Cannes, where it shared the major prize; subsequently it has been shelved in Spain (the censors have not actually rejected it, just deferred consideration indefinitely) and distributed elsewhere in the world after arguments by the Mexican co-producer.

The reasons for official doubts in Spain are easy enough to see, even from a plot summary. *Viridiana* takes up, in a much more direct, unambiguous form, the subject of *Nazarin*: the impossibility of absolute Christianity in the modern world. The film is more explosive than *Nazarin* in that while in *Nazarin* we are permitted to accept completely the hero's purity of motive – the film did not explicitly condemn what he stood for but just said it could not work in the world as it is, a conclusion many of the devout have sadly come to as well as atheists – in *Viridiana* doubt is cast throughout both on the purity of her motives and the worth of her beliefs even if they would work. Viridiana is a girl on the point of taking her final vows and entering a convent. Her mother-superior presses her to visit her only relative, an uncle she hardly knows, before she does so, and unwillingly Viridiana agrees. At first things seem to go quite well, though she finds the closeness of country life to animal realities – cows have to be milked, eggs laid and collected – disturbing. But when her uncle, overcome by her extraordinary resemblance to the wife who died many years before on their wedding night, falls in love with her, begs her to marry him and finally, having persuaded her to dress in his wife's wedding dress, drugs her and all but rapes her, she decides to leave. Before she can get very far, however, she is told that her uncle has hanged himself, and returns, feeling responsible for his death and determined to atone.

Here we reach the main theme of the film. Viridiana and her cousin Jorge, her uncle's illegitimate son, are now left in charge of the house and farm. Jorge sets about getting electricity installed and the farm, long neglected, working again, while Viridiana undertakes 'good works' by taking in a collection of tramps and vagrants, feeding them and making them pray and live an apparently holy life. Eventually the inevitable happens; one day Viridiana and Jorge have to go into town on some business and while they are away the unprincipled vagrants break into the house, stage a feast which develops into an orgy, and when surprised by the unexpected return of the owners disperse into the darkness, the two who remain knocking out Jorge and setting with a will about raping Viridiana, a fate from which only Jorge's quick thinking saves her.

At the last we see her, after a hopeless attempt at taking up again a holy life, coming tentatively into the room where Jorge is playing cards with the housekeeper (with whom, since the departure of his mistress, he has established a liaison). She joins in; she has come over to his side, the side of practical full-blooded materialism which sees that things get done while religion falls back on aimless ritual and denies the body its due.

Even resumed in such terms the story sounds outrageous enough to conventional religious sentiment and *bourgeois* morality, but Buñuel has made it considerably more explosive in the telling. It is hard to think of a film more consistently 'Buñuelian', more packed with telling fragments of observation and perverse, often outrageously funny, asides. In the opening sequences there are all sorts of strange, suggestive moments: the glimpses of the uncle, Don Jaime, trying on various fragments of his late wife's trousseau; the elusive phallic symbols of the cow's udder and the handles of the skipping rope with which Don Jaime eventually hangs himself; the gesture with which Don Jaime, like Archibaldo de la Cruz upon his cure, casually saves an insect from death; above all the wonderful, mysterious scene in which Viridiana, sleep-walking, empties a work-basket into the fire, gathers up the ashes and deposits them on Don Jaime's bed. The rest of the film, too, is full of such effects, often more explicit – the cross-cutting between Jorge's construction work and Viridiana's futile prayers with a bribed congregation, for instance, and the grouping of the beggars round the feast-table into a parody of 'The Last Supper' before they launch themselves into a fantastic ballet-cum-orgy to the strains of Handel's *Messiah*. There is also the curious little scene in which Jorge, on a dusty road, takes pity on a dog trotting pathetically along tied behind a cart which is going too fast for it, and buys the animal, walking off with it as we – but not he – see another cart with another dog in the identical situation pass in the opposite direction. Apart from being a little visual joke – which it is very effectively – the scene is full of meaning, often apparently self-contradictory. Does it mean that it was pointless to save the one dog, because others remain unsaved? Is it an ironic reflection on all human charity? Well, perhaps, but at the same time it conveys something of Jorge's attitude to life as contrasted with Viridiana's: at least he has done something practical; without stopping to bother about principles he has at least saved one dog, whereas Viridiana and her kind would be too busy organizing a campaign to save all the dogs in Spain to do anything much for one dog in particular.

Buñuel's latest film at time of writing, *El Angel Exterminador*, made in Mexico for the same Mexican producer as *Viridiana*, Gustavo Alatriste, and with the producer's wife, Silvia Pinal, also starring, is very much a companion-piece to that film. This time comedy, which is lurking pretty continuously in the background of *Viridiana*, comes unmistakably to the fore, and it is, as was only to be expected, the black, iconoclastic humour of Buñuel's surrealist days. Again, as with *Viridiana*, the subject was chosen by Buñuel himself, the original script, *Les Naufragés de la Rue de la Providence*, being written by Buñuel and Alcoriza (Buñuel was alone responsible for the final version) and very freely adapted from a play by José Bergamin. A group of elegantly dressed, rich and influential people arrive for a dinner party after the opera, and as they arrive all the domestic staff except for the stalwart butler unaccountably leave, impelled by some urge they cannot explain. The dinner nevertheless goes off quite well, though the hostess, a noted practical joker, decides to shelve various jokes connected with a tame bear and a number of sheep when her first joke does not go down well with one of the guests of honour. After dinner the guests retire to the drawing-room, and stay on and on and on, disinclined, it seems, to leave, until finally they settle down to sleep out the rest of the night on the floor. The next morning the butler is summoned to provide breakfast, and he, too, once in the room, senses a curious unwillingness to leave. Indeed, he cannot leave, any more than the rest of them, and no one outside can get in.

This situation persists for days, even weeks perhaps. A water pipe is located in the wall and breached; the wandering sheep make a useful addition to the larder. An old man dies and two young lovers commit suicide; they are unceremoniously bundled into a cupboard, while another serves as an improvised lavatory. Finally one of the guests hits on the notion that perhaps if they all reconstruct the crucial moments in which they first failed to leave, perhaps this time they will manage things differently, and sure enough they do; they hobble out, pathetic exhausted remnants irresistibly reminiscent of the survivors from the Château de Selligny at the end of *L'Age d'Or*. True to the promise someone made, they go to give thanks with a solemn *Te deum* in the cathedral, but after the service is over no one can leave that either – as revolution breaks out in the streets, a herd of sheep are obligingly driven towards the main door of the cathedral, on the assumption presumably that it will be a long time, if ever, before the congregation can get out again.

El Angel Exterminador is inferior to *Viridiana*, if at all, in that it lacks the ruthless logic of that masterpiece: the principal plot devices – the ability to leave taken away, restored and taken away again – are entirely arbitrary, and do not pretend to be anything else. But otherwise the two films form perfect companion-pieces: if *Viridiana* is the summary of Buñuel's ideas on religion, *El Angel Exterminador* is the summary of his ideas on society and social convention: gleefully he watches society, placed in certain test conditions, breaking down from its internal contradictions and falsities, so that these rich, powerful, cultivated people become before long openly no better than the malicious, superstitious savages that, suggests Buñuel, they have always been underneath. The woman who tries to work charms with chicken feet has had them with her all the time (there is a marvellous, at the time unexplained, shot of them early in the film, peeping out of the diamanté evening bag from which she is extracting a dainty lace handkerchief); the petulant boy and his sister are clearly no strangers to the delights of the morphine which the host shamefacedly produces to meet a medical emergency; if the main trouble-maker is capable of throwing away an important box of pills from sheer malevolence after some days in these conditions, he was probably equally prepared to do so before.

As well as being in so many ways a summary of what Buñuel has to say about the Church and society, *Viridiana* and *El Angel Exterminador* show his art as a film-maker *per se* at its highest point, and for that reason, as well as because they are as I write his most recent films, offer a suitable pretext for a retrospective examination of this aspect of his work. There has been a lot in this chapter about what Buñuel is saying, relatively little, explicitly, about how he says it. The main reason for this, as explained at the beginning, is that Buñuel's prime interest in the cinema seems to lie in what he is saying; he does not start with a literary original and make it cinematic; it is simply that he expresses himself in cinematic terms

*7a. Les Dames du Bois
de Boulogne* (Maria
Casarès, right;
Lucienne Bogaert,
left). Dir: Robert
Bresson

*7b. Le Journal d'un
Curé de Campagne*
(Claude Laydu). Dir:
Robert Bresson

8a. *Un Condamné à Mort s'est Échappé* (François Leterrier). Dir: Robert Bresson

8b. Robert Bresson directs *Procès de Jeanne d'Arc*

because he creates films as unselfconsciously as other men write poems or paint pictures. This means that, as in the case of a very different director with whom nevertheless Buñuel has certain affinities, Jean Renoir, there is hardly ever any cinematic effect which forces itself on one's attention and calls for comment, as there is constantly in the work of Welles or Bergman. Effects are achieved instead for the most part with the utmost simplicity; it is simply (in the context that word has an ironic ring) a matter of putting the camera in the right place at the right time. Sometimes, consequently, Buñuel's films, like Renoir's, seem careless from their very ease and informality; he is not, we say, making the most of his material, getting all he can out of it. Ah, but isn't he? Even with his most casual, free-and-easy films like *The Young One*, which looks as if it was made up as Buñuel went along, and probably was, as soon as one comes to consider possible improvements, alternative, better ways of shooting a scene, the complete rightness and inevitability of the way Buñuel has done it is borne forcibly in on one.

Unfortunately (or perhaps not so unfortunately after all) this sort of direction does not make for critical purple patches any more than, say – to take a really unlikely comparison – Evelyn Waugh's prose style does; it does its job of work immaculately well by being unfailingly clear and never standing in the audience's way. It is always possible to pick out exceptions which prove the rule, like the magical slow-motion sequence in *Los Olvidados* in which the young boy dreams of his mother, but in the main the highest tribute one can pay to Buñuel's direction is to say that one is hardly ever conscious of it. All the elements are at least competent, and in *Viridiana*, given a little more time and money (though even so it cost only £80,000, which by normal British or American standards is absurdly little), they are all, but especially the acting and photography, outstandingly good. Yet still the parts are subservient to the whole, and it is the overall effect which one takes away, not the excitements of individual elements. The same is true, despite the perhaps too obtrusive arbitrariness of the plotting – we are really asked to take just a little too much on trust – of *El Angel Exterminador*, and of all Buñuel's best, most personal films before that. (It is, in fact, a sure indicator of Buñuel's lack of involvement with a particular subject, or at least his inability to shape it sufficiently to

C.E.–H

his needs because of outside pressures, if one comes away remembering only isolated 'Buñuel touches', as in *El Bruto*, say, or *La Mort en ce Jardin*.)

Indeed, one might almost carry the argument a stage further and maintain – except that this would seem to devalue the individual films unduly – that Buñuel's total *oeuvre* is greater than the sum of its parts: certainly each addition to it enlarges and clarifies the significance of what has gone before, while the recurrent motifs, though hardly obscure at first sight, take on further layers of significance when studied as they gradually develop from film to film. Buñuel maintains that he never deliberately 'puts in the symbolism': that he lets his instinct carry him along and often does not know why he has done something until someone else points it out to him (Francisco's zigzag walk at the end of *El*, for example, corresponding to that at the height of his insane frenzy of jealousy, was put in according to Buñuel 'just because I liked the effect' – and yet the significance that emerges from it is unmistakable). But whether consciously or unconsciously, Buñuel forgets nothing: even an experience as distant and peripheral as his work on *The Beast with Five Fingers* in Hollywood unexpectedly contributes something to *El Angel Exterminador*, where the same disembodied hand with the same murderous intent turns up in a dream of one of the guests. In a study such as this one can only barely indicate something of the unique coherence of Buñuel's work, which is perhaps more completely stamped with its creator's personality than any other in the cinema. Even less can one exemplify its specifically cinematic quality; there is, happily, no substitute for seeing the films, as only that way can the sublime simplicity and ease of Buñuel's art be appreciated. If I have seemed to concentrate too exclusively on the 'themes' in this chapter, I can only plead that this is the area where written commentary can be most helpful; it can provide a few footnotes, but there is no substitute for the poem but the poem, the film but the film.

Robert Bresson

ALL MAJOR FILM-MAKERS, LIKE ANY OTHER SORT OF
artist, must be to a large extent solitaries, making their own way
towards their own goals. How this works out in practice will vary
enormously, of course, from director to director. Unpopularity and
incompatibility with the normal standards of the commercial
cinema are by no means necessary qualities of the great director;
witness the case of Hitchcock, for example, who has always
managed to make the films he wanted to completely within the
commercial framework, or John Ford, who has worked consistently
on the principle of making two or three films to please other people
in order to obtain the freedom to make one film to please himself;
witness, for that matter, the considerable commercial successes
finally achieved by such an apparently remote, difficult director as
Antonioni. In fact, the one thing that virtually all the directors in
this book have in common is that by pleasing themselves they have
somehow ended up pleasing the public at large; their greatest
artistic successes have often been their greatest commercial successes as well. The major exception to this rule is Robert Bresson.

Bresson has made only six films in a career of twenty years. Two
or three of them have been commercial disasters, and the two which
fairly safely covered their costs, *Le Journal d'un Curé de Campagne*
and *Un Condamné à Mort s'est Echappé*, could not by the remotest
stretch of the imagination be regarded as great popular successes.
Essentially a quietist in the cinema, Bresson has devoted himself
with a quite unworldly dedication to working out and putting on the
screen his own vision, entirely without regard for what is going on
around him in the cinema and the world at large, and it is this
quality of remoteness, the hermetic perfection of the finished films,
which many find off-putting. His films are not easy, they do not go
out of their way to please or attract; they sometimes seem to be
made in complete unconcern over whether anyone will want to see
them or not. In this way they achieve a purity which makes even
Antonioni seem in comparison rather flashy and vulgar; they may
achieve it, however – or so those who do not like them say – only at

the risk of deteriorating from the calm detachment of the philosopher to the mere inertia of a dead object.

Whatever one may think of Bresson's two most recent films, though – significantly, his most popular films were the middle two, made when he had just achieved full maturity and before he had refined his style to a point beyond which many of his admirers, even, were unwilling to follow him – there is no doubt about the consistency of his development and about his unique significance as the extreme example of a particular view of the film-maker's art put into practice. That view might be briefly characterized as the autocratic view: the director is paramount in every area of the film, and all the others involved – actors, cameraman, editor, recording engineer, composer, etc. – are there only as tools to be used by the director, not as collaborators in any real sense of the term.

Bresson has expressed this view most clearly and unequivocally in relation to professional actors in the cinema:

Acting is for the theatre, which is a bastard art. The film can be a true art because in it the author takes fragments of reality and arranges them in such a way that their juxtaposition transforms them. Art *is* transformation. Each shot is like a word, which means nothing by itself, or rather means so many things that in effect it is meaningless. But a word in a poem is transformed, its meaning made precise and unique, by its placing in relation to the words around it; in the same way a shot in a film is given its meaning by its context, and each shot modifies the meaning of the previous one until with the last shot a total, unparaphrasable meaning has been arrived at. Acting has nothing to do with that, it can only get in the way. Films can be made only by by-passing the will of those who appear in them, using not what they do but what they are.

The same, *mutatis mutandis*, might well be taken as true for the other collaborators on Bresson's films: they represent to him only certain talents which he can use as extensions of his own to express his own vision, and this applies even to the distinguished literary collaborators he called on in his first two films – Giraudoux and Cocteau, respectively – to write the dialogue for the screenplays he had already completed.

So, for the final effect of his films Bresson is personally and totally responsible to an extent almost unparalleled in the modern cinema, and his career may be seen largely as a careful and unswerving progression towards this target. Little by little he has managed to dispose of professional actors, to do without literary collaborators on his scripts, to dispense, even, with specially written music: in *Un Condamné à Mort s'est Échappé* and *Pickpocket* the action is counterpointed with classical music (Mozart and Lulli respectively) and *Procès de Jeanne D'Arc* has only some 'orchestrated' drum-beats. Whatever one's ultimate estimate of the films, almost all of it, praise and blame, can be laid at Bresson's door.

Naturally this is less true for the first two films, *Les Anges du Péché* and *Les Dames du Bois de Boulogne*, than for those which come after – 'naturally', because Bresson, like any director who begins his career in the commercial cinema, had less control over the details of his films at the outset than he was later to achieve. In both he wrote the script in collaboration, and in both he was forced to use professional actors if he was to obtain financial backing at all. Up to 1943, when he began work on *Les Anges du Péché* (a silly title imposed by the producers; originally it was to be called *Béthanie*), he had had little experience in the cinema; born in 1911, he had spent most of his life painting (he never was a photographer, as is often reported – this idea probably arises from some confusion with Henri Cartier-Bresson) and had ventured into the cinema only to make a satirical short, *Les Affaires Publiques*, in 1934 – no copy seems to have survived, and he does not choose to talk about it – to work (in name only, he says) on the scripts of two almost equally mysterious films, *Les Jumeaux de Brighton* (1936) and *Courrier Sud* (1937), and to act as René Clair's assistant on his unfinished *Air Pure* (1940). So with *Les Anges du Péché* he was in a fairly precarious position and had to make some concessions if it was going to reach the screen at all.

In the circumstances it is remarkable how much of the future Bresson is foreshadowed in it, though the quality of the film itself has tended, I think, to be overestimated. The weakest element is the basic plot-line, and it is here that the film diverges sharply from Bresson's later works: the ideas may already be, as some critics have maintained, characteristically Bressonian, but they are embodied in a story which is overprodigal of incident and, worse and even less Bressonian, incident tending uncomfortably close to melodrama. This may partly be the result of the way the script was written, in collaboration with a Dominican, Father Bruckberger (who was also, incidentally, Bernanos's collaborator on the *Dialogues des Carmélites*), and Jean Giraudoux. The idea of making a film about the Béthanie order of nuns was originally Father Bruckberger's. Bresson, who had a contract with Pathé, but no subject acceptable to them, agreed, and worked with Father Bruckberger on the scenario, being, apparently, primarily responsible for the story while Father Bruckberger acted as religious adviser. Giraudoux agreed to write the dialogue, and in the process further modified the scenario, while Bresson and Father Bruckberger continued in close collaboration with him. All this means that though Bresson seems to have remained throughout very much in charge of the scripting, it is difficult to know how far he can be held accountable in detail for the result as filmed.

Briefly, the film concerns the intertwined stories of two young women in a convent of the Sisters of Béthanie, Anne-Marie and Thérèse. Anne-Marie is an enthusiastic novice of good family; she arrives at the convent at the same time as Agnès, who has recently left prison (it is part of the order's rule to rehabilitate prisoners and receive into conventual life girls of all backgrounds without distinction). Agnès tells her of Thérèse, another prisoner who is said to be incorrigible. Anne-Marie decides that it is her mission to save Thérèse. Thérèse at first abuses her advances, but when released she goes and shoots the man because of whom she was wrongly imprisoned, then takes refuge in the convent, pretending to have seen the light. Once in the convent Thérèse sets about flattering Anne-Marie's vanity and exacerbates a temperamental incompatability between Anne-Marie and the sub-prioress until it ends in disciplinary action being taken against Anne-Marie, her refusing to do the penance imposed on her (which is to kiss the feet of all the nuns) and leaving the convent. Later, Anne-Marie is discovered in a fainting condition in the convent cemetery where she has been coming every night to pray. She is received back into the convent, already dying, and is tended by Thérèse. When the time comes for Anne-Marie to take her vows she is too weak, and Thérèse does it for her by proxy; at last Thérèse is touched by Grace, and when the police come for her she goes with them willingly, without resisting.

Though one can examine the script in terms of themes dear to Bresson – the anatomy of sainthood, the idea of exchange – there seems little point in doing so. The film remains interesting above all not for the basic material but for the way it is treated -- I deliberately put it that way because here, and here alone in Bresson's work, a clear division between 'form' and 'content' exists; this is the film's principal weakness, but also makes it exceptionally significant in relation to Bresson's work as a whole by allowing us for once to examine his 'style' in isolation, as a thing-in-itself. The first thing to strike one is the extreme rigour of the film's composition. Already elements of the picturesque are cut down to the minimum. There is virtually no background or explanation; all we are permitted to glimpse of the life of Anne-Marie before the convent and Thérèse before prison is the absolute least Bresson can get away with and still make sense. Nor is there more than a hint of deliberate exploitation of the exotic backgrounds; though one may suspect a touch of indulgence in the prison scenes, and the scene in which Anne-Marie is found unconscious on the tomb of the Order's founder is really a trifle too gothick, the convent itself is depicted with remarkable restraint (especially considering that, as Father Bruckberger tells us, it was all quite novel to Bresson at the time). The life of the nuns is never explained or shown for its own sake; we simply see it being lived by the principal characters (effectively, we see it through the eyes of Anne-Marie), and little by little understand it and get the feel of it without further comment.

In other respects, too, the film already anticpates the mature Bresson. It is very tightly constructed, each scene being closely linked to what comes after by a gesture or a line of dialogue, and again Bresson concentrates only on the essential, switching brusquely, for example, from Anne-Marie being expelled from the convent to Anne-Marie in her ordinary day-clothes, as at the beginning. Once or twice his taste for the elliptical seems indeed to be indulged for its own sake: the scene in which Thérèse murders her lover -- just her in the corridor, a shadow in the doorway, a brief greeting and several shots -- sticks out rather too much as a showpiece, in a way which Bresson was subsequently to avoid. The photography, too, is a little too obtrusively beautiful, the contrast of white walls and dark, sculptural habits being clearly irresistible to the cameraman. The acting is mostly excellent and only really arguable in the case of the Anne-Marie (Renée Faure) -- Bresson later remarked blandly that the main trouble with having to use professional actors is that it cuts down so the amount of human raw material available to one, and in the circumstances one should perhaps rather be grateful that for the two other principal parts, the Prioress (Sylvie) and Thérèse (Jany Holt), he happened so fortunately on exactly the right human material. And if the soundtrack is not so meticulously worked out as it is in later films, there are still some very impressive moments, particularly in the use of silence, as when Anne-Marie has to burn her links with the outside world on entering the convent.

So in *Les Anges du Péché* we have hints of Bressonian themes and a sketch of Bresson's way with his performers, his approach to visual style and narrative construction. The film still shows some uncertainties and inconsistencies, but after all remarkably few for a first work, and these disappear altogether in Bresson's next film, *Les Dames du Bois de Boulogne* (1944–5). Where in *Les Anges du Péché*, for all its originality, there are signs of compromise, conscious and unconscious, with the traditional forms of film-making, here there is only one, and that, though tiresome, finally unimportant: the casting, enforced by the producers, of Paul Bernard, the current popular romantic hero of the French cinema, in the leading male role. Otherwise the film is made without any compromise with an audience's conventional expectations. And this explains, as well as its lasting qualities (though Bresson himself does not care for it or *Les Anges du Péché* today, for many critics it remains his greatest film), its almost unqualified failure with the cinemagoing public of the time – a failure which kept Bresson effectively out of the cinema for five years afterwards.

Les Dames du Bois de Boulogne is virtually a manifesto of Bresson's belief in the cinema as an interior art: as he remarked in an interview with Jean Queval, 'It is what goes on inside that is most important. Only the tying and untying of knots inside the characters gives a film its movement, its true movement. It is this movement which I set about making clear by something or some combination of things beyond merely what is said.' And like most manifestoes *Les Dames du Bois de Boulogne* does not exactly make things easy for unprepared spectators. The story concerns a savage and overbearing passion, but the treatment is formal to the point of being glacial; the picturesque and anecdotal are totally lacking, the narrative being stripped to the bone; and the film progresses consistently by a series of ellipses, wasting nothing, elaborating

nothing and calling, at any rate in 1945, for remarkable powers of
concentration from its audience. Moreover, the action is all placed
in a deliberately remote, artificial world carefully abstracted from
all the usual realistic associations on which the viewer might call
for help; perfectly hermetic, closed in on itself, the film seems to be
made in total disregard of its audience, and this the audience,
annoyingly but predictably, tend to resent.

How exactly did Bresson arrive at this extreme position in only
two films? Evidently he did it deliberately, to show precisely what
he was up to, and having shown it he was able in his next two films
to apply the same sort of technique to subjects which allowed
audiences an easier way in by starting from something which might
be expected to arouse an initial stock reaction of some sort (ascetic,
saintly young priest in a hostile parish; young man condemned to
death trying to escape). But in *Les Dames du Bois de Boulogne* the
subject is deliberately chosen to repel this sort of too-easy sympathy, to place the audience willy-nilly on the outside looking in.
Bresson found his subject in Diderot's rambling episodic novel
Jacques le Fataliste. There at one point the hostess of a group of
sophisticates tells a story of womanly revenge and how that revenge
is finally thwarted which, extracted from the interruptions, diver-
sions and critical comments of the hearers with which Diderot
intersperses it goes like this: Madame la Pommeraye, sensing a
cooling in her lover, the Marquis des Arcis, forces him to an
admission of it by pretending first that her own passion has cooled.
Though the pair then apparently settle down as loving friends, she
determines to revenge herself, and for this purpose seeks out an old
acquaintance who has fallen on evil days and lives now on the
highly dubious earnings of her daughter. These two she takes up,
disguises as impoverished but eminently pious and respectable, and
traps her former lover into falling in love with and marrying the
girl. She then takes her revenge by revealing to him his wife's past,
but in the end it slips through her fingers; she has done her work
too well, and the Marquis loves his wife enough to forgive her and
continue happily married.

The precise way that Bresson set about adapting this wandering
and disjointed narrative for the screen makes a fascinating study
and is gone into fully in Jean Semolué's book on his work. It is
enough for our purpose to note that he has concentrated it in time

and made the time scheme explicit – three years since the avenger lost touch with her old acquaintance, two since she began the affair; three months while the trap is set for the ex-lover; wedding, revelation, and forgiveness all in one day – and that he has modified the intrigue in the light of the comments on it Diderot puts in the mouths of the auditors when the hostess has finished, particularly those on the character of the girl, who they suggest would be more sympathetic if she were an innocent dupe rather than an eager collaborator. Oh yes, and that he has 'modernized' the story, re-christening the characters simply as Helène (Madame le Pommeraye), Jean (the Marquis des Arcis) and Agnès and her mother, and placing them in a contemporary setting.

This modernizing, as a matter of fact, is the central problem of the film. A lot of argument has raged round the question of Bresson's intentions in thus moving, almost without modification, a completely eighteenth-century plot to a twentieth-century setting. Even critics, like M. Semolué, who recognize that the issue of credibility on a basic documentary level is not vital to the film have tried to make out a case for it in realistic terms, explaining that in the very highest Parisian society eighteenth-century locutions are still employed, eighteenth-century codes still obtain, women wear their hats at table and so on. All of which may or may not be true, but misses the essential point: that the inevitable impression produced by the film on those who are not so enviably *au fait* with the usages of high society – which is to say, nearly everyone – is one of dislocation between the action and its setting. And this obviously is intended: this is the main thing which abstracts the film from too-ready audience involvement and gives it the timelessness of true tragedy. Great care is taken to see that the action broadly makes sense in twentieth-century terms: for the power of rank in the original is substituted the power of money; for the horror of misalliance the horror of being exposed to personal ridicule. But there is no attempt to make the action conform in detail to normal twentieth-century habits of mind; it remains an eighteenth-century plot set down with artful arbitrariness in a setting of two centuries later, so that we are forced to forget all easy ready-made associations (either with 'modern life' or with our accepted notion of the eighteenth century) and respond freshly and immediately to the particular experience the film offers.

This experience is one of such concentration and intensity that the name of Racine immediately springs to mind for comparison. And undoubtedly the comparison is just, perhaps even intended by Bresson, who has frequently quoted Racine in discussing the film. Hélène in particular is unmistakably a figure from the same world as Phèdre or Athalie, and it was one of those happy chances that she became the first major creation of an actress, Maria Casarès, who was subsequently to prove herself the greatest tragedienne of her day. In *Les Dames du Bois de Boulogne* she gives a performance which succeeds largely by not seeming to be a performance; under Bresson's direction she gives no evidence of 'technique' at work, but simply 'is' the part; he has used her for the qualities he sees in her rather than for her conscious abilities as an actress. The appearance above all is perfect: the long, pale face with the high, prominent brow, the thin, angular body and the mass of dark hair – hardly in any usual sense beautiful, but capable of projecting a strange, esoteric elegance which the bizarre clothes she is given to wear, the long, dark dresses and the towering, Sitwellian hats, perfectly complement and emphasize. Hélène belongs not quite to any outer world; she carries her own world about with her, a dark, passionate, anguished world which comes near to engulfing all those who come in contact with it – so much so that the final salvation from it of Jean and Agnès never rings quite true (here, maybe, the disadvantages of Paul Bernard as Jean are most clearly to be seen).

The film, up to the final sequence, is built entirely around Hélène, and she is the prime mover of the action; each stage in it, up to the last, is the result of a conscious decision by her. The film opens with three brief preparatory scenes which provide, with the greatest economy, all we need to know of what has gone before and set the scene for what is to follow. In the first we see Hélène coming back from an evening at the theatre with Jacques, her oldest friend, who chides her for giving up everything for a lover who no longer loves her. At home, the lover, Jean, is waiting for her and she employs her little stratagem to find out his true feelings. Finally, left alone, she refuses all calls and says simply, with terrible calm, 'Je me vengerai.' We dissolve from Hélène's face straight to Agnès, who is to be the instrument of her vengeance, dancing in a night-club, and from this moment the film moves inexorably forward, without a scene or a word wasted, as Hélène lays her trap and waits for the right moment to spring it. The narrative line is absolutely straight, without detours or gaps, everything is stripped down to the essential. The backgrounds are sketched in boldly and simply, and they are all functional – even the few hints of picturesqueness beyond what was strictly relevant to the story in *Les Anges du Péché* have now been left behind.

Above all it is a film of faces, mostly in close-up or medium close shot. But it does not just depend on faces, in the sense of leaving most of the job to the actors and placing a minimum of interference between them and the audience. It is the way the director treats the faces as merely one element in his 'écriture' which counts. Bresson once defined 'écriture' in these terms:

> The author writes on the screen, expresses himself by means of photographed shots of variable length, and from variable angles. On an author worthy of the name, a choice is imposed, dictated by his calculations or his instinct, never by chance. For him, and for him alone, once he has worked out his decoupage, each shot he takes can have only one definite angle, one certain length of time.

Les Dames du Bois de Boulogne appears now as his first complete and unfaltering attempt to put this into practice: the inherent qualities of the faces, and for that matter the backgrounds as far as we are aware of them – the bare, light flat in which Agnès and her mother are installed, with trees in the square outside; Hélène's dark, richly furnished home; the cascade in the Bois de Boulogne where Jean first meets Agnès – are, of course, important, or Bresson would not have expended so much care on their choice, but more important still is the way these materials are used. In the very first scene, for example, Maria Casarès counts for a lot, but even more telling, finally, is the way the scene is put together, with her pale, tragic mask emerging from the gloom of the car interior while the voice of her unseen companion tells her the things she knows perfectly well and does not want to know at all. In this way throughout the film – though seldom in such an immediately striking way, so impeccably do the various elements coalesce – the images carry at least as much significance as the text, constantly enriching it, adding nuances, complexities and ambiguities, and sometimes taking over all by themselves, as when Hélène watches

Agnès dancing in the cabaret, to tell us something which the words hardly hint at.

The relation between words and images in this film is, in fact, extraordinarily subtle and intricate. It is by no means as some have maintained, taken in perhaps by the 'literary' tone of the dialogue, a writer's film in which what is said is all-important and what is seen remains only an otiose accompaniment. Though indeed the text is readable in a way that few film scripts are, that proves little; by the same token the images would make sense to a viewer who could not understand a word of the dialogue. As often as not the dialogue, being said rather than acted (here Bresson's distaste for acting in the cinema is in evidence), seems like an emotionally neutral commentary on the highly charged images, which suggest something altogether less cool and classical. There is, almost, a counterpoint between the dark, impassioned world which we see and the measured formality of what we hear, even though their intellectual significance is the same. The words act, in a way, as an endistancing agent, helping us (as Bresson puts it) 'to see the characters, as Racine requires, "with different eyes from those with which we normally look at people close to" '.

This effect of endistancement by apparent duplication, and this use of the spoken word in drama virtually as a commentary on the action, is taken up and developed much further, with many additions, ramifications and apparent contradictions, in Bresson's three subsequent films, all of which actually make use of a fully developed commentary, that anathema of the conventional film theorist. The main objection to a commentary, though, seems to be that it detracts from the visual nature of the film; that it is the film's way to make its points visually, with words as an occasional helpmate, not to be too frequently called upon, and in a story film, at any rate, the use of a continuous commentary is felt to be something like an admission of defeat. What, then, should the purist make of *Le Journal d'un Curé de Campagne*, which not only originates in a novel by Bernanos written in diary form, but actually opens with a shot of a notebook and a hand writing in it, followed almost at once by a voice on the sound-track reading what has been written, and returns almost throughout to the notebook, or the voice, or both?

Before we can answer that question, it is necessary to look more closely at what exactly the commentary does in the film. First, it establishes the film's tone and suggests its structure: it will be quiet, intimate, subjective, recording, as the first entry puts it, 'avec une franchise absolue, les très humbles, les insignifiants secrètes d'une vie d'ailleurs sans mystère', and in it events will follow each other naturally, one after the other, as day follows day – carefully-worked-out links of scene with scene which were such a noticeable feature of the previous two films will not be required. Next, it places us in a special, and in some ways a paradoxical, relationship with the protagonist, the young curé of Ambricourt. On the one hand it implies an immediate intimacy, even, one might think, an automatic identification with him, since we are, after all, permitted to see into his mind. But on the other, the device has in practice quite the opposite effect: a barrier, the barrier of what he writes about himself, is put between us and direct imaginative participation in the action. Instead of being presented implicitly with an interpretation of his story which works on us subliminally, we are overtly given his interpretation of what happens and left to judge for ourselves. In the very process of welcoming us into the heart of the story Bresson places us all the more effectively on the outside, seeing it with eyes unfogged by too-easy sentimentality.

All this is done by the narration, and could be done in no other way. If any further justification were needed it is to be found in the detailed relation of narration and what we see. Never does the journal-narration merely duplicate what we see, as in so many films it does. ('I was worried that night', accompanied by a close-up of the speaker looking worried, and so on.) At most it may summarize a whole phase of experience merely suggested by a few shots. ('Nuit affreuse. Dès que je fermais les yeux, la tristesse s'emparait de moi.') More usually a phrase or two introduces a scene (the film's principal overt continuity device) or intervenes during a dialogue to add the Curé's inner voice to the proceedings, commenting on his unexpressed thoughts or feelings. The very regularity of the diary's recurrence also has its place in the scheme, giving the film as a whole a rondo-like structure with a refrain, always different yet always immediately recognizable.

Two French critics, indeed, have hit on and elaborated this idea of a rondo with recurrent themes. René Briot, putting it in purely visual terms, sees the film as a series of variations on three themes, the notebook in which the Curé writes his diary, the Curé's face, and the gates of the château. Jean Semolué, more philosophical, also disentangles three themes, the Curé's illness, his social isolation, and his solitude as a priest. It would perhaps not be too fanciful to suggest a link between these two sets of themes: the book is the repository of the Curé's most private and searching meditations on his priesthood and spiritual life, which he cannot speak to anyone else; his face records more vividly than anything else can the progress of his malady; and the gates obviously stand vividly for the sort of forces which keep him socially isolated.

However, this is really hardly more than an intellectual parlour-game. Both ways of looking at the film are 'true', in the sense that neither falsifies the facts, and both suggest how in different ways Bresson preserves the unity and concentration of what one might at first sight expect to be a rather rambling and formless film. Certainly the book on which it is based is discursive in the extreme, and in most ways, one would have thought, the last thing likely to appeal to a director drawn to the sharp, classical lines of *Les Dames du Bois de Boulogne*'s plot. But again Bresson's adaptation (done largely at the scripting stage, but more than usual in the editing, by eliminating scenes and characters) is a model of clear-headed analytical study. From the variety of incident and reflection in the work he picks out one clear thread of continuity – the progress of the Curé, through trials and doubts, to understanding and acceptance of his role as 'prisonnier de la Sainte Agonie' – and eliminates everything which does not directly relate to this. Every incident in the film, however small and apparently insignificant, contributes in some way to the Curé's realization of his own destiny – a destiny in which his illness and his isolation both as man and as priest all play a part.

In other words, the effect of the journal commentary in making us accept things as they come without inquiring too closely into the logical connexions between them is not finally necessary; it is a device to put us off our guard, if you like, so that the more subtle relationships between the parts may become apparent only gradually, without any too violent schematization. In this way, too, it assists the dramatization of the book in properly cinematic terms by leaving us no excuse whatever for expecting theatrical effects. It remains in form, and so in our expectations, a tale that is *told*, not acted out. This means that none of the scenes have to be played up to their full theatrical potentialities; on the contrary, if one compares the film with the book it often turns out that it is precisely the more superficially 'telling' phrases and actions that have been dropped – great spiritual dramas are not played out in external action, but in the movement of souls, and this, more vividly than anywhere else in the cinema, is what Bresson captures here, in apparently flat, unimpassioned exchanges, while ordinary life goes on all round (a dog barks as the Curé recognizes his true spiritual identity; a gardener mows the lawn outside as the Countess returns to faith).

In *Le Journal d'un Curé de Campagne* Bresson, given a subject perfectly suited to his special talents, achieved for the first time the ideal realization of his concept of cinematic *écriture*; for once, everything, lighting, composition, setting, sound, all contribute to an infinitely subtle, infinitely complex final effect in such a way that not a shot could be removed or changed without the film losing something – indeed, for me this film remains the most nearly faultless ever made. The way the story is told, with absolute economy and simplicity – nothing too much, and yet none of the ellipses obtruding themselves as virtuoso displays – is model, and the sequence of moods as the Curé moves through his unwelcoming parish and his dark night of the soul towards the moment when he can help another – the Countess – and then see his own way and experience his own vision before dying with the words 'Tout est grâce' on his lips is impeccably managed; perhaps nothing in Bresson's work shows his mastery so completely as the conception and placing of the episode when, at his departure from Ambricourt, the Curé rides pillion on a motor-bike, the one sunny moment in an overcast, drizzling world, and for a short space of time we see him as he might have been in other circumstances, we see how far he is just like all other young men, and how, too, he is fundamentally, irrevocably different.

The easy, unobtrusive perfection (so different, incidentally, from the hard, self-conscious glitter of *Les Dames du Bois de Boulogne*) extends to the photography of Léonce-Henri Burel, from this film on Bresson's invariable collaborator, which is throughout grey, pale and diffused, suggesting Corot in many of the exteriors and matching perfectly Bernanos's comment in the book about the apparent weightlessness of the village. The sound-track, with its scrupulously calculated pattern of natural sounds and its tactful use of a score by Jean-Jacques Grünenwald, is a work of art in itself. And the performances – if one can properly use the term – are impeccable throughout; in this film Bresson achieved his ambition of dispensing with professional actors, all the players except two (Marie-Monique Arkell as the Countess and Antoine Balpêtré as the atheist Doctor Delbende, who tells the Curé he comes from alcoholic stock) being amateurs or beginners. But finally there is a limit to what analysis and exegesis can do; the film gives up its secrets only when seen, and when it has been seen all attempts at critical comment are likely to seem, even more than usual, absurdly beside the point.

The same applies, to a slightly lesser degree, to Bresson's next film, *Un Condamné à Mort s'est Échappé* (1956), also known as *Le Vent souffle où il veut*, which for me represents, with *Le Journal d'un Curé de Campagne*, the height of Bresson's achievement to date. It has a number of features in common with the preceding film, and also with the one which followed, *Pickpocket*: they all use a first-person commentary delivered in the character of the protagonist, and they all recount a process analagous to that of spiritual realization after passage through a dark night of the soul, though this theme is disguised in the two later films, which seem at first glance to be something quite different. In the case of *Un Condamné à Mort s'est Échappé* the difference between the two readings of the film are clearly suggested by the two titles; the film which a public otherwise indifferent or hostile to Bresson's films saw and enjoyed was no spiritual drama, but an escape story, a bit on the dry side perhaps, but making up in documentary detail what it lacked in picturesque side-glances at Gestapo torture and all that.

As a matter of fact, the film is genuinely ambivalent. It can be reasonably taken in this way, and if one does not choose to see any more in it one is not forced to – except possibly for a vague uneasiness here and there when the action is accompanied by snatches of Mozart's Mass in C minor. On the other hand, it can be taken equally well as a study in existential self-construction; Fontaine's destiny becomes to escape, and he concentrates all his energies and thoughts on it, sacrificing everything (and potentially everyone) else to it with the same single-minded dedication that the Christian is required to devote to saving his own soul. He manufactures himself in and by the act of escaping, and progresses towards his goal with the certainty of a sleep-walker, knowing that what he needs will come to him, like the gifts of Grace, unasked and unpredictable. The wind bloweth where it listeth, and if the escape attempt of another prisoner had not failed his would not have been able to succeed; if fate had not brought him an ally at the right time he could not have escaped at all; if, even, a spoon had not been left lying around in the courtyard just when he needed it as a tool. . . . All coincidence, perhaps, and Fontaine, on his own admission not religious and entirely self-reliant, simply accepts what comes to him; but in another way – and here the real ambivalence of the film is to be found – all are signs of blessedness in a world where, for one man at least, 'tout est grâce'.

The structure of the film has much in common with that of *Le Journal d'un Curé de Campagne*; the same first-person narrative, flatly and impersonally delivered (the script is based on a newspaper account of an actual escape by André Devigny, later elaborated into a book), the same implication that things are just happening as day follows day, the same scrupulous establishment of an interior continuity, with nothing wasted and nothing irrelevant. The difference between these two films and *Les Dames du Bois de Boulogne*, in fact, is not as at first appears in the care with which everything is related to everything else in the construction, but the degree to which this is allowed to be seen by the audience: in *Les Dames du Bois de Boulogne* a point is made of the extreme neatness of construction, and it becomes a feat of evident artistry; in the two later films much of Bresson's art is devoted to concealing the art with which they are constructed, and thereby allowing the construction to work all the more effectively on us for not being immediately apparent.

Bresson himself has said of *Un Condamné à Mort s'est Échappé* that the problem was 'to make a rapid film out of things slow in themselves, out of the slow, heavy life of the prison. The shooting script consists of 600 shots, but there are no sequences; the whole film is one long sequence.' In this way the cumulative effect builds up gradually, without relief, and all irrelevances are sternly eliminated. Thus we never learn exactly why Fontaine is in prison in the first place; we hardly see the Germans at all, but simply feel them as presences on the edge of the shot, voices rapping out an occasional command – even when Fontaine is briefly interrogated we never see his interrogator's face. Everything is seen from Fontaine's point of view, not so much literally, by liberal use of subjective camerawork (though when this is employed – as Fontaine looks through his window or the peephole in his door, for instance – there is absolutely no cheating, and we see no more than he could see) as by confining us to the world he can see or imaginatively appreciate – even the few shots outside his cell when he is inside, such as that of the guard's key clattering along the supports of the metal rail, or that of Fontaine's improvised brush scooping up fragments of wood from under the door he is dismantling, correspond exactly to the flashes of imaginative vision he must be experiencing at these moments.

On the level of plotting, too, the effect of rapidity is gained by suppressing all except the essential stages of the story – that is, of the escape. The hows and whys are rigidly excluded unless they have a clear bearing on Fontaine's mental evolution: thus, we are never told, for example, exactly how his neighbour in his first cell manages to convey to him quite intricate messages or how, later, he reaches an agreement with the prisoner directly across the way, Orsini, that he will keep watch while Fontaine works on the door – these are merely presented as *faits accomplis*. Some sort of elaboration is permitted only in what mirrors Fontaine's state of mind: in his dealings with Terry, another prisoner who can smuggle messages to the outside and who is the occasion of Fontaine's first act of trust, or with Blanchet, the timorous and despairing neighbour with whom he gradually establishes contact and even a certain friendship. There are also briefly sketched relationships with others whom he meets in the washroom, the only place where the prisoners have even the slightest chance to talk among themselves – with Orsini, the prisoner whose escape attempt fails; with the priest who gives him the text ('Nicodemus saith unto him, How can a man be born when he is old? can he enter the second time into his mother's womb and be born? Jesus answered . . . Marvel not that I said unto thee, Ye must be born again. The wind bloweth where it listeth, and thou hearest the sound thereof, but canst not tell whence it cometh, and whither it goeth' – John III: 4–8). But all reflect back entirely on Fontaine, and no digression, nothing purely anecdotal, is permitted. Even when, near the end, the young prisoner Jost is put to share Fontaine's cell, perhaps to wreck, perhaps at last to make really practicable his escape plans, the camera remains on Fontaine, and the arrival is interpreted entirely through its effect on him.

As ever, therefore – perhaps more than ever – this places a great weight on the shoulders of the central character, especially considering that for a large proportion of the film he is alone on the screen. Here the film is completely successful. One cannot talk of the performance of François Leterrier in the role of Fontaine (as one could, still, talk of Claude Laydu's performance in *Le Journal d'un Curé de Campagne*); he quite simply *is* the part. How exactly Bresson brought this about is a mystery: certainly he chose unerringly someone (a philosophy student in real life) who not only looked the part but brought to it exactly the right qualities of personality, so that by merely saying (not in any normal sense acting) the lines of the commentary, merely going through the actions required of him, he could convey the character with utter conviction. On no one else in the film are similar demands made, but they all – Jost (an apprentice fitter), Blanchet (a journalist), even the German jailers, mostly recruited from among German students in Paris – have the same complete believability, the same air of uncalculated naturalness which enforces acceptance of the film's preface: 'This story is true. I give it just as it is, without embellishments.'

Nevertheless, however meticulous Bresson's documentary reconstruction – much of the film was shot on location at Montluc Fort, Lyons, where the events described took place; the cell reconstructed in the studio was a precise replica of the original, down to the smallest detail; Devigny himself was constantly in attendance to check the film's accuracy – the way the resultant film works on one is the absolute opposite of rough documentary realism. Every detail, when examined, proves to have its clear and deliberate place in the aesthetic system of the whole; nothing happens by accident, or without a specific effect in view. Every sound on the beautifully composed sound-track, for instance, whether something as apparently casual as a distant train-whistle or the clatter of a street-car outside the walls or as complex in its implications as the sections of the Mozart Mass, has its own part to play, reminding us of the world outside, life going on, or separating us from the immediate realities of the situation and enforcing a degree of philosophic endistancement which enables us to judge the action *sub specie aeternitatis*. Equally the pale, diffused photography of Burel, with its avoidance of sharp contrasts, helps to suggest the sameness, the monotony of prison life without ever becoming merely dull and featureless.

All this in *Un Condamné à Mort s'est Échappé* is admirable, and such is the confidence of the *mise en scène* – Bresson seems almost to share his hero's unquestioning certainty that what is needed will be given – that it is hard to think of the style as containing its own dangers. But dangers there certainly are, and in his next film, *Pickpocket* (1959) it seems to me that Bresson has, temporarily at least, succumbed to several of them. The first danger, and one which might seem at first glance relatively unimportant, there proves crucial; it is in the casting of non-actors who can just *be* the part. The part of Michel, the pickpocket, is to begin with more complicated (though not more complex) than that of either the Curé of Ambricourt or Fontaine; at least they, whatever they do or say, are 'sincere', and given an initial spiritual affinity between actor and role the actor has simply to be himself. But Michel is an erratic character, a *poseur* in some respects, and in others (his self-conscious conviction of his own superman status, for instance) hopelessly self-deceived. When questioned about the film now Bresson maintains that ideally he was right in choosing Martin Lassalle (a nephew of Supervielle) for the role, but admits that the spiritual affinities of actor and character may not have come through because of Lassalle's lack of ease with the French language (his background is Uruguayan). However that may be, it is noticeable that he does not manage just to say the commentary – again by the principal character, in the first person, and quite extensive – but tends to put expression into it, to act it even, and thereby weaken its effect. So, too, in the scenes where he is called on to speak – those with the enigmatic police inspector, his best friend, and the girl Jeanne – which contrast strongly with the much more convincing scenes when he says nothing. The girl who plays Jeanne also seems infected with his awkwardness and self-consciousness, and their scenes together have a quality which, within the rarified terms of reference of Bresson's cinema, one is tempted to call frankly hammy.

Thrown off-centre in this way, the film fails to rivet attention to the extent that the two previous films do, and we have time to notice other characteristics which are not entirely advantageous. For in works so closely knit as Bresson's, where no single aspect is allowed to obtrude itself, once things begin to fall apart the subordination of the parts to the whole becomes positively irksome, because it means that if the whole does not stand, the parts do not in themselves amount to much in the way of compensation. One cannot, for instance, say, 'Well, it doesn't quite come off, but at least it's beautifully photographed', or 'the music is marvellous', or something of the sort. In *Pickpocket* everything is carefully devised to set off the central spiritual drama in which Michel finds his way through petty crime to self-discovery and life, but when this fails to emerge it is left looking rather like *Hamlet* without the Prince of Denmark. Burel's photography is admirably unobtrusive: flat, diffused, almost newsreel in its plainness and determination not to be marked for irrelevant graces, it would be perfect, as the photography of *Un Condamné à Mort Échappé* is perfect, provided we were not compelled by the failure of the central matter to mark it only too well. The music this time is from Lulli, and seems pretentious in a way that the Mozart in *Un Condamné à Mort s'est Échappé* never does, for the same reason.

And so on. It all comes back to the casting of the central part. Bresson's '*écriture*' is a matter of fusing all the elements of the cinema together; 'writing' the film in the normal sense of the term enters into it very little. The stages of Michel's spiritual progress are never explained literally: we have to see them happening on his face. The human face, the expressive human face, is more than anything else the foundation of this *écriture* and when it is not present, when the face resolutely refuses to let us see into the soul, the whole point is gone. This, for me, is exactly what happens in *Pickpocket*: Martin Lassalle goes through the whole thing as though ill at ease and puzzled by what he is called on to do, and no sort of inner progression is evident from his first amateurish attempt at picking pockets, through his conversations with the police inspector (in which he gets involved in a sort of *Crime and Punishment* situation in which he is impelled to give himself away), his collaborations with professional pickpockets (including technical notes which are the most interesting part of the film) to his eventual, inevitable capture (almost deliberate, it seems), and when suddenly at the end he comes together with Jeanne and says simply 'What a strange way I have travelled to find you at last' there is no sense of a process completed, but only of an inexplicable change of character.

Technically *Pickpocket* is considerably rougher than the previous films, perhaps because much of it was improvised during shooting. Curiously for so meticulous a director, Bresson claims to do a lot of improvisation on the set; he usually knows, he says, what he is going to shoot, but not how he is going to shoot it until he starts the day's work. In his next film, *Procès de Jeanne d'Arc* (1962), this means even more than in *Pickpocket*, since the text is given rather than written. In *Pickpocket*, it is reasonable to suppose, some of the way of shooting was clearly in Bresson's mind even before the words to be used were down on paper – entirely his own words this time, with no literary original, no pre-existent story even. But in *Procès de Jeanne d'Arc* the text comes entirely from transcriptions of Joan of Arc's trial, selected, it is true, by Bresson, but not otherwise tampered with. All of Bresson's vision, his 'treatment' of the subject, must be in the precise way he puts it on the screen – the critical fidelity to the originals of *Les Dames du Bois de Boulogne* and *Le Journal d'un Curé de Compagne* carried, if you like, to its logical conclusion by treating historical *faits divers* with fidelity so severe that nothing at all is allowed to come between the event and its literal re-enactment; if Bresson's adaptation of Diderot is a critique of Diderot, his adaptation of Bernanos a critique of Bernanos, taking them apart in order to re-create them in a different medium, so his treatment of the facts in *Procès de Jeanne d'Arc* is a critique of the facts, taking them apart in order to re-create them in their own terms. Nothing is done to explain Joan of Arc, to render her sympathetic or unsympathetic, to colour our view of her; as it is in the spirit of Diderot or Bernanos that we should see things from a certain angle, in a certain light, and Bresson makes sure that we do, so it is, if one can speak so, the 'method' of a piece of literal reporting that we should just see them, in no particular light, from no particular angle, and that is what Bresson allows us here. We must judge the maid not from what we are told about her, but from what she – or the girl playing her – is.

Certainly everything else in the film is unhesitatingly subordinated to that end. It is a film totally without *complication*:

everything is shot in plain medium shot, from eye-level (sitting or standing according to circumstance), and the same set-ups constantly recur – the same angle on Joan as seen from the judgement-seat, the judges as seen by Joan, and not even the luxury of a variation from a simple to-and-fro alternation between these that a shot showing, say, Joan and her judges in the same frame, from the point of view of a spectator in court, might provide. There is no Mozart or Lulli or indeed any music at all to distract us from the central action; only some drumbeats at the beginning. There is not, even, any drama in the usual senses of the term: there is conflict, of a sort, between Joan and her judges, but the conclusion is foregone and we are not even permitted the sentimental anecdotism, as Bresson would probably see it, of a Joan in herself divided and torn by doubt. Bresson's Joan is smooth and unruffled (in accordance with Bresson's view that the records show her as no country bumpkin but a literate, soignée, even rather elegant figure), answering her judges with unswerving confidence and some asperity, betraying no half-stifled desire to live at any price or doubt that heaven awaits her. Even her retraction and retraction of that retraction seem merely a matter of form, an acting-out of what must happen, rather than evidence of a real division of mind. If one may use the word of something so muted and unassertive, the film is a paeon, and like all paeons has a way of seeming more than a little inhuman.

In what, then, resides its quality? It lies, I think, chiefly in its extreme interestingness. It does not involve one, it does not seem in itself to move one (though it is always difficult to keep separate in one's mind the emotions which come from associations and received ideas and those which are excited directly by the object before one). But it is interesting: interesting to hear the exact words which were used; interesting to learn the brutal details of the tortures, the examination of Joan's virginity; interesting, too, to see style pared down to an absolute minimum, where it borders on total non-existence. Bresson's art has always been one of elimination, of seeing what can be left out, what effects can be dispensed with; little by little he has trained himself to do without one resource of the cinema after another, just as before him the Japanese director Ozu gradually eliminated from his films moving-camera work, the dissolve, the fade, and nearly all variations of *cadrage*. It amounts, in a way, to a reduction of the external forms of the cinema in order that the content shall shine through the more clearly, which is all very well except that it ignores the fact that ultimately form and content are the same thing, single and indivisible. If you take away too much of what we for convenience' sake choose to call 'form', you may well find in the end that you have thrown the baby out with the bathwater; that the 'content' you were striving so scrupulously to preserve in all its integrity has somehow disappeared altogether in the process.

Procès de Jeanne d'Arc has, as I say, the interest of any theory carried to an ultimate extreme. It is more of a piece, more coherent by far than *Pickpocket*: it is indeed, I think, in its own terms a remarkable success. The only thing is that those terms may well be such that there is really almost no perceptible difference between success and failure, triumph and disaster. *Procès de Jeanne d'Arc* is so rigidly defined in its own terms, so totally pure and free from any human adulteration whatever, that finally it may mean everything or nothing entirely according to the temperament of the viewer, or indeed the mood of any particular viewer at any particular time – and this goes for every aspect of it from the presence – one can hardly say 'performance' – of Joan herself down.

One thing seems clear, though; that it is a *ne plus ultra*. Still, many people thought that of *Pickpocket*, and were proved wrong, so Bresson may still have some further revelations for us, some ultimate refinements in cinematic ascetism. But whatever may befall, it remains an inescapable fact that he has made in *Le Journal d'un Curé de Campagne* and *Un Condamné à Mort s'est Échappé* two of the supreme masterpieces of the cinema, and in *Les Dames du Bois de Boulogne* one of the most remarkable of *films maudits*. He has revolutionized our ideas – though not, alas, our practice – of literary adaptation in the cinema, and has been an important technical innovator, particularly in his use of commentary. And all this in a mere six films. Few film-makers can claim as much; none, I think, can claim more.

Ingmar Bergman

PERHAPS CRITICISM CAN HARDLY HELP BEING CONFES-
sion, but often the confession is too deeply embedded for the reader
to extract without difficulty and be reasonably sure of its significance. Basically, I believe, we start with an intuitive reaction of
favour or disfavour, a warming or a cooling towards the artist as
present in his work, and then we find reasons to back this up, or at
least we explore the reasons which, rightly or wrongly, we suppose
to lie behind this intuitive reaction. The confession of emotional
compatibility or incompatibility should, however, be made at some
stage, since our feeling the one or the other is bound to colour all
our specific opinions, and it is only fair that the reader should be
aware of this colouring when he comes to evaluate what we write.
I suppose the implication of emotional compatibility, of a general
sympathy with what the artist is trying to do, is pretty clear in
nearly all the chapters of this book, since I have naturally chosen to
write as far as possible about the directors I personally think worth
writing about and hope therefore I have a fair chance of writing
illuminatingly about. With Ingmar Bergman, however, the case is
different. I find Bergman disturbing not so much because I feel a
hostile reaction, a positive dislike of his work, but because I have
no general reaction at all. Some of his films I like very much, others
not at all, and there seems to be no overall view into which these
isolated reactions fit: I go to a new Bergman film not unwillingly,
but with none of the pleasant anticipation I would feel at the prospect of a new Buñuel, a new Fellini, a new Hitchcock. Maybe this
involuntary open-mindedness is an advantage, maybe not; I don't
know. But anyway it seems good to declare it at the outset. The
reader is warned.

Well, then. Ingmar Bergman, who was born in Uppsala in 1918,
is one of the key figures in our study of the evolution of the complete film-creator. Unlike most of the other people in this book,
who seem to have hit on the film as their medium at once and stuck
to it (like Buñuel) or to have drifted, finding nothing satisfactory
until they began film-making, Bergman is a man of many and dis-

parate talents, a writer and dramatist as well as a film-maker, a man
of the theatre as much as of the cinema. Formally, all is in order for
classing him as a film-creator in the fullest sense of the term: he
writes, produces and directs most of his own films, and in those
which he does not himself write he has a completely free choice of
writer and subject. And yet the suspicion persists, still, that it is
possible to be a brilliant *metteur-en-scène*, a sensitive interpreter
and first-rate technician in the cinema (as Visconti is, for example),
and at the same time a gifted creator of literary material in film
form (like Zavattini or Prévert), without the two talents being quite
fused into one; and that if it is possible, this may be precisely the
case with Bergman.

The distinction is subtle: too subtle, probably, to be suceptible
of demonstration. And yet if we could postulate two Bergmans –
Bergman the writer and Bergman the director – co-existent but
distinct, this might well help to clarify an occasional slight sense of
discomfort we feel in Bergman films which in any other circumstances we would put down to a director's determination to 'make
something' of the script which was not present in the original conception at all – as often occurs, for better or for worse, in the
theatre, and as surely should not happen when writer and director
are literally as well as metaphorically of one mind. Even this is to
oversimplify, though, for even if we agree that such a separation is
in theory possible and perhaps present in Bergman, we cannot
assume that the functions will be equally separate on all occasions,
in all films; or, indeed, that they will always be separate at all.
There is, above all, no simple formula to tie up so complex a figure
as Bergman, and at this stage one can only throw out a few general
ideas which may help to clarify our consideration of the individual
films as they come up.

Bergman was the son of a pastor, and has frequently remarked
himself on the significance of the religious background in his childhood, both in the development of his ideas and in the encouragement it offered to express abstract ideas in literal, visual terms (the
young Bergman would seem, to judge by his later testimony, to
have been particularly preoccupied with the visual presentation of
the devil; an interest which has never ceased to haunt him one way
and another). During his studies of art, history, and literature at
Stockholm University he became very interested in stage production,

and acted in and directed a number of student productions.
From these he went on to become a trainee-director at the Mäster
Olofsgärden Theatre and at the Saga-Theatre, where he put on a
spectacularly peculiar and disastrous production of Strindberg's
Ghost Sonata. At this time, too, he wrote a lot of plays, novels, and
short stories, mostly unpublished; one of the stories later provided
the idea for *Sommarlek*. In 1944 he met Carl-Anders Dymling,
head of Svenskfilmindustri, who encouraged his interest in the
cinema and persuaded him to write an original screenplay, *Hets*
(*Frenzy*), which was directed in 1944 by the leading Swedish
director of the day, Alf Sjöberg. In the next year, moreover,
Dymling gave him his first chance to direct a film, *Kris* (*Crisis*), his
own adaptation of a play by Leck Fischer. Bergman's next four
films were also adaptations, and he did not direct an original screenplay of his own until *Fängelse* (*Prison*) in 1948.

Of the films of this early period in Bergman's work I have little
to say, first of all because I have not had the opportunity to see
several of them, and second because there does not seem much to
be said of those I have seen, *Musik i Mörkar* (*Music in the Dark*)
and *Hamnstad* (*Port of Call*). Both are simple, unaffected pieces of
film-making – no tricks, no intricacies and, truth to tell, no interest
very much – based on rather novelettish stories about the troubles
of the young (a subject regarded rather as Bergman's speciality at
that time and also handled, in much the same way it would seem, in
Kris, Det Regnar på vår Karlek (*Love in the Rain*) and *Skepp till
Indialand* (*Boat to India*) the other films he directed at this time). In
Musik i Mörkar a young man is saved from despair by the love of a
girl he meets shortly after being blinded on manœuvres; in
Hamnstad a young nymphomaniac is saved from despair by the
love of a young sailor who prevents her from committing suicide
and listens to her sad story of a broken home and a period in a
reformatory. Neither film, taken by itself, would suggest any very
interesting talent at work either in writing or (more significantly at
this stage) in direction, though they are competent enough as far as
they go.

Rather more interesting from all points of view, in fact, are
Bergman's original scenarios for other directors, *Hets* (directed by
Sjöberg) and *Kvinna utan Ansikte* (*The Woman Without a Face*)
and *Eva*, both directed by the veteran Gustav Molander. In these,

at least, some of Bergman's real creativity emerges, particularly the
first, which by virtue of its international success – and, of course,
basically of its imaginative power – became for many years virtually
the Swedish film on which most people's idea of the Swedish
cinema was based. It remains even now the most forceful expression
of Bergman's youthful preoccupations with the situation of the
young in an old world and their need to rebel against their surroundings: more so, certainly, than any of the films he directed
himself at this time. It concerns the intricate relations of three
people: a sadistic teacher, the pupil who becomes his chief victim,
and the young prostitute the boy turns to for consolation. The girl
has a secret terror she will not confide to the boy, though he suspects it to be an older man, and finally with the girl's death it is
revealed to be the teacher, 'Caligula'. The boy turns on Caligula,
accusing him of the girl's murder; the teacher, by virtue of his
seniority and privileged position, is able to defend himself and
wreck the boy's school career in the process. But at the end, after a
nervous breakdown, the boy meets Caligula again, now lonely and
broken, appealing to him for aid and companionship, and is able (in
a perfect piece of adolescent wish-fulfilment) to refuse him and
walk out into a symbolic dawn. The story is in a sense naïve, but by
its very *naïveté*, its uncomplicated truth to the adolescent's subjective view of the world, it retains the power and validity of a document, and its virtues in these terms are reinforced by Sjöberg's
sympathetically atmospheric direction.

The two Molander films lose somewhat by comparison, though
they, too, have the advantage over Bergman's own films of this
period in that they do not hesitate to go to those extremes from
which a highly personal art is more likely to emerge than from all
the quiet competence and good taste in the world. Both, like *Hets*,
are studies of young men (both of such an age that they are involved
in compulsory military service) in exceptional psychological states.
In *Kvinna utan Ansikte* a young father is lured to leave wife and
child by an obsessive passion he conceives for a woman met by
chance in a florist's. She – the 'woman without a face' – is determined to retain her freedom and refuses to become involved with
him except physically. He sacrifices everything for her, even
deserting from his military service to rejoin her, and is only finally
saved by his best friend after a suicide attempt which somehow

seems to exorcise her influence. In *Eva* a young man is obsessed
with guilt feelings after accidentally causing the death of a childhood playmate. He becomes convinced that he is fated to bring
disaster to all those he is involved with, and when he falls in love
runs away to Stockholm to become a jazz trumpeter before resolving to marry the girl. Even then his obsession keeps recurring until
ultimately exorcised by the vision of his wife with their first child.
Both scripts represent further actings-out of adolescent fantasies,
though slightly more mature than in *Hets*; both take us into
neurotically subjective private worlds and only at the last, with
perhaps more determination than real conviction, bring us back to
normality with a reassuring picture of family life and adult responsibility; both conclude, significantly, with a quasi-symbolic
putting-away of childish things. The line of continuity runs
through them from *Hets* to *Fängelse* far more appreciably than it
does through *Musik i Mörkar, Hamnstad* and Bergman's own first
attempts at direction.

Fängelse (1948) is a highly significant work in many ways. Not
only is it the first complete Bergman film, directed by Bergman
from his own original screenplay at the end of a period of intense
creation in the theatre (three original plays – *Rakel och Biografrakt-
mästaren, Dagen Slutar Fidigt, Mig Till Skräck* – written and staged
in two years), but it has all the marks of a key work in his career,
wildly bundling together any number of themes which are to recur
later and, it seems, just had to find expression at this time in some
form. Moreover, it is the first of Bergman's films which demonstrates any real desire (or possibly, since we know little of the
circumstances in which the early films were made, any real freedom) to experiment with the medium, to use it positively as a
means of expression in itself, rather than merely recording with
competence but no special aptitude. In *Fängelse* already Bergman
is reaching out towards the highly personal style of his later work,
integrating the rather faded studio romanticism (derived,
apparently, from an enthusiastic study of the works of Carné)
which marked his earliest films and the rather hesitant touches of
neo-realism in *Hamnstad* into a newer, more complex and, in the
first instance, more theatrical style of direction. In *Fängelse*, indeed,
the theatrical origin of much in the later films which one would not
instantly think of as theatrical, especially where the direction of

actors is concerned, is still clearly visible. And in general the main interest of the film now is a by-product of its crudities and awkwardness: it is situated at the vital juncture in Bergman's career when he has found his feet and struck out on his own, but not yet had a chance to cover his tracks: most of what he says, crudely and directly, in the screenplay recurs in an infinitude of transformations and transmutations in later works, elusively difficult to pin down exactly; much of what he does with actors and camera shows in a raw and unformed state the procedures which will underlie his mature practice.

The story of the film is at once complex and obvious: complex in its interweaving of different strands, simple in that its general significance is directly stated in the sequence before the credits and summarized in rather different terms at the end. At the beginning a professor, recently released from an asylum, goes to visit Martin, a former pupil now a film director, and suggests to him as a film subject the idea that the Devil rules the world and Hell is already here. Everything which follows arises out of and returns to this basic theme, directly or indirectly. First Martin recounts the meeting to his friend Thomas, a journalist, who in answer tells him of a girl he met a little while before who lived as a prostitute with the encouragement of her fiancé and his sister, and suggests this subject would form a good illustration of the professor's idea; he himself could write the script. Six months later the prostitute, Brigitte-Caroline, has an illegitimate child which is disposed of by her fiancé, Peter. Six months later still, when we next see the characters, Thomas and his wife Sophie reach a crisis in their marriage, and Thomas suggests a double suicide; Sophie knocks him out and disappears. Meanwhile Brigitte-Caroline and Peter are arrested, and arrive at the police station at the same time as Thomas, who is convinced he has killed Sophie. When the two cases are cleared up to the police's satisfaction, Brigitte-Caroline and Thomas meet in the street and go off together to a strange lodging-house where they find a brief and desperate love, though constantly haunted by the lives from which they have come. Finally Brigitte-Caroline goes back to Peter, and Thomas, eluding Martin and Sophie, who are looking for him, goes after her, but she rejects him. Her prostitute's life is beginning again, but after her first customer, a sadist who burns her badly with a cigarette, she creeps away to the cellar and kills herself. Thomas, as hopeless as ever, returns to Sophie, and when at the end the professor comes back to hear Martin's opinion of his film-idea, Martin, who has observed all that has happened, replies simply that the film could not be made: 'It would end with a question-mark. If one can believe in God there is no problem; if not, there is no solution.'

The 'message' of the film, if one seeks a message, is blackly pessimistic: 'L'Enfer, c'est les autres'; 'And this is Hell, nor am I out of it'. There is no God, only the Devil, and the Devil rules: the only possibilities are death and vaguely stoical endurance of an almost insupportable life. It is, in fact, all very neatly epitomized in the only relatively light-hearted, even comic episode: that in which Thomas and Brigitte-Caroline, in the attic of their hideaway, come across some old silent films and a projector, and run a short farce in which the characters, in the midst of frenziedly persecuting each other, are suddenly threatened by a skeleton and vanish. The fact that the message can be so simply and completely epitomized suggests one of the film's weaknesses: it is very much a *film à thèse*, and in its determination to put over its creator's ideas it tends to adopt an almost didactic tone, with things happening, one sometimes cannot help feeling, more to demonstrate a point than from any appreciable dramatic necessity. Given this reservation, however (and a further reservation about the crudeness of the means sometimes used) the fault is disguised with considerable virtuosity. The structure of the film itself, a simultaneous demonstration of certain ideas and assertion that a film on these ideas could not be made, suggests an obvious parallel with *Six Characters in Search of an Author* and prefigures the strong influence of Pirandello in many of Bergman's later films, notably *The Face* and *The Devil's Eye*. And the subsidiary themes represent a very interesting mixture of 'early Bergman', in the shape of Brigitte-Caroline, a characteristic young misfit, and her doomed love for Thomas, and later Bergman in the Thomas-Sophie scenes, which take up for the first time the question of marital relations which was to obsess him in subsequent films.

The style of direction, too, gives hints of the future, as yet not at all integrated: the scenes involving Brigitte-Caroline and Peter are made in a harsh, realistic style a little reminiscent of *Hamnstad*; the scenes between her and Thomas are given a hazy romantic quality

which looks forward to, ultimately, *Sommarlek*; and Brigitte-
Caroline's dream, with its forest of human trees, its mysterious
woman in black offering a stone which she says is 'the most valuable
thing in the world', and its heavily symbolic play with a doll (representing Brigitte's dead baby) which turns into a fish and is killed by
Peter, is conceived in terms of an all-out theatrical expressionism
which later will apparently disappear, but actually be completely
integrated into Bergman's mature work. Even the little silent film
in the attic (notice, by the way, a further piece of heavy-handed
symbolism: nearest approach to Heaven in the attic, final suicide in
the cellar) looks at once back to Bergman's own childhood magic-
lantern and forward to the *bourgeois* farce of *A Lesson in Love* and
the stern morality play of *The Seventh Seal*. At this stage in
Bergman's career the precarious mixture is held together – if,
indeed, one feels it is held together at all – only by sheer force of
personality and the author's own desperate involvement in what he
is saying. But before very long the raw materials will be fused
together into one coherent and immediately recognizable style, in
which such violent changes of tone are child's play. *Fängelse*
already looks forward to the bravura of *Smiles of a Summer Night*
and *Wild Strawberries*; Bergman may not yet know how it is to be
done, but *Fängelse* is an unmistakable earnest of his determination
to find out.

For the moment, however, after having got *Fängelse* out of his
system (and possibly to some extent because of its commercial
failure), Bergman concentrated on less complex themes and less
intricate structures. In the two films which immediately followed
Fängelse, *Törst* (*Thirst*) and *Til Glädje* (*To Joy*), he takes up the
subject of marriage, as sketched in the Thomas-Sophie relationship in *Fängelse*. The couple in *Törst*, for example, might be
Thomas and Sophie immediately after their precarious reconciliation at the end of the film, and not only because they are played by
the same actors, Birger Malmsten and Eva Henning. Bertil and
Rut, as they are called in *Törst*, are a married couple also in the
uncomfortable mid-passage of their life together, bored with each
other, irritable, but still with enough vestiges of passion left to
make them unable to lapse either into comfortable affection or into
formal indifference. The outward movement of the film is forward
in the most obvious fashion possible: its framework is a journey

C.E.–K

from Basle northwards through Germany, into which are inserted a number of flashbacks and fragments of parallel action (a procedure used with infinitely greater finesse in *Wild Strawberries* and, more relevantly, in *A Lesson in Love*, which is in effect a comic remake of *Törst*, ludicrously reversing its progress during a journey southward).

On their way back from a holiday in Sicily shortly after the end of the war, Bertil and Rut stay the night in Basle. While Bertil is sleeping Rut remembers her first affair, a 'summer interlude' (this flashback might almost be a sketch for *Sommarlek* and *Summer with Monika*) which ends with the discovery that her lover is married, a pregnancy and an abortion which leaves her sterile for life. When Bertil wakes up they quarrel, and on the train Rut taxes him with his infidelities with a girl called Viola. Bertil starts to think of Viola, and as he does so we see in parallel action what is happening to her meanwhile in Stockholm: first a psychiatrist tries to seduce her and when he fails contemptuously tells her she must go into a mental home, then a schoolfriend meets her and offers her comfort but proves to be a lesbian with designs on her, and finally Viola drowns herself in despair. Back on the train a further flashback from Rut tells us something about her earlier, more carefree life as a chorus-girl, and she resists all Bertil's attempts to patch up their quarrel, until eventually the cumulative effect of the misery and devastation they see in the war-torn Germany they are passing through convinces them that companionship, any companionship, is preferable to a desolate solitude.

The film has intermittent power, but mainly because of this, the force of personal anguish applied rather irrelevantly to a novelettish plot (adapted by Bergman in collaboration from a novel), the final result lurches once or twice dangerously close to self-parody, particularly in the Viola episode, when the proliferation of horrors and miseries finally becomes just absurd. Bergman tries, also, to make full use of his new stylistic discoveries from *Fängelse*, constructing the film in long, elaborately worked-out scenes, employing a lot of murky low-key lighting, and calling on the brief glimpses of haggard faces and shattered buildings to carry a weight of symbolic significance which, at any rate for an audience without Sweden's pronounced guilt-feelings about neutrality, they just cannot support. In consequence only the young-love sequence, in

which Bergman's warmest romanticism for the moment takes over
without complication, really comes alive at all, and *Törst* is a film to
be seen, perhaps, but if possible not re-seen.

Til Glädje is rather better, if only because it has an original
Bergman screen-play and marks a return to relative simplicity. It is
the story of two musicians who marry and live happily until the
husband has a spectacular failure. While he is upset about it the
young wife of an old actor acquaintance makes advances to him,
but he is too upset to respond. Years later, when he has two children and his marriage, despite his failures, has settled to a comfortable habit, he meets the girl again and this time she becomes his
mistress. His wife leaves him, he realizes how much she really
means to him and implores her to come back, but when she does
she and one of the children are killed in a domestic accident.
The husband is heartbroken, and takes refuge in his art;
the final sequence shows him at last transfigured and finding
a sort of tranquillity while taking part in a performance of
Beethoven's Ninth Symphony, with its last choral movement 'To
Joy'.

The story sounds like an irresistible appeal to the stock responses
of the sentimental filmgoer, and that it might well have been in
other hands. But Bergman, by filming it with the utmost clarity and
simplicity (the heaviness and pretention of *Törst* are mercifully
absent), manages to make it something very different, cool, classical
and precise. The *clou* of the film, though, is the climactic scene in
the concert hall, which becomes a musical documentary of dazzling
brilliance and penetration (the elaborate camera-movements are
both beautiful in themselves and elucidate unfailingly the structure
and feel of the music) but at the same time symbolizes perfectly the
mental development of the principal character. The ruins and dis-
placed persons in *Törst* which both symbolized the mental world
the principal characters lived in and motivated the change in their
attitude towards it, seem in comparison an empty literary device;
with the music in *Til Glädje* one senses instead a real involvement
on Bergman's part, a realization perhaps that the artist-hero's position in relation to his art can stand for that of any artist in relation
to any art, even that of the Bergman who said 'For me making films
is a necessity of nature, like eating and drinking. Some express
themselves in writing books, climbing mountains, beating their

children, dancing the samba. I express myself making films',
towards the art of his choice.

After these two studies of marriage, *Sommarlek* (*Summer Interlude*) looks at first glance like a throwback to Bergman's problems-
of-youth phase: a story of a light-hearted summer romance between
two young people, a dancer and a student, which ends tragically
when he is killed in a swimming accident. But this time the story is
not told for its own sake, as an end in itself; it is seen as an incident
in the past, thirteen years in the past, which nevertheless still has
the power to determine the present, for good or ill. It is told in two
long flashbacks, symmetrically disposed in the film. First we meet
Marie, a mature and beautiful dancer, the star of the ballet and, in
her early thirties, still mysteriously unmarried. She receives at the
theatre a packet containing a diary, and when rehearsals are interrupted by a lighting failure she leaves, escapes the company of an
attentive journalist, and catches a boat to an island near Stockholm.
Here she goes to a small cabin on the shore, and starts to relive in
her mind the affair between her and Henrik, the author of the
diary. We see their meeting and their first halting steps towards
each other and love during the summer holidays, when she is staying with her uncle and he is living near by.

A visit paid by the two of them one evening to the uncle's house
brings us back to the present. Marie rouses herself from her reflections and goes up, in the gathering dusk, to her uncle's house to
thank him for sending the diary, which he recovered from the
hospital where Henrik died. 'When I think of Henrik I can't understand why I let you touch me,' she says suddenly. On her way back
to Stockholm on the boat she returns to her reverie, and we see the
rest of the story, ending suddenly when a day or two before the end
of the holiday Henrik strikes his head diving from a rock and dies
later in hospital without recovering consciousness. On her return
Marie gives David, her journalist suitor, Henrik's diary to read,
and says that when he has read it they can have their first serious
conversation; at least he is alive, and she has now realized the
pointlessness of living for ever in the dead past; by reliving the
experience she has begun to exorcise it.

Seen in these terms *Sommarlek*, one of Bergman's own favourites
among his films, comes to represent not so much a harking-back as
a deliberate farewell to the theme of young love. Marie, as is made

clear in the opening sequence where she has an odd and elusive
conversation with her slightly sinister ballet-master, is not so much
living in the past as not living at all because of the past. She has not
been obsessed with her tragic love for Henrik, but on the contrary,
as far as her conscious mind is concerned, she has forgotten it and
lived in a void until the diary brings it all back. The point of the
film is not the story in the flashbacks, but Marie's remembering of
and coming to terms with it; she has to face it in order to dismiss it
from her mind and start again.

This idea of death-in-life and a return to the past from which the
central character arises reborn is reinforced in all sorts of ways
within the film itself. In the sequence leading up to the first flashback the accent is entirely on darkness and decay: the lights in the
theatre fail; the ballet-master asks her if she is sad because autumn
is coming on; her journey to the island is accomplished as dusk
falls with a few spots of rain, and under the distrustful eye of an old
crone in black. From this the first flashback switches us at once
into a world of light and colour – the gleaming summer days are
lyrically evoked in Gunnar Fischer's photography, and everything
except for the brief incursions of Marie's uncle and Henrik's guar-
dian is fresh and young and gay. Back in the present night is falling
and Marie's uncle is alone, drinking in the deserted house; the
glittering blacks and whites of the flashbacks are replaced by a dull
diffused grey and return only when from the present we move back
into the past. But even here shades of the prison house are closing
in; just before Henrik's accident an owl frightens Marie, and after
his death the world of clear contrasts is already being invaded by
drab greys of apathy. Only at the very end do we find a return in
the present to the mood of the past, though deepened and enriched,
as the ballet performance begins and David watches Marie from
the wings with almost the same rapture that Henrik had shown
thirteen years earlier.

Technically *Sommarlek* is relatively unadventurous, except for a
brief and not very successful interlude when some doodles by
Marie take on a life of their own and start to move and gesticulate
like something from one of Emile Cohl's early animated films; a
sort of equivalent to the play with the silent projector in *Fängelse*.
It is content to use the normal repertoire of film technique simply
and directly, with a strong feeling for sympathetic natural

backgrounds and a lavish, perhaps on occasion rather facile, use of visual symbolism derived from nature, both of which characteristics hark back more clearly than anything in Bergman's previous work to the early Swedish cinema of a temperamentally very different director, Victor Sjöstrom. After the uncertainty and sometimes rather wild experiment of Bergman's previous films, it looks very much like an expression of confidence; confidence that his material could, if he wished, stand up on its own without extraneous tricks. Unsuccessful some of his later films might be, but never in quite the way that *Fängelse* or *Törst* failed; at least the later films, when they are wrong, are confidently wrong, not just awkward and fumbling.

This is not to say, though, that the full fruits of Bergman's new-found maturity are immediately to be seen after *Sommarlek*; first came a political thriller based on a script by Herbert Grevenius, *Sånt Händer Inte Här* (*It Couldn't Happen Here*), which I have not seen but seems not to be very interesting, then, in 1951, a crisis in the Swedish cinema which virtually stopped production and reduced Bergman to filming soap commercials. When things started up again in 1952 his first film was the lightweight but interesting *Kvinnors Vantan* (*Waiting Women*); before we consider that, however, we may as well dispose of the following film, *Sommaren med Monika* (*Summer with Monika*), both because its subject-matter allies it closely with *Sommarlek*, to which it is considerably inferior, and because it represents in many ways a throwback to Bergman's early style. This time the story of a summertime affair between two young people is told for its own sake, without any endistancing framework; a shopgirl and a workman pick each other up, fall in love (supposedly, though the girl is shown throughout as a complete bitch incapable of loving anyone but herself) and run away for the summer to live an uncomplicated, irresponsible life on the islands. But when autumn comes she is pregnant and bored, and does not want to return to ordinary life with him; indeed, after she has had her baby she leaves him and goes off with an old flame. The story (drawn from a naturalistic novel by Per-Anders Fogelström) takes us back to the world of *Hamnstad*, and so, for that matter, does the treatment, which is firmly direct and realistic, almost documentary, with none of the richness and complexity of *Sommarlek*. Indeed, the film stands quite outside the course of

Bergman's development from *Sommarlek* on; it can well be left out of account, especially since even on its chosen level it is not really very good.

With *Kvinnors Vantan*, on the other hand, we are in a quite different world, the world of Bergman's first maturity already hinted at in *Sommarlek*. And this, even though the film seems consciously designed as a sort of résumé of Bergman characters and themes to date. It consists essentially of three long flashbacks as three of a group of four women married to four brothers talk about their marriages as they await the men's return. After some short comments on the difficulties of marriage from the eldest, the first flashback, filmed in a fairly straightforward realistic style heightened with free use of visual symbolism, tells of the crisis in the marriage of a couple very reminiscent of the couple in *Törst*, childless and empty, when the wife takes a lover, the husband threatens to commit suicide, and finally both, with no illusions, set resignedly about the business of living together again. The second flashback shows us a couple much like the young lovers in *Sommarlek* (and played, in fact, by the same actors) meeting in Paris, where she is a student and he a painter; they have an affair, then he is called home and shortly afterwards she finds she is pregnant and returns to Stockholm too, but refuses to see him until she has had the baby; then, quite lucidly, she decides to marry him. This episode, a flashback within a flashback (from the nursing-home where the baby is being delivered), is treated in more highly coloured, expressionistic style, as befits something meant to be a dream under anaesthetic, and contains in addition one or two allusions (which cannot be wholly accidental) to the Paris of Bergman's early idol Carné.

The third episode, the famous 'lift sequence', brings in something new in Bergman's work – comedy – and looks forward rather than back, to his studies of maturity and its problems. It also unites for the first time two of Bergman's most attractive regular actors, Eva Dahlbeck and Gunnar Björnstrand, as a married couple of some years' standing, whose interest in each other has dwindled to remote politeness. But then they are trapped in a lift one night on their way home, and find themselves discussing their lives together and apart, their affairs with others, and finding in the process a new community of interests, a new interest in each other – until the

morning brings them both very much to where they started. From
the director's point of view the episode is a challenge to virtuosity,
demanding the utmost variety and fluidity in shooting in a confined
space, and Bergman carries this off triumphantly. But what is
chiefly remarkable – and a little surprising considering his previous
work – is the natural flair for sophisticated comedy the episode
reveals; the timing is impeccable and both writing and playing
reach a high level of wit and elegance. Moreover, the writer-
director's attitude, if not positively optimistic – the ending throws
an ironical light on the good resolutions of the previous half-hour –
is at least life-accepting; the adolescent rebellion which was already
being moderated somewhat in *Sommarlek* has now virtually disappeared, to be replaced by an adult understanding of how things
really are and what (little perhaps) one can really do about them.
This new understanding is also reflected in the conclusion of the
whole film. Listening to these stories of marital problems has been
a young girl, sister of the wife in the second episode. She is shocked
by the revelations of the older women, but at the end, without telling anyone, she slips away to meet the boy she loves, son of the
oldest couple; hope springs eternal, and whether or not they can,
each generation will believe profoundly in their ability to avoid the
mistakes of their elders – that is the way life goes on.

   With *Kvinnors Vantan* Bergman came to the threshold of
maturity, both in his materials and in the manner he treated them.
After his brief return to troubled youth in *Sommaren med Monika*,
already mentioned, he went on to make the first work of his
maturity, *Gycklarnas Afton* (*Sawdust and Tinsel*). The progress in
this case is not so much in the material as in the treatment; the view
of life put forward in the film is as gloomy and anguished as anything that has gone before, but the style in which it is treated is
complex and magisterially confident; for the first time Bergman
manages to unite in one film the disparate influences which have
appeared in his work – from early Swedish cinema (Sjöström's
feeling for landscape, Stiller's flair for bitter erotic comedy), from
the French cinema of the 1930s (especially Carné's elegantly artificial studio-bound studies of fate and its workings) and German
silent cinema, with its obsession with mirrors and staircases, with
hysteria and humiliation. All these combine in a film which is not,
perhaps, without its absurd side – it is a little too much like a con-

coction of absolutely everything the foreign filmgoer might regard as 'typically Swedish' in the cinema – but which still holds together its diverse elements remarkably well and achieves a rich, elaborate, and unmistakably personal style of expression.

Moving for the first time into period settings (the time is some-where in the early 1900s) Bergman suddenly finds the visual style which, variously modified to suit the subject-matter, is to serve him well throughout his mature career. Whereas before the purely visual side of his films had often lacked any special distinction, and those distinctions it did have had usually been a matter of good isolated ideas rather than any overall quality, in *Gycklarnas Afton* the style all at once becomes rich and strange. Compositions are intricate and bizarre, with much play of reflections, harsh, crisp contrasts of light and shade, and an almost continuous use of deep focus to give the whole thing a powerfully sculptural quality, emphasizing textures and effects of perspective. And this style is used consistently throughout the film, except for a flashback near the beginning, which is set apart from the rest of the film in that it is filmed silent, with a musical accompaniment, as the narrator tells the story, and is photographed in a wan, flat, overexposed fashion to give it the remoteness and insubstantiality of a dream.

The flashback in question relates how the clown Teodor inter-rupts his wife in the middle of a shameless flirtation with soldiers on the shore and carries her back naked to the circus they both work for, pursued by the jeers of the onlookers. This sets the tone of the story: all is humiliation, all love unsatisfactory and leading to suffering; life is a trap and there is no way out, not even death, for those too cowardly to do anything decisive. The main plot concerns the attempts of the circus-owner and his mistress to escape from each other and the circus, he to his long-deserted wife, who now does not want him back, she to an affair (very brief, as it turns out) with the handsome young leading man at the town theatre. Neither attempt leads anywhere, and to make matters worse the leading man publicly humiliates the circus-owner at the evening perfor-mance. The circus-owner cannot even manage to shoot himself, and in the cold dawn the cavalcade moves off, a little more dis-illusioned, a little nearer the complete hopelessness which, Berg-man clearly indicates, is the only realistic reaction to their position.

Depressing, obviously; superficial very probably; highly

mannered without a doubt. But with this film Bergman established himself fully for the first time as what the French call an *auteur*; someone whose films, for better or as it may sometimes be for worse, have to be judged all of a piece. No longer is it possible to talk of an interesting script uninterestingly directed, or vice versa. The film is 'written' from first to last completely and unalterably in film terms, and most of the significant content is, in fact, the form – not the words on paper, but the way it is all put on the screen.

This is equally true of the otherwise totally different first-fruit of Bergman's new freedom and confidence, *En Lektion i Kärlek* (*A Lesson in Love*). Having touched on comedy before, most notably in the lift sequence of *Waiting Women*, in *A Lesson in Love* Bergman makes a thorough-going comedy, still on the marriage theme which obsesses him at this period, but turning without a moment's hesitation from its blackest aspects, as shown in *Sawdust and Tinsel*, to its sunniest and even at times its most farcical.

A Lesson in Love has not on the whole been a popular film with the critics, but to me it seems almost wholly delightful; I am not even worried by the naked Cupid who seals the couple's reunion at the end. Bergman has a real flair for stylish comedy – there is, after all, more of Stiller than of Sjöström in his temperament – and *A Lesson in Love* is something of a *tour de force*, reconciling the most apparently disparate elements with the greatest ease. Its plot, as has been remarked, is a sort of ironic mirror-image of *Törst*: whereas that showed an estranged married couple reminiscing grimly about their earlier life and loves on a train travelling northward, and finally achieving a gloomy, *faute-de-mieux* sort of reconciliation, *A Lesson in Love* shows an estranged couple travelling southward, reminiscing, but this time almost entirely in humorous terms, about their meeting and earlier life together, and finally coming together again quite simply from the realization that after all they are still very much in love.

The ways by which the film brings them, and us, to this conclusion, are devious but telling. For some time we are kept in the dark about the real subject of the film: we see David, a gynaecologist, hurrying to catch a train and as he does so recalling the beginning of an affair with a patient who threw herself at him. On the train he shares a compartment with a commercial traveller and a beautiful blonde, and we have another flashback, in which he

recalls a strange conversation with his teenage daughter, who wants
to be changed into a man, is revolted by the idea of sex, and
incidentally informs him that her mother has a lover, Carl-Adam
(this scene, an intense, Strindbergian set-piece, should be completely out of key with the rest of the film, but somehow fits in
without any jolt, perhaps because it is placed so early that we are
not yet very clear exactly what sort of film we are seeing). Meanwhile, on the train, the commercial traveller is making advances to
the blonde and being sharply rebuffed; from the conversation
which ensues between her and David we realize that she is, in fact,
his wife, Marianne, and that they have much in common with the
couple in the lift scene of *Waiting Women*; they are even played by
the same actors, Gunnar Björnstrand and Eva Dahlbeck.

Once we know the identity of the mysterious blonde we can see
more, in flashback, of the couple's marriage. First a flashback
shows how the wife, Marianne, discovers that her husband is
deceiving her and turns up at the hotel the next morning with a
breakfast tray for David and his mistress. Then back on the train
Marianne helps David to win a bet he has made with the commercial traveller that he will succeed in kissing her before the next
station, and on this note we go back to a light-hearted flashback
which tells us how they came to get married when Marianne, due
to marry Carl-Adam, refused to go through with it and ended by
marrying David, who was sent to persuade her. Back in the present
again, the train arrives at Malmö and a surprised Carl-Adam meets
husband and wife together. That evening in Copenhagen they all
go to a night-club, and David finally wins back Marianne by the
oldest of tricks, making her jealous by pretending to pay attention
to another woman. The whole thing ends in a general mêlée from
which David and Marianne extract themselves and set off together
for their hotel room as the dawn breaks.

A Lesson in Love, as will be apparent even from this summary,
treats of the same sort of themes as Bergman's more evidently
serious films of this period, and reaches many of the same conclusions about marriage and the need to compromise a little in order to
live at all. Nevertheless – and despite unexpected touches of bitter-
ness from time to time in the dialogue – it remains a comedy, and a
light comedy at that, often veering towards farce. In many ways it
stands as a sketch for Bergman's finest comedy – and for me his

finest film – *Smiles of a Summer Night*, which again takes up the obsessive theme of marriage, and also renews the Gunnar Björnstrand-Eva Dahlbeck partnership, this time as lover and mistress. Before that, though, Bergman made another film with them both in, *Journey into Autumn* (*Kvinnadröm*), though unfortunately on this occasion they appear in different stories; one of Bergman's slighter works, it concerns two unfortunate affairs, one between a fashion photographer (Eva Dahlbeck) and a married businessman, which is ending, and the other between one of her models and an older diplomat (Gunnar Björnstrand) which never gets started because of the girl's inexhaustible energy, because of the old man's daughter, and because anyway the model has a lover of her own age back in Stockholm.

With *Smiles of a Summer Night* (*Sommarnattens Leende*) in 1955 we finally see for the first time, and virtually for the last, all Bergman's diverse talents together in a single film. It is an intricately constructed high comedy for nine characters, whose positions are modified and rearranged with the utmost elegance and precision during the course of a single week-end. First there is the lawyer Fredrik Egerman (Gunnar Björnstrand), who has Anna, a wife of sixteen, still virgin; a son a year or two older by a former marriage; and an actress-mistress (Eva Dahlbeck). Or at least he had a mistress, but broke off with her when he remarried and is now regretting it. An attempt to renew relations ends in temporary defeat when he meets at Desirée's house her new lover, a fiercely military count called Malcolm, who frightens him off the premises. Subsequently we meet Malcolm's almost equally savage wife, Charlotte (a character straight out of Strindberg), and then see Fredrik's young wife at home, romping with her maid, scolding her stepson, being rebuffed by her husband and exchanging gossip, sometimes too pointed for comfort, with Charlotte.

That week-end all these characters are gathered together at Desirée's mother's house in the country. Desirée plots with Charlotte that things shall be arranged so that Charlotte gets back Malcolm and Desirée gets back Fredrik. Up to this point the tone has been consistently that of artificial comedy with an occasional dash of bitters, especially when Charlotte is expressing her disgust with men and her passion for her husband; rather as though Strindberg had taken it into his head to adapt Marivaux. The Marivaux side is stressed by the backgrounds – mostly graceful Swedish rococo – and the elegant period costumes (*c.* 1901), and by the cool formality of the *mise en scène*, which is of an almost obtrusive neatness and clarity. From this point of the film on, though, the mood suddenly changes as though by magic – literally as well as metaphorically, for Desirée's mother announces at dinner that the wine they are drinking is reputed to be a love potion. During the enchanted night that follows the various loves, potential or actual, sort themselves out of their own accord. First, on the basic animal level, there are the Egermans' maid and the major-domo of the house romping in the hay. Then Henrik and his youthful step-mother discover their love for each other and leave together in the first false dawn (the first smile of a summer night is for young lovers). Then Desirée's plot goes into action: she tells Malcolm that Charlotte and Fredrik are alone together in the summer-house. He rushes out and challenges Fredrik to a duel by Russian roulette, but when finally the gun goes off against Fredrik's temple it proves to have been loaded with a blank. Charlotte reminds Malcolm of a bet she made with him at dinner that she could seduce Fredrik in fifteen minutes, and forces a *rapprochement* between them (the second smile is for the clowns, the fools, the unredeemable), while inside the summer-house Fredrik ends up being comforted on Desirés's maternal shoulder (the third smile is for the sad, the depressed, the sleepless, the confused, the frightened, the lonely).

It is difficult if not impossible to explain how exactly this curious *mélange* of comedy and drama, dry wit and poetic fantasy, manages to hold together in the cinema. Essentially, one suspects, it is a matter of conviction: conviction on the creator's part that naturally anything that he thinks of is related to anything else he thinks by the simple fact that it is he who is doing the thinking. The over-riding unifying factor here is the sheer force of Bergman's per-sonality; the film is the product throughout of a single idiosyncratic imagination working at full pressure and never for one moment playing safe (anyone else, for instance, faced with Charlotte's out-burst to Anna about the ignominy of love, would surely have guyed it a little to fit in with the rest of the comedy, but Bergman shoots it straight and dramatically in harsh close-up, and somehow, inexplicably, it works). In any case, the film is an almost total success, with neither Bergman nor his cast (brilliantly directed, incidentally; the acting in Bergman's films is generally so good that one comes to take it for granted) putting a foot wrong.

Even though his next film, *The Seventh Seal* (*Det Sjunde Inseglet*), was responsible more than any other single work for Bergman's international vogue, and was at its first appearance in 1956 generally hailed as a masterpiece, it is difficult now to feel anything like the same degree of enthusiasm for it. In *The Seventh Seal* Bergman turns from marriage and the relations of man and woman and takes up instead the relations of man with God and with death – a theme which has continued ever since at the centre of his work, though sometimes more evidently so than at others. Unfortunately in doing so he does not escape pretentiousness, perhaps because in his eagerness to make a statement of universal validity he has separated himself too far from the clear observation of believable human beings which had always given strength to even his most melodramatic earlier pieces.

This time what we are offered is a full-scale allegory, based on a one-act play Bergman had written a couple of years earlier. It is a morality about a knight's battle with Death, represented by a chess game. The knight, played by Max von Sydow (an actor subsequently, and understandably, almost inescapable in Bergman films), has just returned from a crusade and meets Death at dawn on the shore. The whole action of the film takes place in twenty-four hours, and is made up of a series of encounters involving the knight and his squire (Gunnar Björnstrand) as they make their way across country to the knight's home and the inevitable final reckoning with death. The knight is racked with doubt, unable to live either with God, as the simple players they meet on their way do, or without him, as his squire does. During the day he finds little enough to bolster his belief. Plague is ravaging the land, the Church offers no help (when the knight tries to confess he finds it is Death he is confessing to; the principal clerical character is first seen robbing the dead and raping the defenceless; the Church as an organized body contributes only to the general misery, by organizing roaming bands of flagellants and burning supposed witches), and humanity is utterly brutal and depraved except for the 'holy family' of strolling players (significantly, the parents are called Jof and Mia) who live in innocence and are the only ones to escape when Death comes at last to lead the knight, his lady, his squire and their guests over the hill in a grotesque *totentanz*.

Technically the film is impeccable. The black-and-white photography of Gunnar Fischer is constantly striking (it is the sort of film which yields excellent stills, which may or may not be a good thing), with its crisp, clear deep-focus work, its very black blacks and very white whites. The story is told with admirable economy, no detail being wasted or missing its effect. The acting, when acting is called for (mainly from Max von Sydow and Gunnar Björnstrand), does perfectly everything required of it. And yet the film, despite all this and some genuinely enthralling moments, seems somehow too pale and remote, too patently composed as an illustration of its thesis. Its final effect, when all has been said in its favour, is rather lifeless, and lacking as it does the power of a completely realized work of art to sweep aside objections, *The Seventh Seal* strikes one as making implicit claims for itself out of all proportion to its actual achievements. If a film-maker sets out to make a cosmic drama of Life and Death, with a lot of Christian symbolism thrown in, he must expect to be judged by the most rigorous standards, and by such standards *The Seventh Seal* fails. It never finally convinces us, as it obviously intends to, that all its horrors, the rapes, tortures, flagellations, burnings, are valid expressions of a pessimistic world picture only lightly touched with hope; they remain, if not exactly sensational, at least rather pointless, overstating a case that should not need such determined emphasis.

As if realizing his mistake, Bergman returned at once to modern life and the sort of intricate structure of flashbacks, dreams, and visions which had so often before brought out the best in him. The result was the only one of his films worthy to stand by *Smiles of a Summer Night*, *Wild Strawberries* (*Smultronstället*). The action of *Wild Strawberries*, like that of *The Seventh Seal*, *Sawdust and Tinsel* and several of Bergman's lesser films, all takes place within twenty-four hours, in the course of which a character (in this case a 78-year-old professor called Isak Borg) is brought to a clearer realization of his own character and situation by what happens to and around him. This time, too, as so often in Bergman, the external sequence of the plot is provided by a journey; Isak Borg is going to the University of Lund to receive an honorary doctorate

for his services to science. The film actually starts with a dream:
the previous night Isak dreams that while he is walking in a
deserted town (evoked very much in the style of German expressionism) he accosts a man who proves to have no face, and then,
in a coffin which has fallen from a hearse, sees his own body, which
tries to drag him into the coffin. So, right from the start, we understand that Isak is near death, and that his own subsonscious realization of this is prompting him to look back over his own life.

Everything else in the film contributes directly or indirectly to
this self-examination. His relations, for example, with his daughter-
in-law, Marianne, who is travelling with him in the car after leaving
her husband; and even what we see of this couple's relations with
each other, since Isak's son Evald fully shares the coldness and
selfishness of which Marianne accuses Isak. The landscape, too,
plays its part: a brief halt near the former home of one of Isak's
uncles sets him off remembering his youth and his first love, Sara,
who found him too dull and studious and preferred his brother
instead. At the end of this dream-recollection (it is half one, half
the other, since in it Isak as he is now sees events from which he
was absent at the time) a new Sara, like a reincarnation of the old,
intrudes on his thoughts; she is hitch-hiking to Italy with two
young men and wants a lift. It is Sara, prattling thoughtlessly on as
they drive, who gives expression to one of the dominant ideas in
Isak's mind, 'How disgusting it is to get old', and at this very
moment the car is nearly in collision with another car, from which
eventually they pick up the two occupants, a husband and wife who
are so savagely, exhibitionistically at each other's throats that
before long they are dropped again (an image, as it later transpires,
both of Isak's unhappy marriage and that, equally unsatisfactory,
of his son).

After this climax of unpleasantness comes a relatively calm
sequence: a brief interlude at a garage when the owner will take no
money, remembering what Professor Borg once did for him (to
everyone, clearly, he has not been merely a monster of selfishness
and egotism), and a happy dinner in the open air at which everyone
relaxes and just enjoys the cool evening and the company. Then
again we return to the past, physically as well as mentally, with a
brief visit by Isak to his mother, now 95 and virtually a living
mummy ('I have been cold all my life,' she says). Back in the car

9a. *Sawdust and Tinsel* (Ake Grönberg). Dir: Ingmar Bergman

9b. *The Seventh Seal* (Bengt Ekerot; Max von Sydow). Dir: Ingmar Bergman

10*a*. *The Virgin Spring* (Birgitta Pettersson). Dir: Ingmar Bergman

10*b*. *Winter Light* (Gunnar Björnstrand; Ingrid Thulin). Dir: Ingmar Bergman

there is a little scene between Isak and Sara, who in her indecision
over which of her two escorts she should marry recalls the other
Sara, then we go off into the most complicated of Isak's dreams. It
starts with Isak as he is now meeting the Sara of his youth by the
wild-strawberry patch: she holds up a mirror to him and says,
'Look at yourself, Isak; how old and ugly you are', then tells him
that she is going to marry his brother and carries back to the house
a baby she is minding, leaving Isak alone with the empty cradle.
He approaches the house and sees through the window a loving
scene between Sara and his brother; then the mood suddenly
changes. As the moon clouds over the house takes on a different
aspect. Isak knocks and is let in by someone looking like the
motorist he picked up earlier in the day, and is led into an
examination-room, where he fails to answer three questions
correctly; he cannot do an experiment required of him because the
microscope will not work for him; he cannot say what a text written
on the blackboard means, and he cannot tell his interrogators what
the first duty of a doctor is. Worse, when asked to examine a woman
who looks like the motorist's wife he says she is dead, at which she
bursts into harsh, mocking laughter. Finally his examiner tells him
his wife also accuses him, and then with him we witness his wife's
adultery in the woods, at the end of which she speaks bitterly of
him and how he will loftily forgive her, as though she was of no
importance whatever. Sentence is pronounced on Isak: it is solitude.

This is the turning-point of the film: the worst that Isak can say
of himself, or that anyone else can say of him, has been said, and
from now on his actions are directed towards reintegrating himself
with the world of men before it is too late. First he extracts from
Marianne the real reason for her journey: her husband (his son)
has brusquely rejected her when she has told him she is pregnant,
and told her to choose between him and the baby; she is choosing
the baby. At Lund, Isak goes through the ceremony, now fully
conscious of its total irrelevance to his life and achievements; he
has already attempted, maladroitly it is true, to bring together his
son and daughter-in-law, and will continue with his attempt. And
at the last the young people come to serenade him and the young
Sara bids him affectionate farewell; as he sinks into sleep we are
back again in his youth, but this time without torment: his father

and mother wave affectionately to him from the other side of the lake; time is at last completely regained.

The space that it takes to tell the story of this relatively short film (only ninety-three minutes) gives some idea of its compression and complexity. Technically it is a *tour de force*, uniting into one coherent unit an even wider variety of styles than *Smiles of a Summer Night*: the Germanic expressionism of the opening dream and the weird atmospherics of the visit to Isak's mother and the interrogation dream, rather suggestive of Cocteau: the basic realism of the scenes in the car, with conversations largely put together by the simple expedient of moving the camera from face to face; the lyrical feeling of the dinner scene and the childhood flashbacks, which call to mind Renoir more than anyone. A whole repertoire of foreign styles, one might say, and yet all working together in such perfect harmony that one never for a moment questions that they are the natural and inevitable form of expression for a single highly individual creator.

The principal unifying factor is the determination to show everything through the eyes of one man, Isak Borg. His voice on the sound-track introduces us to him with cool objectivity in a brief pre-credits sequence, and recurs every so often throughout the film to remind us that what we are seeing is his selection of those events during the day which seem to have some relevance to his persistent quest of his own true nature. This makes sense of the changes of style and preserves a consistency beneath the seeming inconsistency, colouring the most apparently objective sequences with the subjectivity of Isak's own selecting mind. Everything that he records assumes its own special significance in relation to his own life: the young people who represent his young self, his brother and the first Sara; his son and daughter-in-law; his own wife seen in flashback; the couple they pick up on the road, who all represent different stages of his own marriage; his mother and the people he encounters in his first dream, who represent the extremes of solitary old age, a death-in-life, and death itself.

Clearly, the performance of the central role is of vital importance and Victor Sjöström, the great director of the silent Swedish cinema, here gives the most remarkable performance of his long career, capturing to perfection the old man's fluctuations of mood behind his urbane façade, the pride and the fear battling for the upper hand in his mind as death approaches. Sjöström's performance is supported, too, by most of the 'Bergman stock-company' at their very best: Gunnar Björnstrand as Isak's son, Ingrid Thulin as his daughter-in-law, Max von Sydow as the garage proprietor, Bibi Andersson as both Saras, Naima Wifstrand as Isak's mother. From all points of view *Wild Strawberries* must rank as one of Bergman's best works, showing his complete mastery of the medium, his sheer genius as a director of actors, and some of his most mature and subtle observations of character: it is, as Ravel once said of his musical ideal, 'complexe mais pas compliqué'.

After this Bergman's two subsequent works, *Nära Livet* (*So Close to Life*) and *Ansiktet* (*The Face*), come as respectively a slight and a considerable anti-climax. *So Close to Life* is at least relatively unpretentious: a study of three women in the same maternity ward over twenty-four hours, two of whom lose their children, one by miscarriage and one when the child has to be sacrificed to save her, while the third, who does not want her illegitimate child, bears it successfully and is reconciled to her situation by the sufferings of her two companions. The direction here is starkly simple and severe, and performances of the three women (Ingrid Thulin, Eva Dahlbeck, and Bibi Andersson) are remarkable; indeed, the film is marred only by the obtrusiveness with which everything clicks neatly into place – the plot is so schematized and predictable that one tends to lose interest.

The Face, on the other hand, is highly pretentious, and an almost total disaster. It is nominally a comedy about a hypnotist in mid-nineteenth-century Sweden who is largely but not perhaps entirely a charlatan; in the course of the film he undergoes a long interrogation by a sceptical Royal Counsellor on Medicine, but finally manages to terrify him and then drives off in style to perform at court. It is difficult to convey, or indeed to account for, the curious heaviness and suffocating boredom of this film in the cinema; I suspect it is something to do with the way absolutely everything is crammed into it – Bergman's attitude to life, to women, to his art and the role of the artist; even to religion, since Vogler, the magician, has a disconcerting habit of turning into a Christ-figure every so often. The style used to convey all this is Bergman's most intricate and baroque, full of enormous, significant close-ups, involved compositions, bizarre effects of light and shade and a battery of special effects, reaching its climax while Vergerus, the Medical Counsellor, performs an autopsy on a body he believes to be that of Vogler. Nothing in this film is quite what it seems: truth may be trickery, apparent trickery may be truth; Vogler's boy assistant is, in fact, an attractive girl, while Vogler's own beard and black hair peel off in his room to reveal a clean-shaven blond. In short, there is just too much of everything, until the slight scaffolding of comedy creaks and finally collapses under the strain.

One wonders whether the basic trouble may not be that what Bergman is saying about the relation between truth and trickery in the magician's act (and by extension, surely, in his own) is really rather bogus, so that when he ultimately finds himself debunking the magician's art by way of an unassailable magician's art, the cinema, his conviction fails him. He has been carried too far, it appears, in the elaboration of his original thesis, and what looks in the script a fairly coherent piece of dramatic fantasy is just not intuitively true for Bergman the film-maker. Where another director working from Bergman's script might somehow have glossed this over, Bergman cannot; all his technical resources cannot carry him over something in which he has, subconsciously at least, lost belief, and so the virtuosity stands out with something like the uncomfortable extravagance which characterizes lies told by a usually truthful man.

Perhaps it was in tacit recognition of his errors in *The Face* that for his next film Bergman decided not to write the script himself, and turned instead to Ulla Isaksson, author of the original story of *So Close to Life* and his collaborator on its screenplay, to write him an original screenplay based on an old Swedish ballad, 'The Daughter of Töre in Vänge'. The result was *The Virgin Spring* (*Jungfrukällan*), one of Bergman's most controversial, and to me one of his most remarkable, films. The story has a stark and classic simplicity. A pure young girl, on her way to early Mass, is captured, raped, and killed by three brigands in the woods. Her father takes ruthless vengeance on the assassins and then begs God's forgiveness and promises to build a church on the spot where she died. As he does so a spring of fresh water miraculously gushes forth under her head. In the film it is given a context of the battle between Christianity and paganism, with some characters, such as Karin's jealous half-sister, Ingeri, still calling on Odin to curse, and others, like Karin's father, still instinctively acting, despite their nominal Christianity, according to pre-Christian codes of behaviour.

Bergman's handling of the story is unflinchingly simple and direct; the technique is hardly ever obtrusive (in this there is a striking contrast with *The Face*), and the film is built on strong, obvious juxtapositions of day and night, white and black, instead of on the intricate chiaroscuro of the last few films. *The Virgin Spring*, in fact, is an extraordinary – and to my mind an extraordinarily successful – attempt on Bergman's part to strip himself of all his twentieth-century sophistication and enter completely into the imaginative world of the middle ages. I have slight doubts about his success with the new character, Ingeri, who sometimes seems, as directed and as played by Gunnel Lindblom, to have wandered in from another century, but for the most part Bergman achieves an astonishing feeling of strict literalness, of telling the story and telling it all just because that is the way things happened, which removes from the rape scene and the destruction of the assassins – the two savage climaxes of the film – all feeling of sadistic gloating or sensationalism. Instead Bergman manages to show us rape and slaughter with the simple directness of

> *He cut her paps from off her breast;*
> *Great pity it was to see*
> *That some drops of this lady's heart's blood*
> *Ran trickling down her knee*

or

> *And he pull'd out his bright brown sword*
> *And dried it on his sleeve*
> *And he smote off that lither lad's head*
> *And asked no man his leave.*

and that, in a director of his culture and sophistication, is a rare achievement indeed.

After *The Virgin Spring* Bergman projected an ambitious trilogy which would deal directly with the subject which has lurked in the background of so much of his work, the relations of man and God. Before undertaking it, though, he made another diversion, conceived mainly in terms of comedy and called *The Devil's Eye* (*Djävulens Öga*). The screenplay, again Bergman's own, is suggested by the Swedish proverb 'A chaste woman is a sty in the Devil's eye', and concerns a mission to earth by Don Juan, sent from Hell at the Devil's behest to seduce the innocent daughter of a pastor before she goes chaste to her wedding. Predictably, Don Juan's mission fails, since the girl feels only pity for him, while he falls in love with her, and even his servant's success with the pastor's wife rebounds, because in the long run it only brings the pastor and his wife closer together. In fact, the only solace for the Devil's sty is the little white lie the girl tells on her wedding day when she assures her groom that she has never been kissed by another man. The film looks as though it was made hurriedly and has a scrappiness one would not expect from Bergman (his notoriously shaky taste does its worst with a pseudo-eighteenth-century pasteboard Hell), but it also has some excellent scenes, notably those between Don Juan and the virgin and his servant and her mother, and personally I even rather enjoy the encounters between the lesser devil who attends the intruders and the pastor, who finally manages to shut the devil in a cupboard. Anyway, the whole thing is rather engaging, and is patently not intended to be more.

Would that one could say as much for the trilogy, which consists of *Through a Glass Darkly* (*Såsom i en Spegel*), *Winter Light* (*Nattvardsgästerna*), and *The Silence* (*Trystnaden*). The three films are quite separate in plot, though the same actors recur in them to some extent (as, indeed, in most of Bergman's films) and they are related in theme. The questions: Does God exist? If he exists, what is he like? What should our relations with him be? have preoccupied Bergman the pastor's son throughout his creative career, explicitly or implicitly: God is either present in the films, or his absence is in itself an important factor. As with so much of what has come after, the germ of the trilogy primarily devoted to this question is to be found in that central earlier work *Fängelse*: the concept, in particular, of a Manichean world in which God may be a monster, permitting for his own unknowable ends things of (by human standards) the utmost horror and evil to occur, which recurs forcefully throughout the trilogy.

In the first there are only four characters: a middle-aged novelist, his daughter, recently released from a mental hospital, his son-in-law and his younger son. They are all on a small island where the novelist has a summer house. David, the novelist, has just come back from Switzerland, having completed a new novel there, and is about to set out on his travels again. He is, like Isak Borg, a cold, self-centred man, and both his children feel abandoned by him; the main thing that keeps him in Sweden at the moment is the rather morbid novelist's fascination he finds in watching the progress of his daughter's schizophrenia, which, he confides to his diary, is incurable. When his daughter, Karen, reads this note in his diary she slips further and further into insanity, quite beyond the help of her simple, loving husband: she seduces her brother, and as her voices become more insistent has a final vision of her God, so long expected and eagerly awaited, as a monstrous spider. In a state of complete and presumably permanent mental collapse she is taken off in a helicopter, accompanied by her husband. But at the end there is a note of hope: David has learnt through all this something of love and humanity, much as Isak Borg did in his day of reflection, and has similarly determined to do something before it is too late: he turns to his son at last in a feeble but real attempt to make contact.

Winter Light has much the same sort of structure. Again Gunnar Björnstrand, who played David in *Through a Glass Darkly*, is at the centre of the drama. He appears as a village pastor who has lost faith, and the film shows a series of encounters he has between Communion and Evensong with various parishioners: the village schoolmistress with whom he has had a loveless, desperate affair; a fisherman who is in despair at the idea the Chinese, 'taught to hate', may get the atomic bomb, and who commits suicide after an interview with the pastor which turns more into a confession of the pastor's failure and loss of faith than an application of spiritual consolation; his crippled sexton who meditates on Christ's despair on the cross because no one, not even the disciples, understood him. And again there is a vague touch of hopefulness at the end, when before an almost empty church the pastor begins the evening service with 'The earth is full of the glory of God'.

At the time of writing the third section, *The Silence*, has been held up for some months in Sweden as a result of troubles with the world's censors, but enough is known about it to show that it differs considerably in its subject-matter and approach from the other two. It is the story of two sisters (who Bergman at one time suggested might symbolize Flesh and Spirit respectively) travelling in Eastern Europe. They have had a lesbian relationship, but it is breaking up, and the younger turns for purely physical satisfaction to a waiter with whom she cannot communicate in words as they have no language in common. Their scenes of physical passion are elaborate and explicit, and are witnessed by both the older sister and the younger sister's little boy. Finally mother and son set off alone for Sweden. How exactly all this fits in with *Through a Glass Darkly* and *Winter Light* is not quite clear, and presumably will not be until we can see it for ourselves; meanwhile Bergman has already completed yet another film, his first in colour, *Not to Mention All These Women*, which he describes darkly as 'a comedy to bait the critics' and will say nothing more about.

Not to Mention All These Women is the twenty-sixth feature film Bergman has directed in eighteen years; in addition he has written four screenplays for other directors, and had a career in the theatre which would more than occupy the entire attention of almost anyone else. There is no doubting, at least, his immense fertility; especially considering that not one of his films has been a straight commercial assignment. Evidently there must be films among the twenty-six that he felt less personally involved with than others, but since *Sommarlek* in 1950 there is not one, major or minor, scripted alone or in collaboration, which does not have the air of being in some way a personal statement. After that, if a film misfires, as for me *The Face* and the first two of the trilogy do, at least it is a failure on the highest level, judged by the highest standards, while from his greatest successes – *Smiles of a Summer Night, Wild Strawberries* – one can hardly withhold the word masterpiece. Why, then, should any doubts remain about Bergman's right to the vague, ambiguous title of *auteur*? I think because the feeling remains that though at his best he has all the gifts of the outstanding screen-writer and the outstanding screen-director, they are not for the most part inseparably fused, but merely subsist in an uneasy alliance. In *Smiles of a Summer Night* and *Wild Strawberries*, and sometimes elsewhere, sheer force of inspiration fuses them into one complex, indivisible gift, but often in his work one remains conscious of a gap between conception and realization; an attitude, one might say, rather similar to that usual in the theatre, where an author may sometimes direct his own play but no necessary connexion between the two activities is assumed. Too often in Bergman's films one senses the writer doing a good imaginative job on the script, working with complete mastery within the chosen medium, and then the director taking over and setting out to 'do something with' what has been written, to make the most of it, to choose the most telling way of realizing it for the screen.

The fact that writer and director are the same man has little to do with it if there is no essential connexion between their functions; as Bresson has said, 'on an *auteur* worthy of the name a choice is imposed . . . for him, and for him alone, once he has worked out his *decoupage*, each shot he takes can have only one definite angle, one certain length of time'. With Bergman it seldom seems that the choice is *imposed*; one could conceive of a dozen ways, more or less good, of shooting the same material, and the very ease and naturalness with which one finds oneself thinking in these terms indicates the gap which exists between script and finished film. Admittedly Bergman has made some very remarkable films, and will no doubt make more. When they come one will enjoy them and recognize their merits. But a coolness persists in my, and I suspect other filmgoers', relations with Bergman and his work; perhaps because he has, in the last analysis, failed to give himself completely to the film while working in it, we still, however great our admiration for isolated achievements of his, draw back ultimately from giving ourselves completely to him.

Alfred Hitchcock

THE APPEARANCE AT ALL OF ALFRED HITCHCOCK IN A BOOK
devoted to cinema since 1950 and the dominating figures of that
period may seem at first glance decidedly incongruous. One of the
other directors I have dealt with, Buñuel, admittedly goes back to
the silent era, but before 1950 he had been inactive and virtually
forgotten for nearly twenty years, his early achievement misunderstood and in general attributed to someone else. Bresson and
Bergman began in the 1940s (1943 and 1945 respectively), but
undoubtedly reached their maturity in the 1950s; Fellini and
Antonioni effectively began their careers after 1950. But what of
Hitchcock, who was born in 1899, began directing his first film (the
unfinished *Number Thirteen*) in 1922, and has been directing almost
without a break since 1925, with a total of forty-eight feature films
to his credit up to and including his most recent, *The Birds*
(1963)? Evidently he can hardly be claimed as a discovery of the
1950s.

And yet after all his inclusion in this group is not merely wilful.
To begin with, quite simply, he has made his best films since 1950.
While virtually every other director who has been making films
since silent days has declined in this period (witness Clair, Pabst,
Wyler, Capra, even, though less disastrously, Ford; Renoir is
perhaps the only important exception), Hitchcock remains as
masterly and unpredictable as ever, with no sign of stiffness in the
joints and always ready to experiment, to conquer fresh territory.
Then, almost equally important, it is only in the last few years that
Hitchcock's influence on other film-makers has really taken full
effect; there have always been occasional pseudo-Hitchcock films,
as we would expect with a director so commercially successful, but
it is only since 1950 that he has become the god of young film-
makers, had his films anatomized in exhaustive detail (sometimes,
especially by the French critics connected with the magazine
Cahiers du Cinéma, rather dementedly, but always with devotion),
and exercised real influence on the films of serious directors.
Whichever way you look at it, Hitchcock is a man of here and now,

and a more commanding figure in world cinema now than ever before.

Hitchcock's career to date falls neatly into four phases: the silent period (nine films); the 1930s in Britain (fourteen films); the 1940s in America and Britain (thirteen features and two shorts); and the period since then, beginning with *Strangers on a Train* (twelve films). To indulge in drastic oversimplification, these phases represent respectively: apprenticeship; the perfection of a style; appreciation of the limitations of that style and an erratic quest for a new style; and final maturity. Hitchcock was born in London, brought up and educated as a Roman Catholic (his Jesuit training has been made much of by French critics and no doubt counts for more than English critics generally suppose), and got into the cinema by way of brief engineering studies and a period in an advertising agency. His first film job was designing titles, and after a couple of years around the studios he stumbled into direction when the director of a Seymour Hicks vehicle, *Always Tell Your Wife* (1922), fell ill and Hicks, suddenly called on to finish the film himself and with no idea what to do, gladly accepted the young Hitchcock's enthusiastic assistance. His appetite whetted, he formed a company with the actress Clare Greet to produce and direct *Number Thirteen*, but ran out of money before it was finished; however, almost at once he was hired by Michael Balcon as assistant director (and sometimes script-writer, art director and editor as well) on five films directed by Graham Cutts.

This extensive practical experience meant that by the time Balcon entrusted him with his first solo job as a director in 1925, with an Anglo-German co-production called *The Pleasure Garden*, Hitchcock was technically well prepared. The result is remarkably polished for a first film, and still quite enjoyable, perhaps more because than in spite of its nonsensical plot about two chorus-girls and their tangled relations with two men bearing (in one case none too well) the white man's burden in the tropics. At least, it was successful at the time, and from then on Hitchcock was rarely idle. There is no point in dwelling on most of his other silent films, though; several of them were tasks in which he had no special interest, and it is difficult to imagine that one has missed much in, say, *Easy Virtue* (after Noel Coward), *The Farmer's Wife* (after Eden Philpotts) or even, despite the praises of the French critics,

Downhill (after Ivor Novello). In all his work at this time Hitchcock was an able, sometimes a brilliant craftsman, and both *The Ring* (1927) and *The Manxman* (1929) have excellent things in them, particularly the former and less pretentious, but coolly considered there is little in them really to suggest the future greatness of their director: some imaginative touches lift them out of the rut of British cinema at the time (things of the order of the shot in *The Ring* which shows the face of the boxer-hero's rival superimposed on the punch-bag he is savagely attacking), and in *The Manxman* there is the theme of transfer of guilt, which the *Cahiers du Cinéma* critics find so significant, while the melodramatic plot of Hall Caine's novel (a variation on the *Enoch Arden* theme) is certainly dealt with in an admirably, restrained, and severe fashion.

If it were not for his later reputation, however, it is unlikely that these early efforts of Hitchcock would still be remembered today; the only possible exception among the silent films is *The Lodger* (1926), based on Mrs Belloc Lowndes's novel, which is, significantly, a thriller in much the same mould as his most famous films of the 1930s and also the first of Hitchcock's films in which he had a credited hand in the scripting (the only other silent film of which this is true is *The Ring*, for which he wrote the original scenario). Even for *The Lodger* allowances have to be made; to enjoy it fully requires an exercise of deliberate 'thinking-back', to see it in the context of the British cinema of the time (not to mention a willingness even in this context to disregard the hamminess of Ivor Novello's performance in the principal role of the mysterious young man unjustly suspected of being Jack the Ripper). In itself the film is clearly something of a declaration of independence: deliberately showy in style, it leaves no one in any doubt that its maker is a director to reckon with, even to the extent of being over-rich and weighed down with set-pieces of technical bravura such as photographing the lodger's nightly pacings in his room through a glass floor, the elliptical treatment of the murders (right from the opening, where a murder is evoked by a close-up of a hand, a shot of a fitfully illuminated staircase, and an anonymous figure, disappearing into the night, followed by a newspaper headline about the latest crime) and the supposed murderer's pursuit by a vengeful crowd near the end, which leaves him trapped in a Christ-like attitude against a grating he cannot open (the crucifixion symbolism, naturally, being found very significant in France).

For all that the film has perhaps, retrospectively, been overrated; it is all rather too self-conscious, too determined to impress, and therefore finally less fresh and appealing than *The Ring*, arguably Hitchcock's best silent film, since there at least the technique is all properly functional and the aim unpretentious. The suspicion of technical indulgence for its own sake recurs in Hitchcock's first sound film, *Blackmail* (1929), which he originally completed as a silent film and then synchronized and partially reshot as a sound film. This again is something of a declaration of independence; again it is a thriller and again the technical set-pieces stand out: the famous scene in which, after the heroine has knifed a man in self-defence, the word 'knife' keeps stabbing at her from the conversation of those around her; the cut on a scream from Alice, after the murder, seeing a tramp lying in the same position as the dead man to the murdered man's char finding his body; the shattering effect of the bell on the shop door to the ears of Alice distraught at the realization that her policeman fiancé suspects her. And, of course, for a very early sound film these effects are remarkable, though not enough in themselves to save the film now, where the slowness and heaviness of the synchronized dialogue scenes ('The actors sound as if they are reciting the titles,' Hitchcock later remarked) inevitably induce some boredom and irritation on the audience's part.

But these technical defficulties were only temporary and no doubt unavoidable given the circumstances of production; just as Clair showed a rather similar maladdress with *Sous les Toits de Paris* and immediately afterwards an extraordinarily complete understanding of the possibilities of the sound film in *Le Million*, so Hitchcock showed an enormous leap forward, technically speaking, in his next film, an otherwise thoroughly uncharacteristic version of O'Casey's *Juno and the Paycock*, and by the time we get to his third sound film, *Murder* (1930) he is completely in control of the medium. *Murder*, in fact, is his first fully mature and characteristic film, full of little tricks and ingenuities, of disturbing overtones of all sorts; of the mixture of cheerful brutality, sexual innuendo, and black humour which makes up so much of 'characteristic Hitchcock'. It concerns an actress found unconscious beside the body of a murdered girl friend, tried, found guilty and condemned, despite the efforts of one of the jury, and then proved, as a result of his investigations (he has, of course, fallen in love with her) to be shielding her fiancé, an equivocal figure who does a circus high-wire act in women's clothes. The opening shot, showing a black cat prowling while cries and footsteps are heard on the sound-track and the scene of the murder finally revealed, pitchforks us straight into the drama, and other scenes stay vividly in the memory: the famous finale in which the murderer, about to be unmasked (as a pervert perhaps as well as a murderer), kills himself by jumping from the high wire; the clamour of the jury breaking upon the one member hesitant (for no very good reason other than intuition) to bring in a verdict of guilty; the grotesque and often wryly amusing sidelights on show-business behind the scenes. Already, too, the subject-matter, starting from a basically banal story-line, is developed to imply much that is normally far outside the range of the thriller (even now, and much more so then); the implications of homosexuality in the case of the real murderer are carefully placed for anyone with an eye to see, though subtle enough presumably to get past the censor and go over the heads of most contemporary audiences (a very similar way of approaching the same subject is to be seen in the much later *Rope*).

After this striking presage of the shape of things to come Hitchcock lapsed during the next four years – for reasons at this distance of time a little difficult to decipher – into a variety of hack works: an adaptation of Galsworthy's *The Skin Game*; a highly enjoyable nonsense called *Number Seventeen*, about some stolen jewels and a strange assortment of characters gathered together in a deserted house to battle over them, ending in a spectacular if unlikely train wreck at the Channel terminal; and worst of all *Waltzes from Vienna*, a musical starring Jessie Matthews and full of Strauss music and Old Vienna atmosphere for which, reputedly, Hitchcock expressed the utmost contempt to the assembled cast half-way through production. The only interesting film from this barren period was *Rich and Strange* (1932), certainly one of Hitchcock's strangest, and to some observers also his richest, works. Apparently a subject which he had very much at heart (and still, it seems, Hitchcock's favourite among his British films – or so he tells French critics), it was made largely silent on locations from Marseilles to Colombo, and concerns the trip taken by an ordinary married couple when an unexpected legacy permits them to do exactly what they want. It is half grotesque comedy, half morality: the humours on shipboard are often pushed up to and over the edge of caricature, with sea-sickness, unhappy encounters with the natives, and a bizarre selection of fellow passengers. But gradually the tone grows more serious; under the strain of all this the couple's marriage is beginning to break up, and when their ship is wrecked and they seem doomed to die, trapped in their cabin as the water rises, this theme comes to the fore. The rest of the film is drama, and sometimes pretty harrowing drama: they are rescued by some Chinese and see such horrors – one of them drowned without anyone doing anything to help or showing any concern; a cat tortured and crucified – that they are only too happy to return home to safety, security, and the middle way. It is difficult to go all the way with those critics – Eric Rohmer and Claude Chabrol, for instance – who regard this film as one of Hitchcock's masterpieces: it is too muddled in execution, too extreme in its fluctuations of tone, for that. But it is interesting as one of his most immediately personal, 'felt' films; one suspects that in it, unselfconsciously and even perhaps a trifle naïvely, the young Hitchcock was wearing his heart on his sleeve, and when the reaction of critics and public was thoroughly unfavourable he decided to set up securer defences the next time. Hence, perhaps, his decision to throw himself instead into the series of thrillers which are the chief glory of his period in the early British sound cinema – films in which ideas close to his heart could be touched on more safely, under the guise of popular entertainment, than when left to speak out for themselves in films like *Rich and Strange*.

When one talks of Hitchcock's 'ideas', though, it is important to be clear about what one means. I cannot myself follow the critics who see him primarily as a philosopher-filmmaker, conveying regularly a certain specific view of the world and human life (a view, no doubt, strongly influenced by his religious training). Certainly it is more possible in Hitchcock's case than in that of most of the directors to whom *Cahiers du Cinéma* apply the same approach (Raoul Walsh, Alan Dwan, etc.), since while they, like most Hollywood directors of their generation, are content mainly to do a good craftsman's job on any script which is handed to them, Hitchcock always plays an important part in the scripting of his own films (a part seldom signified on the credits: since *Number*

Seventeen he has taken screen credit only for the original story of *Notorious*, though the name of his wife, Alma Reville, appears frequently from *The Pleasure Garden* up to *Stage Fright* in 1950). If there is any overall significance in the subjects chosen and the way they are put on the screen, it can fairly be attributed to Hitchcock himself. But I do not really see his films in this way: rather, I think, Hitchcock has interests which recur, sometimes in the situations he likes to treat (yes, undeniably confession and the transfer of culpability is one of them), and sometimes in the way stories are put together – in his passion, for instance, for the intricate red-herring which leads when the audience least expects it to the real trail and the real thrill; in his taste for shocking juxtapositions of comedy and horror, of the unimpeachably normal with the extravagantly abnormal – a reminder that in the midst of life we are in death or that murder can happen to the nicest people, depending on how 'philosophically' you like to interpret things.

All this has up to now been merely implicit in most of his films – perhaps there to be winkled out with powerful aid from hindsight, perhaps not – but in the great sequence of six films which began in 1934 with *The Man Who Knew Too Much* it all comes to the surface and becomes instantly recognizable as 'the Hitchcock touch', that invaluable commodity which made his a box-office name when most filmgoers never noticed the director's name and had little or no idea what exactly he did in a film. (Here, incidentally, Hitchcock's weakness for 'signing' his films with a brief appearance also had a considerable effect, since it gave audiences an added element of puzzle working out exactly where he was to be seen, and made him a physical reality to millions while all other directors remained faceless and unknown.) This series of films – *The Man Who Knew Too Much, The Thirty-Nine Steps, The Secret Agent, Sabotage, Young and Innocent*, and *The Lady Vanishes* – all made within a space of four years, established for ever the conventional image of Hitchcock which underlies the ideas even of many younger filmgoers who have never seen one of them, and is handed on, in Britain at any rate, from critic to critic as part of a national myth. The other part of the myth – that he has never been so good again – we shall deal with in due course, but for the moment let us look carefully at what the image entails.

First of all, they are, of course, all thrillers. Whether they are

11*a. Blackmail.* Dir: Alfred Hitchcock

11*b.* Alfred Hitchcock directs Anne Baxter and Montgomery Clift in *I Confess*

12a. *The Wrong Man* (Henry Fonda, left). Dir: Alfred Hitchcock

12b. *Psycho* (Anthony Perkins). Dir: Alfred Hitchcock

'just' thrillers or thrillers plus is another matter, and one which has caused a lot of argument, with those who think that some of them at least are more than thrillers ranged both against those who say that they are just thrillers and therefore much inferior to his later, more complex works and against those who say they are just thrillers but so what; provided they are good thrillers why should we ask for anything more? With this last point of view I must confess I have much sympathy; I am disturbed by the to me quite irrelevant pseudo-moral judgement implied, that something which is 'just' a thriller or 'just' a musical or 'just' one of the other less pretentious forms has to be rejected as not worthy of serious consideration, or apologized for, or worst of all has to be built up into something it is not in order to justify our enjoyment of it. I believe that Hitchcock's thrillers of the 1930s are essentially just thrillers, exceptionally cunning, complex, intelligent thrillers, full of personal preoccupations and unexpected sidelights, but for all that thrillers with no real pretension to be regarded as anything else.

Take the first of the series, *The Man Who Knew Too Much*. Here everything depends on the cunning with which the involved story is timed, so that we are kept absorbed by the most basic desire to know what happens next and don't stop to question too closely what we are seeing (when Hitchcock came to remake the film twenty-two years later in Hollywood he himself complained of the troubles a more critical, prosaic age had given him in filling up the gaps in the story). A perfect Hitchcock opening shows off admirably one aspect of his way with a story: it all begins a light comedy, with some amiable rivalry during a Swiss shooting tournament and a little joke at the celebration dance, when a bit of wool is attached to the back button of the winner's tails on the dance floor, everyone gets tangled up and starts laughing and suddenly a shot rings out and the victor falls dying, with only the time to mutter something about a planned assassination in the Albert Hall. This plunge from carefree amusement to violent action in a split-second is an effect which Hitchcock uses again and again in his films of this era, and in quite a few subsequently; it is part of the popular image of Hitchcock's style and critics are still disappointed when it does not come, when Hitchcock turns, as he has increasingly of late, to an inextricable mixture of comedy and horror which manages to leave us most amused even as we are most shocked.

C.L.–M

Other characteristic Hitchcock ploys of which this film offers classic examples are the double bluff and the waiting game. The double bluff's most usual form is that a situation is built up for horror or excitement, then proves, actually or apparently, to be quite harmless and mundane, and then, while we are still relaxing, ruefully aware that we have been taken in and resolving not to be again, suddenly, before we can take breath, the real horror or excitement is upon us. In *The Man Who Knew Too Much* two such sequences follow closely on each other: the hero's daughter has been kidnapped to ensure his silence about whatever he may have learnt, and he and a friend set out to track her down. First there is a scene in a dentist's where he goes in search of information and we are kept in horrifying suspense, undecided whether this is a red herring or the real thing, whether the dentist is a villain, has tumbled to his game and has him completely in his power (what more potent image for anyone than a dentist with evil designs on a patient helpless in the chair?) or is simply getting on with a routine job. From this encounter a real lead is obtained (the equivalent episode at a taxidermist's in the second version is by comparison irrelevant to a disappointing degree) and the next sequence takes place in a Mission Church of some eccentric sect. Here we expect it all to be very sinister, and instead the hero and his friend arrive in, apparently, a normal, harmless religious meeting attended by perfectly ordinary people. Relaxation; relief. And then suddenly we realize that something is wrong; as the congregation file out our heroes' way is barred; they are after all trapped in the headquarters of the international spy ring. As for the waiting game, that comes when the heroine (the kidnapped girl's mother) makes her way to the Albert Hall, where the assassination is timed to take place on the third cymbal crash; as we work slowly towards the music's climax, the will-she, won't-she, what-will-she-do suspense is built up in a way which for some mysterious reason the second version, though closely similar and using the same score, does not begin to equal.

No one, I think, doubts that *The Man Who Knew Too Much* is just a thriller, but things get more complicated with *The Thirty-Nine Steps*. Very freely adapted from John Buchan's novel, this again involves an international spy ring, the 'thirty-nine steps', and a more or less innocent bystander who becomes involved by a confidence on the point of death (the famous transfer theme can be forced into service here for both *The Man Who Knew Too Much* and *The Thirty-Nine Steps*): a Canadian who pursues information given to him by a murdered chorus-girl to Scotland, finds the villain of the piece, a respectable-looking professor called Jordan, tries to tell the police who won't believe him, escapes handcuffed to another innocent bystander, the heroine, and in the end breaks the organization by finding out their secret, a scientific formula carried in the brain of a music-hall memory-man who dies in peace once he has told it (the theme of confession hovering in the background). Again, I think it is just a thriller, full of eccentric humour, human observation (hero and heroine, manacled together, trying to pass a fence, he over, she under), sexual innuendo (the idea of two virtual strangers inescapably linked together has obvious possibilities, further reinforced by such details as the hero suggestively filing his nails as the heroine tries, at least partially, to undress) and cunning play on our nerves; any idea of the film's being an allegory of good and evil – any more than any conflict between hero and villain, us and them, can be interpreted in this light – seems to me quite unnecessary and at odds with the general impression the film creates on the mind.

Such serious considerations look much more justified, though, in relation to *The Secret Agent*, which is in this sense the most substantial, though not necessarily therefore the best, of Hitchcock's films of the 1930s. The construction rather resembles that of *Rich and Strange*, the whole film resolving itself into one enormous instance of the abrupt change of tone which, as we have remarked, occurs more usually and generally more satisfactorily within individual scenes. The first half is an almost farcical picture of a group of British spies (or at least one spy, one apprentice spy assigned the role of his wife, and one comic-opera double spy) out to dispose of an enemy agent in Switzerland; then all at once the man chosen has actually to be killed, and after he has been killed proves to be the wrong man (another variation of the transfer theme, the substitution of innocent for guilty, which finally receives its definitive treatment in the film actually called *The Wrong Man*). Thereupon, *The Secret Agent* becomes very serious indeed; the double agent is quite undisturbed by the error, but the two others recognize explicitly that by killing an innocent man, with whatever motives, they have made themselves little if at all better than their real enemy, and accept responsibility for their actions. It is all done within the thriller mould, of course, and quite successfully, though the rupture of tone is disturbing and the film consequently fails to match the achievement of either of its predecessors as a successful work of art on its own chosen level. One or two bravura touches might be mentioned in passing though, particularly such little triumphs of springing the extraordinary on us in ordinary surroundings as the discovery of the dead organist in the Swiss church, propped on one key of the organ which sends out a single note to resound maddeningly through the building, and the surprising location of a secret service centre in a scrupulously hygienic chocolate factory.

It is precisely for its glimpses of the extraordinary which may lurk behind the ordinary that *Sabotage*, the next film in the series, is mainly remembered; adapted from Conrad's novel *Secret Agent* (confusing; Hitchcock's *Secret Agent* is based on Somerset Maugham's *Ashenden* stories), it yet again concerns an international spy ring in unlikely surroundings: a saboteur who runs a small London cinema; a bomb manufacturer who sells birds in Islington. And it has one of Hitchcock's classic waiting games, complicated by a double bluff, when the saboteur's young brother-in-law is sent off to deliver a time bomb in a package by a certain time, but delays and delays until the deadline is reached and then passed; we relax in relief – the bomb will not explode after all; at which precise point it does, blowing the boy and the bus he is riding in sky-high. Otherwise the film is enjoyable and fairly unpretentious; only perhaps the scene in which the saboteur's wife sets out to kill him for killing her brother and he accepts this like a lamb to the slaughter is perhaps a shade too 'significant' for comfort. *Young and Innocent* lacks even this touch of pretentiousness; it is entirely an entertainment, taken at breakneck speed with absolutely shameless model-work and slapdash continuity, and climaxed by one of Hitchcock's most stunning pieces of bravura technique: we know that the wanted man has a twitch in one eye, and in one continuous shot the camera narrows down our field of vision from a whole crowded *thé-dansant* to the band at the far end, then to the drummer, disguised in black face, and then finally, inexorably, to his right eye, twitching.

And so to *The Lady Vanishes*, with *The Thirty-Nine Steps* the most famous of Hitchcock's British films and a worthy climax to his second period. Here the tone is predominantly comic, although again spies are involved (and in the world of Munich perhaps more immediate, believable spies than before) and strong drama always lies in wait just around the corner. The most striking and attractive thing about the film is its insolent ease and gusto; with never a pause the intrigue unrolls, the various groups of characters on the middle-European train from which an apparently harmless old lady has inexplicably vanished are placed with the minimum of to-do, the clues are fairly planted, the surprises just surprising enough (well, yes, of course the harmless old lady would be a vastly efficient spy; anyone could see that!) and the resolution comfortingly neat. When asked later what happened to a group of characters locked in the luggage van and subsequently dismissed from mind, Hitchcock replied blandly that for all he knew they were still there, which sums up the mood of the film very satisfactorily and leaves little else to say.

The Lady Vanishes was really Hitchcock's British swan-song. Immediately afterwards he made an uncharacteristic costume drama based on Daphne du Maurier's novel *Jamaica Inn*, with nothing much to recommend it except a bizarre performance from Charles Laughton, then packed his bags and did not return, except for a brief interlude in 1944 when he made two shorts in French for the Ministry of Information, until 1949–50, when another brief sojourn produced two films, *Under Capricorn* and *Stage Fright*. But in 1939 the die was cast, and from then on Hitchcock, despite his cockney accent and his unchanging Britishness, belongs irrevocably to the American cinema. This, with the tiresome chauvinism of many British critics towards anyone who in their opinion 'abandons' Britain, meant that his subsequent work was for long under a critical cloud in this country, and only comparatively recently has a willingness been shown to forgive and forget, though even now occasional nostalgia is expressed for the good old days and the good old Hitchcock of the uncomplicated prewar thriller.

But this last remark shows exactly why the break was inevitable and in the long run a good thing. In making the six great thrillers Hitchcock had achieved perfection in the genre and had become typed to it. Everyone knew what to expect from him and tended to resent it if they got anything else. But the genre is limited and the dangers of self-repetition or falling back on an increasingly sterile search for new ways of extracting thrills and surprises from the same small round of basic situations are all too clear. Evidently they were clear to Hitchcock and he did what he had to: he got away to entirely new surroundings and started again. The next ten years or so, despite regular (though not quite invariable) commercial successes and some outstanding individual films, among them one (*Shadow of a Doubt*) which Hitchcock still names as his favourite of all his films, is mainly, on the artistic level, a record of trials, false starts, and disappointments, but from the experience he emerged with a new maturity and a new vitality which have made him, and kept him, one of the most dynamic forces in the cinema today.

One of the problems which beset Hitchcock all through this period, it seems to me, is that of coming to terms with the heavier, more fully worked-out style of the expensive Hollywood production in the 1940s as compared with the slight, swift, corner-cutting style he had perfected in his British films of the previous decade. This is not necessarily to say that either style is generally or automatically preferable to the other, but merely that a difficult adjustment is necessary if the films of a director schooled in the latter approach are not to be smothered altogether under the glossy production-values of the former. Hitchcock's first Hollywood film, *Rebecca* (1940), is, seen in this light, a doubtful precedent. Based on Daphne du Maurier's best-selling novel about a timid second wife who is nearly driven to despair in her attempts to emulate the totally dissimilar dead first wife she mistakenly believes her husband still loves, it is superbly professional, well acted, smoothly put together (here the technical resources of Hollywood studios are a clear advantage, allowing Hitchcock to carry much further his former experiments, especially with the moving camera) and thoroughly enjoyable. And yet I cannot help finding it always just a little disappointing; superbly machine-finished, a trifle heavy but intimidatingly efficient, it might, save for one or two small touches like the scene in which the happy couple show home movies of their honeymoon, have been directed by any of a dozen able, anonymous Hollywood directors.

In three of his four subsequent films (the fourth, *Mr and Mrs Smith*, was a curious and not at all successful essay in an alien genre, screwball comedy) Hitchcock returned with varying measures of success to suspense more or less *à l'anglaise*. *Foreign Correspondent*, like the British films, is a thriller about spies, constructed in a series of set-pieces cunningly joined together into a rather picaresque narrative of the adventures of an American reporter with some secrets and some Nazis eager to keep them secret. Memorable scenes include a clumsy attempt to kill the hero by pushing him off the top of Westminster Cathedral tower (the fact that it is a Roman Catholic cathedral seems, oddly, to have escaped French commentators), which concludes with the would-be assassin himself plunging over the edge; a characteristic torture scene in which the victim's cries are covered by loud jazz; and a final climax in which all the principal characters are involved in a plane crash in mid-Atlantic. *Suspicion* is less successful on the whole. It is all built on one situation: a rather naïve young woman (Joan Fontaine doing something like her *Rebecca* role all over again) marries a plausible young man and then gradually comes to suspect him of wanting to murder her and in the end, realizing that even if he does mean to murder her she still loves him and has no desire to live without him, drinks the poison he offers her without demur. Or at least, that is how it ends in the book, and how the film would have ended, with a slight modification to satisfy the Hays office that the murderer would after all be punished. But front-office pressure intervened and forced on Hitchcock a happy ending which makes what has gone before a rather silly much ado about nothing. In *Saboteur* we are back again to the picaresque, with a man on the run after being unjustly suspected of sabotage and experiencing a variety of adventures as he uncovers the real culprits. The film is a sort of minor Hitchcock festival, with scenes strongly (and surely deliberately) reminiscent of *The Thirty-Nine Steps*, *The Man Who Knew Too Much*, *Sabotage* and even *Jamaica Inn*, and constantly hovers on the verge of self-parody. The scenes everyone remembers are the charity ball at which the hero and heroine, oddly dressed for such smart surroundings, have to dance in a crowd of socialites who remain totally unaware of the danger menacing the couple as soon as they leave the floor, and the finale on top of the Statue of Liberty in which a man held by one arm falls to his death after we have watched the sleeve of his jacket giving way stitch by stitch.

These films were all quite successful as far as they went, but that was not very far and they did not do much for Hitchcock's reputation except as a reliable commercial director. *Shadow of a Doubt*, though, which he made from a subject of his own choice in 1943, was a very different matter. It is a very curious, complex film, on the one hand in many ways Hitchcock's most scrupulously realistic, almost documentary in the care and precision with which its small-town background is established (it was even – a great rarity in Hollywood films of that epoch – shot largely on location rather than in the studio), and on the other in construction it is one of his most intricate and artificial, with shot answering shot and idea answering idea down to the smallest detail (what François Truffaut analysed as a regular principle of duplication and reflection; what Chabrol and Rohmer call visual rhymes). It concerns a man, Charlie, who makes a living by murdering rich widows for their money. Under suspicion, he decides to visit his sister in California, and settles down in the family, forming a particularly close relationship, almost telepathic in its intimacy, with his niece and godchild, also called Charlie. He is totally cynical and corrupt, she totally pure and innocent, and Chabrol and Rohmer suggest, with some show of reason, that they are in effect two aspects of the same character, the good and the evil, locked in conflict. However that may be, before long she begins to suspect him, and though the police's attention is lifted and the case closed when an alternative suspect is accidentally killed in the East, she soon ferrets out the truth and confronts him with it. He refuses to do anything and realizing the danger in which her continued existence puts him (she has meanwhile fallen in love with a policeman) tries twice to kill her, without success. Eventually he leaves, however, and is in his turn accidentally killed while making another attempt at murder. He is given a splendid funeral, while his niece and her fiancé wonder how such monsters come to be born into the world.

Apart from the ending, which cannot but seem a little flat and moralistic – it would be better if Uncle Charlie were just to disappear as unexpectedly as he came, or, since the censors would not allow that, if both Charlies, inextricably linked as they are, should die together – the film is uniformly brilliant, a splendid beginning for the new, American Hitchcock which was not, alas, to find really free expression again for some years afterwards. It gains particularly over the other films of this period in two respects. The first is the extreme neatness and ruthless logic of the script's development, with everything in its place in a perfectly ordered, morally ambivalent world where everything goes by twos – Chabrol and Rohmer detail two scenes in a church, two scenes in a garage, two visits of the police to the house, two meals, two attempted murders, and a number of identical shots of the two Charlies, uncle and niece: two close-ups of the back, two travelling shots from in front, two shots from below, and so on. The second is in the use of locations, which lets air into the airless world of Hollywood studio realism, where all too often in other films Hitchcock's special talents seem to suffocate and droop.

In the next film, *Lifeboat*, there is quite a lot of drooping; a drama which takes place entirely in a lifeboat, it has been (deliberately one supposes) denuded of all external reality to put the abstract moral issues posed by the lifeboat's occupants the more clearly in relief, and the studio tank never looks like anything except a studio tank. The characters are all more quasi-allegorical abstractions than believable human beings, and the debate they engage in is all talked out in a heavily literary fashion (Steinbeck was responsible for the original treatment). A German submarine sinks an American transport, and then itself sinks, and a group of survivors from the transport pick up one Nazi. What to do with him? Especially since he alone knows how to steer the boat and will certainly steer it to a German port. In the end he is disposed of, but another U-boat sinks, another German is rescued, and they are back where they started: 'What should we do with these people? Only the dead can tell us.' Ambitious, pretentious, at once too schematic and too ambiguous morally, *Lifeboat* is a worthy failure, no doubt, but a failure none the less, and only went to confirm those who thought that Hitchcock should stick to uncomplicated thrillers in their overhasty judgement.

If *Lifeboat* is overwhelmed by its Hollywood gloss, the next two films, *Spellbound* and *Notorious*, set out apparently to outdo the gloss-merchants at their own game. Stunningly proficient, they are both very fair entertainments and if, to my mind, the better of them, *Notorious*, still fails to reach the highest class of Hitchcock, it is only by a certain deadness in the execution, a fatal heaviness which makes it, for all its brilliance, just a tiny bit boring.

Spellbound is all in line with the contemporary Hollywood vogue for psychiatry on the screen; an unlikely tale of a dried-up woman doctor (Ingrid Bergman!) who flowers under the influence of the love she feels for a new-comer at the asylum, Dr Edwardes, who proves to be not Dr Edwardes at all, but an amnesiac and possibly a murderer. Of course, she saves him, restores his memory and un-masks the real murderer, the head of the asylum. The direction is again, as in *Rebecca* and *Lifeboat*, smooth and solid, with one or two imaginative touches (though not the grotesque dream sequence concocted by Dali, and not particularly the most famous, the 'sub-jective' suicide with a red flash from a gun pointing straight at the spectator), but in the main rather impersonal and characterless, and nothing is done to alleviate the improbability that anyone could believe, even for a moment, in Gregory Peck as a dangerous lunatic.

Notorious, though usually bracketed with *Spellbound* (both are scripted by Ben Hecht, both star Ingrid Bergman) is a far better and very different film. It is the film, in fact, which comes nearest to justifying the wilder claims of the *Cahiers du Cinéma* critics, especially when we remember that Hitchcock himself, excep-tionally, takes responsiblity for the original story. It is an intricate and subtle love story set in the familiar surroundings of spy adven-ture but showing just how far Hitchcock has travelled since *The Lady Vanishes*. This time the spy intrigue counts for little, the relationship between the principal characters for almost everything. The daughter of a Nazi spy who has just been executed is approached by the American secret service and asked to help them in a matter which requires contacts with the Nazis now settled in postwar Brazil, and the easy virtue her way of living already testi-fies. She accepts, and sets off with a handsome American agent rendered cynical by his police experience. They fall in love, and have an affair, but neither will be betrayed by an avowal; when the mission turns out to be that she should seduce a prominent local Nazi she waits for the agent to forbid her and prove his love, while he waits for her to refuse to prove hers. Consequently she does what is required of her, even to the point of marrying the man, while he, illogically, feels that her willingness to do all this merely confirms what he has known all along; once a tramp, always a tramp. But finally, when she fails to turn up at their rendezvous, he gets worried to such an extent that he goes to look for her, thereby placing their whole enterprise in jeopardy, and arrives just in time to save her from the slow poisoning by which her husband and his mother, realizing what she is up to, are trying to dispose of her before she can do any more harm.

The whole story, in fact, is whichever way you look at it based on the importance of an explicit avowal, a confession if you like, as liberating factor: the action turns entirely on the unwillingness of either party to say the necessary word. Moreover, the theme is developed with extraordinary concentration; there are no irrelevant extravagances of any sort (even the famous travelling shot which sweeps down from the top of the grand staircase and finally comes to rest in a close-up of a key in the heroine's hand can hardly be described as irrelevant, though in its context undeniably a little showy) and the big scenes – the bravura display of physical passion near the beginning, the scene in which the heroine realizes that she is being poisoned – are all managed with the utmost directness and simplicity. *Notorious* is also perhaps the most visually ravishing of all Hitchcock's films, certainly of all those in black-and-white; the blacks of Ted Tetzlaff's photography have a rich velvety quality and the whites a distinctive luminosity which give particular value to the texture of objects and materials and make the comparison with Murnau (again a favourite with *Cahiers du Cinéma* critics) almost inescapable. In fact, virtually the only thing to be urged against the film is its ponderousness and claustrophobia – a quality often justified by the story but sometimes, as in the scenes on the hotel balcony against a very hazy back-projection of Rio de Janeiro, certainly not. It is a gallant battle against the steam-rollering impersonality of Hollywood production values, but the danger is there, and one senses that only a small relaxation of resistance and they will flatten all before them.

This is exactly what happens in Hitchcock's next film, *The Paradine Case*, which was the last made under the seven-year contract with David Selznick which had brought him to Hollywood in the first place. Admittedly in this instance Selznick, who scripted as well as producing, no doubt had a more evidently baleful influence than he had had on the two other films Hitchcock had made directly under his aegis, *Rebecca* and *Spellbound* (all the rest were on loan-outs to other companies), but even so it must be admitted that *The Paradine Case* is quite the worst film Hitchcock has made in the

last thirty years, and this despite a story with possibilities, particularly in the character of the vicious judge, spectacularly played
by Charles Laughton. But the treatment is so slow, heavy and
academic that it weighs almost physically upon the senses, reducing
the best moments to nothing and making the shortcomings of most
of the cast (notably Gregory Peck, Alida Valli and Louis Jourdan as
the central romantic triangle, handsome young lawyer, beautiful
client, and client's secret lover) painfully evident. *Rope*, which
immediately followed *The Paradine Case*, is hardly better; indeed,
if the plot were not more interesting, it would be decidedly worse,
being the occasion of one of Hitchcock's unhappiest technical
innovations, the ten-minute take. This means that editing is
eliminated, and instead the camera, perpetually on the move,
follows the action round and tracks dutifully into a back or a piece
of furniture when the reel-change is due, or at least indulges in a
very simple and almost imperceptible cut to facilitate focusing at
the changeover. The technique enforces – or at least here results in
– a uniformly slow tempo unrelieved by any variations in pace from
a pretty stodgy cast, and since Hitchcock plays it straight, without
any zoom-lens trickery – all apparent moves are, in fact, real moves
of the camera – reactions take an age while the camera trundles in
to show us a significant detail. Given that Patrick Hamilton's piece
(here adapted to an American context and made even more suggestive than before of the Leopold and Loeb case) was bound to be
fairly talky on the screen, this is the last way to minimize the effect,
especially considering that much of the talk is half-baked anyway,
particularly from the theoretically Neitszchian college professor
who undergoes a sudden change of heart on first contact with his
ideas in action and instantly starts preaching good old democracy
in the most tiresome manner. The film has, too, its mildly daring
side, suggesting that the two young murderers are a homosexual
affair, or at least not saying they are not (a nod, presumably, being
as good as a wink in this world of rarefied depravity), but on that
perhaps Renoir should have the last word: 'I thought it was a film
about homosexuals, but you don't even see them kissing.'

    After *Rope* comes what is perhaps the most controversial of all
Hitchcock's films, and in a way the summary of this third period
rather as *The Lady Vanishes* is of the second: *Under Capricorn*.
Under Capricorn has in an extreme form both the virtues and the

vices one has come to expect of his films since his arrival in America. It has an interesting, substantial plot, full of the themes and situations which go to make up the 'univers hitchcockien' of the French critics, and we know that filming Helen Simpson's novel had been an ambition of Hitchcock's for some time, so it is reasonable to suppose that, for whatever reason, Hitchcock found something in it specially congenial to him. The plot turns, like that of *Notorious*, on saying the word, on making the avowal or admission that sets free, and without which nothing can happen. In *Under Capricorn* it is, specifically, a confession: Harrietta, beautiful wife of an Australian businessman, seems for no apparent reason to be becoming an alcoholic; a visiting cousin, in his attempts to rescue her from this state, falls in love with her and eventually, after a public scandal, she confesses to him that she committed a murder (that of her brother) for which her husband took the blame; after another quarrel between husband and cousin, in which the latter is wounded, Harrietta and her would-be saviour renounce their love and she stays on with her husband. The crucial position of Harrietta's confession in the story is evident even in summary, and is made more so in the film by being the occasion of a ten-minute take à la *Rope*; evidently Hitchcock knows precisely what he is up to. And yet, far from being the masterpiece Jacques Rivette, Jean Domarché, Eric Rohmer and Claude Chabrol claim it to be, the result is one of Hitchcock's dullest films. Again the tempo is terribly slow, and inartistically so, since the inner tensions and complexities which might justify this are totally lacking. The acting is almost entirely undistinguished, and even Ingrid Bergman, Hitchcock's favourite actress at the time and one with whom he had done wonders in *Spellbound* and particularly *Notorious*, here seems lifeless and abstracted. Moreover, the colour is sludgy and the visual side of the film generally flat and unappealing, and even the points of interest in the direction – the confession scene, the enormous close-up of Harrietta's eye opening to discover an attempt on her life by the wicked governess – are so ponderously introduced that all the excitement they might provide tends to evaporate before we reach them.

Rebecca, Lifeboat, Spellbound, Notorious, Rope, Under Capricorn: these are the characteristic Hitchcock films of the 1940s, and there is no escaping the fact that they suggest a spectacular decline in his talents as a director. The increasing heaviness of the direction, the general humourlessness, the pretentiousness of many of the subjects, the tendency of glossy impersonality to take the place of individual invention, the evident loss of the zest and gusto which used to characterize even Hitchcock's feeblest works before: these damage all of them, including the best (*Notorious*), and give rise to the gravest doubts about Hitchcock's future. Admittedly to set against them there is one unexpected, idiosyncratic masterpiece, *Shadow of a Doubt*, which is exempt from all these criticisms and at the same time quite different from the pre-war British Hitchcock, but in 1950 that was seven years and seven films away, and Hitchcock's latest, an attempt to return to the straightforward thriller entertainment in *Stage Fright*, was hardly more encouraging than his preceding heavyweight flops.

Then, suddenly and quite unexpectedly, another masterpiece, *Strangers on a Train*, and the new, dazzling, mature Hitchcock of the 1950s was upon us before we knew it. How to explain this astonishing transformation? Partly, of course, and very importantly in this particular case, a really brilliant script (Raymond Chandler, who worked on the adaptation, was obviously the ideal writer to bring out the best in Hitchcock, so much in their outlook – the preoccupation with morbid psychology, the black humour – corresponding closely), but also, and I think in the long run more importantly, the reaction against studio realism instituted by the really-shot-on-the-street-where-it-happened school of semi-documentary thriller makers who came to prominence in Hollywood at the end of the 1940s. Hitchcock's response to the spirit of place is highly developed, and he has always drawn strength from it. In the British thrillers, however studio-bound they might be, he was re-creating places and people he knew well and could evoke vividly without too much effort. In the characteristic products of his first American period, though, the predominant feeling is airless, timeless, placeless, however much we are told about the where and when of the action. It is as though, cut off from his roots in familiar surroundings, Hitchcock had lost his power to re-create with any immediacy the semblance of life as it is really lived, and this, however fantastic the plot structure of his films, has always been a necessary constituent, the context of ordinary everyday existence in which the extraordinary can so startlingly and yet for all that so believably flower. In *Shadow of a Doubt* he was able, for once, to get out of the studio and draw strength again from real places, real people, but elsewhere in the films of his first American decade the old power appears only in brief flashes, which get fewer and fewer as the years pass and real inspiration is increasingly replaced by the sterility of technical innovation for its own sake.

In *Strangers on a Train* at last we are back in the open air. With a story after his own heart (involving again, let us note in all fairness, the famous transfer of guilt) about a tennis-player who meets on a train a strange young man who proposes an exchange of murders – he will murder the tennis-player's wife if the tennis-player will murder his father – does not take it seriously, but then finds that 'his' murder has been done for him and he is expected to perform his part of the bargain or else, Hitchcock makes full use of outdoor locations – the stations, the tournament tennis-courts, the funfair where the wife is murdered – and succeeds in making his interiors and studio scenes match them closely in life and verisimilitude. The effect is instantaneous: the *mise en scène* loses the ponderousness of the last few years and becomes light and adventurous, full of little inventions (like the murder reflected in the victim's broken glasses) and elaborate set-pieces, like the climactic cross-cutting between Guy frantically trying to win a tournament in record time and Bruno desperately battling to retrieve from a grating a lighter which he intends to plant as the last piece of incriminating evidence against Guy at the scene of the crime – all leading to a final battle on a merry-go-round run wild. Seldom if ever had Hitchcock's sheer technique been more dazzling, but, significantly, this time it was not technique in a void, as in suspense-machines like *Saboteur* and *Stage Fright*, but technique used to create an atmosphere, advance a coherent narrative and put before us believable characters: some of the most telling scenes in the film, in fact, are from the technical point of view the most unobtrusive, like that in which Guy's fiancé goes to visit Bruno's mother and little by little discovers that she is madder than her son.

Once started off again on location shooting (and with a sympathetic cameraman, Robert Burks, who would continue to work with him uninterruptedly for the next nine films), Hitchcock proceeded to go still farther along the same line in *I Confess*, a thriller-cum-problem picture about a priest who receives the confession of the man who committed a murder he is himself accused of. Shot almost entirely on location in Quebec, this film is, of course, an ideal hunting-ground for critics determined to discover religious preoccupations in everything Hitchcock does, but essentially it is simply a thriller in which the inviolability of the confessional is one of the principal *données* (though the reasons the story appealed to Hitchcock – confession, the word that kills or gives life, transfer of guilt – are obvious). The special atmosphere of the film's locations –the narrow, mysterious streets, the wild nineteenth-century gothic turrets, the gigantic sculptures of the Stations of the Cross which survey the action – accounts for much of its fascination, a fascination intensified by the extraordinary beauty of some of the images (the beginning, for instance, of the long and rather awkwardly placed flashback in which a married woman, attempting to clear but actually further incriminating the priest, tells of their affair before he entered the priesthood: the shot in slow motion and soft focus, from below, of Anne Baxter coming down an iron stair to meet her lover must be one of the most exquisite in the whole of the cinema). The priest's ordeal is worked out with rigorous logic, and permits much to be read into it, though whether the film really resolves itself into a drama about the will to martyrdom, the temptation of doing the right thing for the wrong reason, is highly questionable; to me it seems that the film simply accepts that he is acting properly and heroically, and that is the end of it. But either way – tragedy of conscience or off-beat thriller – *I Confess* is further evidence of the remarkable revival Hitchcock's talents and reputation have achieved in the 1950s.

Since *Strangers on a Train*, in fact, Hitchcock has made only one film, the remake of *The Man Who Knew Too Much*, which seems to me undeniably an artistic failure (though even here some critics have attempted to deny it). It is noticeable, and perhaps symptomatic, that during this time he has turned more and more to comedy, though sometimes very black comedy indeed, and that for four successive films – *Rear Window, To Catch a Thief, The Trouble With Harry* and *The Man Who Knew Too Much* – he worked with the same script-writer, John Michael Hayes, who is known primarily as a specialist in sophisticated comedy writing. Before embarking on this cycle, however, Hitchcock took time off to make a fairly close adaptation of Frederick Knott's stage success *Dial M*

for Murder, the chief interest of which, apart from some excep-
tionally neat plotting, was the use of the 3-D process, at that time
(1953) the main hope of Warner Brothers in the 'battle of the
processes' which threw up in quick succession Cinemascope, Vistavision and Cinerama, among others. The vogue was so short-lived
that in Europe *Dial M for Murder* was never, as far as I can discover, shown in the 3-D process at all, but as a normal two-
dimensional film. Nevertheless one can see what Hitchcock is
trying to do: there are none of the usual gimmicks of throwing
things at the audience, but a strong emphasis on analytical shots
from above, the angle, after all, at which the relief of things is most
marked. In general the film rather resembles *Rope* – both are
adaptations of one-set stage plays observing the unity of time more
or less closely, and do not depart far from the original conception –
but is infinitely more lively and imaginatively handled. It also
introduces into Hitchcock's work another actress, Grace Kelly,
who was to become a favourite of his – to such an extent that she
starred also in his two subsequent films, *Rear Window* and *To
Catch a Thief*.

In these two films and *The Trouble With Harry* Hitchcock's
passion for tantalizing his audience reaches its climax. In the first
we are given a characteristic technical problem: that of showing a
whole complex action from one point of view, the window from
which a newspaper photographer with a broken leg spies (aided, of
course, with a variety of telescopes, lenses, etc.) on his neighbours
around a Greenwich Village court. This is, so to speak, the technical *raison d'être* of the film, the same sort of challenge that
Hitchcock has sought out before by confining the action of a film to
a lifeboat or to a single flat, and the ingenuity he uses to solve the
problems is one of the principal pleasures of the film. There is
virtually no cheating; I remember only one shot from an angle
impossible to the hero, though no doubt there are one or two more
which pass unnoticed. But if the prominence of the technical
problem and the confinement of the action to a large studio set look
like danger signals, in *Rear Window* the dangers are speedily dismissed. What we find instead of a sterile technical exercise is one of
Hitchcock's most complex and teasing films, full of black humour
and disturbing ambiguities. Most striking among the ambiguities is
the position of the hero, with whom we are virtually compelled to

C.E.–N

identify, seeing everything through his eyes, and yet whose motives and behaviour are highly dubious to say the least. It is really the story of a heartless fantasy which becomes a reality, of humans reduced by a human mind to conventional puppets who suddenly reassert their humanity and get terrifyingly out of the puppet-master's control. The photographer deduces, as an intellectual game, that one of his neighbours has murdered his wife. His deduction is only a fantasy to while away a boring convalescence – you don't really expect your neighbours to be murderers, even in Greenwich Village – but little by little it becomes a reality, and he becomes obsessed by it to a point where he nearly gets his own fiancée murdered in the course of the investigation and finally – the implication is clear – becomes little if at all better than the criminal he is tracking (compare particularly *The Secret Agent*). All this is told with a dry, caustic humour which makes the film a uniquely disturbing experience: Hitchcock's alleged misanthropist tendencies have seldom been more clearly in evidence.

After this, *To Catch a Thief* makes an agreeable interlude of fairly uncomplicated relaxation. Warm, sunny and expansive, for much of the time it is hardly a thriller at all, though some vestiges of the thriller form remain and the retired cat-burglar does in the end manage to unmask the impostor whose methods so tiresomely recall his own. For the most part, though, the film is all a huge joke at the expense of the audience, building up our expectations of a suspense situation only to throw it away with a shrug – a pursuit of the hero ends when he is cornered by a tiny, irate old woman whose flower-stall he has overturned; a car chase ends unpredictably in a scatter of chickens – and throwing in odd shocks to the nervous system like the highly coloured image of a cigarette being stubbed out in a fried egg. Comedy, too, is the note uppermost throughout *The Trouble With Harry*, a sparkling *jeu d'esprit* about a body found lying out on a Vermont upland in the middle of a glowing, golden autumn and the various people who come into contact with it, three at least of whom quite happily assume that they are, in fact, the murderer. The story, told with perfect directness and simplicity, is totally amoral, and, though very closely based on Jack Trevor Story's novel, totally Hitchcockian in its insolent humour, its blandly persuasive assumption of the audience's complicity in something which in normal circumstances normal audiences would be likely to reject *in toto*. One of Hitchcock's most masterly works, it has a unity and simplicity which almost defy analysis; like *The Lady Vanishes* it is just a film to be seen.

Very different indeed is the major work which followed it, *The Wrong Man* (leaving out of consideration, that is, the remake of *The Man Who Knew Too Much*, which seems to me, apart from an intriguing new introduction where sightseeing in Morocco replaces shooting in Switzerland, an almost complete disaster). Here we are back to location realism with a vengeance (*The Trouble With Harry* is carefree location fantasy), comedy, colour and John Michael Hayes being abandoned in favour of strict verisimilitude in the reconstruction of events which actually happened. The extreme example of Hitchcock's interest in the position of the innocent wrongly accused, it tells the story of Mannie Balestrero, a double-bass player who is one day arrested and charged with committing a number of hold-ups. Numerous witnesses identify him, everything stacks up against him, the two people who could provide him with alibis die, his wife goes mad. All this, as Hitchcock himself assures us in a brief prologue, is *true*; it all really happened that way, though if such a collection of coincidences were offered to us in a purely fictional narrative we would never believe them. At long last, released on bail while awaiting a retrial (his first trial has been invalidated on a point of order), Balestrero is reduced to despair and prays, at which moment the real criminal – whether by chance or by divine intervention we are left to judge for ourselves – is found, arrested and confesses. In putting this story on the screen Hitchcock uses his most severe and rigorous style (indeed, treating a subject which might have appealed to Bresson he sometimes comes close to Bresson in final effect); the camera relentlessly pursues the hero through his ordeal, and much of the film is constructed in a series of harsh, searching, black-and-white close-ups with no room for intrusions of the irrelevantly picturesque. Only when it moves briefly away from the central character does the film lose its grip a little (even if it did happen just like that, it is asking rather much of any actress to go mad convincingly in the course of one short sequence), but elsewhere, as we go through Balestrero's experiences with him, spared nothing of the exhausting formalities of the process of law, watching with him, in the hallucinatory clarity of a bad dream, the faces of the jurors as the trial grinds on, there is not even a momentary slackening of the film's power over us.

Of the four films Hitchcock has made since *The Wrong Man* (since his great burst of creativity in 1954–6, when he made five films in under three years, his films have been fewer and farther between) one, *North by Northwest*, seems to me diverting but unimportant, a return to the style of *Saboteur* with at least two classic suspense pieces, an auction in which the hero, surrounded by the enemy (spies again), bluffs his way out with extravagant ingenuity, and a sequence in which he finds himself alone in the depths of the country, far from cover, with a pest-spraying helicopter spraying him with bullets instead. The other three, though, *Vertigo, Psycho* and *The Birds*, are all major works, and indeed *Psycho* and *The Trouble With Harry* remain for me the masterpieces of Hitchcock's whole career, with *Vertigo* only a fraction behind because of an unnecessary expansiveness in the exposition.

Vertigo, nevertheless, is perhaps the most haunting of all Hitchcock's works, the most subtly disturbing in its atmosphere. This is hinted at in the title of the Boileau and Narcejac book on which it is based, *D'Entre les Morts*, which also gives the clue to the real subject of the film, so surprisingly misunderstood by nearly all the critics, who tended to treat it as a suspense piece in which Hitchcock, for some extraordinary and inexplicable reason, chose to throw away the suspense half an hour before the end. It concerns a private detective who develops a paralysing fear of heights as a result of an accident in the course of his work. Restored to health, he is hired to keep an eye on a woman who is said to suffer from suicidal tendencies, and on one occasion actually rescues her from what he takes to be a suicide attempt. They fall in love, but the next time she tries to commit suicide it is from a high tower, and his helplessness under the effects of vertigo prevent him from saving her. Some time later, though, he sees in the street a girl just like her, though the hair is a different colour and the personality, when he approaches her, tough, brassy and totally distinct. All the same, the attraction is irresistible.

At this point comes the controversial flashback: through her eyes we see what really happened that day at the tower, and learn that, in fact, the whole thing was an ingenious murder plan; the story of a suicidal temperament was an elaborate cover, and the woman that the detective followed and fell in love with was not the real wife at all, but a hired substitute; the two women are, in fact, one and the same. End of suspense, beginning of real story: as we watch, fascinated, the detective sets about remoulding the new girl in the image of the loved and lost. If we were not given the necessary information right away, we would merely be waiting for the unexciting resolution of a simple question – is she or isn't she the same person? But as it is we are given instead a human drama of extraordinary subtlety and suggestive power, tending towards only one possible, bitterly ironic conclusion. Again the realization of it all is extremely pure and simple: the familiar San Francisco locations, so matter-of-factly dismissed in most films, here take on a misty, ghostly quality in Robert Burks's exquisite Technicolor photography, and the whole thing is given a strange, dreamlike atmosphere in which people can appear and vanish mysteriously and nothing is quite what it seems. No displays of technical bravura break the illusion (on the contrary, some of the process work looks rather ropy and amateurish); instead a careful unity of tone is maintained, compelling our acceptance of the hero's vision of the world, up to the moment (at the flashback) when we enter instead the inscrutable heroine's mind and from then on see the reverse of the picture, from her point of view.

This construction of a film on a sudden change, not so much of mood (as in *Rich and Strange* and *The Secret Agent*) as of viewpoint, is carried a stage further in *Psycho*. Here we are 'with' a character – a young woman who has committed an ingenious robbery and is on the run with the loot – for about half the film, seeing everything in effect through her eyes, and then with a violent rupture of mood she is brutally murdered and disposed of – for reasons totally irrelevant to the load of money she carries – and we start to see things instead from a coolly objective standpoint as the action is carried through to its relentlessly logical, unforeseeable conclusion. *Psycho* is the most thrilling of thrillers; even Hitchcock has never bettered some of its shock effects, like the murder through a plastic shower curtain (the shower, like the dentist's chair, is an archetypal position of vulnerability) or the attack on the intruders in which the camera plunges pell-mell down a flight of stairs. It is also the most savagely amusing of *comédies noires*, balancing us, even at its most horrifying, on the knife-edge where there is almost no distinction between a laugh and a scream. Only at the very end does it falter slightly, while a psychiatrist pains-takingly explains that the mother-dominated central character has developed a split personality after his mother's death so that one side of him can continue to be dominated by his own persisting image (fancy dress and all) of a jealous mother who would brook no other force in her son's life than herself. But even here Hitchcock retrieves matters with a shattering final scene showing the subject of these observations, curled up as though in a womb, retreating completely into the fantasy world where no one can get at him any more.

After this peak *The Birds* comes as something of a relaxation, if anything so sinister can reasonably be described in such terms. It is a planned crescendo based on a single idea: what would happen if the birds suddenly turned on the rest of the world. Not the big, frightening, menacing birds of prey, but little, fluffy insignificant birds; wrens and starlings, seagulls, doves. A perfect example of that extraordinary from the heart of the ordinary, that menace lurking in the most unexpected and apparently inoffensive objects, which has been a constant of Hitchcock's work from the earliest days, the film, after an opening three-quarters of an hour of sophis-ticated comedy with hardly a hint of suspense, resolves itself largely into a special-effects man's dream as the attacks start, first here and there, with a few glancing blows, and then all over, as masses of birds descend on isolated humans and peck them to death. On this level at least it is masterly, even if there is a slight tendency for the birds to overshadow the mere humans in the picture; one suspects that the film is an interlude in Hitchcock's career, but what will come next from this most inventive, un-predictable of film-makers is anyone's guess.

Whatever it is, though, one can predict with reasonable safety that it will be brilliant of its kind. Since *Strangers on a Train* Hitch-cock's unmatched expertise has never deserted him (even the despised remake of *The Man Who Knew Too Much* is unshakeably adroit), and in his full maturity and confidence he has been ready to tackle almost anything. The sheer variety of his films in this period is staggering: from the macabre comedy of *The Trouble With Harry* and the romantic comedy of *To Catch a Thief*, through the light-hearted thriller-entertainment of *North by Northwest* and the neat mechanics of *Dial M for Murder* to the unsettling ambiguities of *Rear Window* and *Strangers on a Train* and the rigours of *The Wrong Man*, all are encompassed with equal ease and success. And, more astonishing still, they all come out unmistakably as 'Hitchcock films'; one is never tempted even for a moment to wonder if they could be the work of a technically brilliant but quite impersonally eclectic talent. Throughout his career Hitchcock has used his collaborators to the full, and often they have been collaborators who brought to the work a marked individuality – not only among the warranted greats like James Bridie (*Under Capricorn* and *Stage Fright*), John Steinbeck (*Lifeboat*), Maxwell Anderson (*The Wrong Man*) or even Dorothy Parker (*Saboteur*) and Robert Benchley (*Foreign Correspondent*), but capable professional script-writers like Ben Hecht (*Spellbound, Notorious*), John Michael Hayes or Charles Bennett, whose way with a red herring has been evident elsewhere than in his pre-war Hitchcock thrillers (there is a perfect 'Hitchcock' red herring, for instance, in his *Night of the Demon* (Jacques Tourneur, 1957)). But always the special qualities of these writers, and of his cameramen, designers, editors, etc. – and even of his actors, whom he tends to regard as puppets – have been used, ruthlessly and quite properly, entirely for what in them could be turned conveniently to Hitchcock's own personal ends. Themes and attitudes recur constantly in his films, tying them into a web of references and reflecting, evidently, Hitchcock's own interests and preoccupations, though not, I think, anything like a coherent personal philosophy. It is rather a question of mental furniture, 'keepings', to use Hopkins's word for it, which somehow crops up in everything that passes through Hitchcock's hands. If Hitchcock does not have 'a style', in the way that, say, Ophuls or Minelli does, so that a few feet extracted from any film would be constantly recognizable by a certain way of moving the camera, of lighting, of composition, he has nevertheless something much less self-conscious: a personal *écriture* which comes, like Buñuel's, simply from trusting to his personality to colour all his work (or, perhaps, from not considering such matters at all, but just unself-consciously following his own bent wherever it may take him). Like Buñuel, Hitchcock achieves his style by an inspired absence of style; of him perhaps more unarguably than of anyone else in the cinema can it be said quite simply 'le style, c'est l'homme'.

The New Wave

By the end of the 1950s all the directors dealt with up to now in this book had become firmly established as leading figures in world cinema, the last to do so being Antonioni, whose decisive success with the world at large did not come until 1960, with *L'Avventura*. But even before this people began wondering, with the restlessness characteristic of the film enthusiast, where the next excitements were to come from. As ever, what was needed primarily to focus attention on a new area or group of film-makers was a label, like Neo-Realism, which brought a whole generation of Italian film-makers to attention just after the war, and around 1958–9 such a label began to be generally applied to a number of young French film-makers, many of them still in their twenties, who directed during these years their first feature films. They were *la nouvelle vague*, the new wave the French cinema had been waiting for since the last generation of film-makers – Jacques Becker, René Clément, Yves Allégret and others – had emerged during the tensions and troubles of the Second World War.

Like most such labels, 'New Wave' was most useful when it meant nothing very specific; when it meant simply a conglomeration of new directors with for the most part no particular affiliations one with another, and only related by the incidental fact that conditions in the French film industry at the time permitted, indeed encouraged, them all to break into the commercial cinema during the same relatively short period. Some of them – in most respects, certainly, the most interesting of them – were film critics turned creator; virtually all the founders and regular early contributors to the monthly review *Les Cahiers du Cinéma* have directed at least one feature film, and three of them, François Truffaut, Jean-Luc Godard, and Claude Chabrol, have become dominating figures in the new French cinema. But others have come from documentary, like Alain Resnais, Agnès Varda, and Georges Franju, yet others, like Chris Marker, Jean Rouch and the proponents of 'cinéma-vérité', have stayed with documentary, and others again have come up during the 'New Wave' period by the most traditional route in the French cinema, graduation to full directorship after a period as 'apprentices' learning the craft by assisting already established directors.

More recently attempts have been made to define the New Wave, to itemize its qualities and discriminate between those who 'belong' and those who don't. To do this is to imply a coherence which the movement never had to begin with and certainly does not have any more. It began – to oversimplify drastically – because one young man, Roger Vadim, happened to be married to an up-and-coming starlet, Brigitte Bardot, and, after a respectable period as assistant director, was allowed by an enterprising producer to direct a film himself, starring his wife. The result, *Et Dieu créa la femme* (1956), was an enormous commercial success, especially abroad, and from then on producers were that much more willing to gamble a little on young directors, young stars, in the hope that youth itself would prove saleable. As it happened a supply of really young directors was to hand, many of them, like the *Cahiers du Cinéma* group, already experimenting with privately financed shorts, documentaries, or even in one or two cases whole feature films from which their potential talents and assimilability into the commercial system might reasonably be gauged.

The whole explosion of talent which resulted is obviously much too large a subject for a single chapter, and in any case there is no point in considering many of the directors who have emerged under the banner of the New Wave with any great seriousness. There have been a few (though on the whole surprisingly few) incompetents who have crept in, shielded by the temporary readiness of some critics to accept anything new just because it was new. There are many, many more who have proved themselves capable technicians, sound commercial directors who would probably have found their opportunities anyway, sooner or later, and as a result of the New Wave's vogue just happened to find them sooner. And there are a number of genuine, personal talents at work who are unlikely ever to change the world or revolutionize our way of seeing things, but will certainly continue to make outstandingly good films. Jacques Rivette, for instance, whose strange, elusive, haunting film *Paris Nous Appartient* stays obstinately in the memory, even if it is difficult to decide how much of it was initially intended and how much was created by the editor in the

cutting-room. Jacques Demy, whose *Lola* was a uniquely elegant and
subtle charade full of charm, wit, and genuine feeling. Marcel
Moussy, script-writer of Truffaut's *Les Quatre Cents Coups* and
Tirez sur le pianiste, whose own *St Tropez Blues* caught with the
least apparent effort the sort of free-wheeling youthful grace and
freshness so many more pretentious films have striven for and
signally failed to achieve. Agnès Varda, distinguished documentarist who in *Cléo de 5 à 7* achieved that rare thing, a film by a
woman which is neither defiantly masculine nor self-consciously
'feminine', but simply and movingly the natural expression of its
creator's temperament. Marcel Hanoun, who in his television film
Une Simple Histoire carried Bressonian asceticism to its logical
conclusion with a subtlety and restrained power which made it in
the opinion of many a better Bresson film than Bresson himself has
managed to produce for some years. Or Jean Rouch, whose
Chronique d'un Été hit for the moment a happy balance between
mise en scène and the arid ramblings which later proponents of
cinéma-vérité have sought to palm off as the last word in unvarnished documentary truth.

And there are more. But for the moment I shall concentrate on
three leading figures, Truffaut, Godard, and Resnais. The choice
seems right today for a number of reasons even apart from their
relevance to the central theme of this book, the relationship of
writer and directors at this stage in cinema history (Truffaut and
Godard being examples of the complete film creator, like Buñuel,
Bresson, Fellini, Antonioni, Bergman and Hitchcock, and Resnais
an interesting example of the pure *metteur en scène* who seeks to
collaborate with a series of notable writers on absolutely equal
terms). But it is early days yet; far too early to prophesy about
which of these bright new talents will ultimately prove to have the
staying power and the range of a really great director. The following pages can be regarded, at best, as a very tentative interim
report.

François Truffaut

Like so many of the most interesting New Wave directors,
François Truffaut first made his mark as a critic. He was born in
Paris in 1932, had a disturbed and stormy childhood which at one
stage brought him to confinement in a reformatory, and was work-

ing by the age of 15 in an office and then in a factory. His main spare-time occupation even then was attendance at and organization of local ciné clubs, and he soon attracted the attention of the critic André Bazin, who saved him from the reformatory and after his military service introduced him into the staff of the monthly *avant-garde* film magazine *Les Cahiers du Cinéma*. Here, for some eight years, he showed himself one of the most implacable enemies of all that was stale and conventional in the French cinema of the period, ever ready to condemn the 'tradition of French quality' in favour of the 'politique des auteurs', and one of the enthusiastic supporters of film-makers at that time little thought of in France, especially the veteran American commercial directors like Howard Hawks, Raoul Walsh, and even Hitchcock, and of the low-budget American B-feature, all the more estimable in his eyes for not being tarred with the brush of phony 'art'.

Thus Truffaut was already an 'influence' in the French cinema some time before he ever made a film. In 1954 he made a 16 mm. short, *Une Visite*, which no one seems to know anything about, but his effective début as a film-maker was with another short, *Les Mistons*, in 1957. The effect of this was quite unexpected. Whatever might have been anticipated from a wild young critic of revolutionary tendencies, it was hardly this, a quiet, graceful, even, one might say, romantic evocation of childhood and far-off innocence. In it Truffaut seemed to owe more to Renoir than to any other director, the feeling for place and atmosphere (Nîmes in summer) is very suggestive of Renoir, and so is the mingling of the evocative and the nostalgic with occasional outbursts of unpredictable knockabout humour. In most ways the story is told fairly straightforwardly. A group of boys at the dawn of adolescence eye an older girl with intense juvenile excitement and interfere, rather ineffectually, in her romance with their P.T. master; when the master is killed in a mountaineering expedition they feel temporarily a little guilty at their behaviour, but not for long, and it is all long ago. . . . Only occasionally does the film betray the film critic, the intellectual theorist, working hand in glove with the romantic artist: odd, unexplained moments like the teacher's encounter with a man in the street who refuses furiously to give him a light; the lightning reconstructions of moments from other films, like Lumière's *L'Arroseur Arrosé*. But these in context suggest only youthful high spirits, an enjoyment of and at-homeness with the medium which augur well in a first film.

The beginning, once made, was followed up almost immediately with a short slapstick comedy, *Une Histoire d'Eau*, put together by Godard from material previously shot by Truffaut, and then with Truffaut's first feature-length film, *Les Quatre Cents Coups* (literally *The Four Hundred Blows*, but more accurately something like 'Living It Up'). This again, perhaps even more than *Les Mistons*, was not a revolutionary's film, or not anyway in the method of its putting together. It may be revolutionary in what it has to *say*, but then that is something quite different. Essentially it is an autobiographical document, a longer and far more realistic evocation of a young adolescent's world than *Les Mistons* (no attempt here to make us believe that the most scurrilous thing a 13-year-old could think of to say about a courting couple is that they are engaged!). Antoine, the hero, is a Parisian boy of $12\frac{1}{2}$, dividing his life between a school made up of boredom and petty tyrannies and a home overshadowed by his parents' mutual resentment and distrust. His own private world is, like that of most children, one of idols and fetishes: he even builds a little altar in his room to one idol, Balzac, and then gets into trouble by nearly setting the flat alight with a candle he lights to its deity. But then he is always in trouble, one way or another: at school he is punished for cribbing an essay from Balzac, at home he gets into trouble for playing truant and petty pilfering, and the whole thing comes to a head when he is caught with a stolen typewriter (he intended to sell it and go to the seaside with the proceeds) and taken to the police station by his father.

Up to this point the film is built up in a succession of small touches, little scenes conveying the character of Antoine, his father, his mother, and his best friend René, and the curiously contradictory quality of his life, with his parents alternating between affectionate understanding and unconcealed resentment, his own feelings veering from unexpected, unaccountable joy to equally little motivated desperation. The film, in fact, achieves the same sort of objective-subjective balance that Shelagh Delaney achieved in *A Taste of Honey*: looked at one way it is a wholly clear-eyed, unsentimental, objectively believable picture of an adolescent, a specific adolescent in a specific situation; but in another way it gives us the curious feeling of seeing everything from the inside outwards. It is not so much that our sentimental participation is demanded in the hero's sufferings – quite the reverse; we are allowed to see round him and criticize him even as we sympathize – but that the life around him is shown only in so far as it impinges on him, and is coloured by his view of it. Antoine is, like all of us, a mass of contradictions, and so are those about him; he is in many ways responsible for what happens to him, he almost deliberately precipitates the events which finally bring him to reform school. Everything he does seems to be informed with a strange subdued frenzy which is only partially, if at all, 'explained' by his family difficulties; there is no facile attempt to place the responsibility for his 'delinquency' on his parents or his environment. He is always a free agent, living while still a child the independent life of an adult, taking his own decisions – often the wrong ones – and standing by them.

From Antoine's arrival at the police station the tone and method of the film gradually change, and it concludes with two sustained sequences of great power, his interview with a psychiatrist and his escape from the reformatory and long run towards the sea, symbol of freedom which has been hovering in the background throughout the film as a far-off, desirable goal. The interview is shot entirely in one set-up, showing us only Antoine as he answers the questions of the unseen psychiatrist, and might almost be seen as the germ from which the whole of 'cinéma-vérité' sprang; it was improvised on the spot and has at once its functional part to play in the film as a sort of epitome of what has gone before and all the fascination of personal revelation which the best television interviews possess (*Les Quatre Cents Coups* is very much a film 'about' Jean-Pierre Léaud, the boy who plays Antoine, as well as about the young François Truffaut). After this the long run, with its light and air (instead of the darkness and claustrophobia of the interview), its dazzlingly free and mobile camerawork, comes as a blessed relief, a final assertion of Blake's principle 'Damn braces. Bless relaxes' all the more telling for being made entirely in film terms. And at the last, when on the fringes of the sea Antoine turns questioningly towards us, the gesture is stripped of sentimentality by Truffaut's inspired use of a 'freeze' to leave him still, haunting, immobile, caught for ever on the edge of a new life like the lovers on Keats's Grecian Urn.

As has been said, the film is not for the most part technically adventurous. There are things in it which are novel and exciting, like the treatment of the interview. But in general Truffaut is content to use traditional technique in order to express his call to arms. For *Les Quatre Cents Coups* carries in many ways a revolutionary message; it is as joyfully, uncompromisingly against authority of any sort as *Zéro de Conduite*, the work of one of Truffaut's idols, Jean Vigo, with which it has most often been compared. It is a celebration of the health, independence and right-mindedness of the child, as against the adult's slavery to formula and protocol, which must stir romantic sympathy in the heart of any adult. For Truffaut is above all a romantic, fascinated by the state of innocence before shades of the prison house begin very literally to close about the growing boy. Not the obvious sort of innocence; he is not sentimental about the adolescent's interests and desires. But innocence of adult accommodations with the world, of compromise, of premeditation, of the sort of betrayal supposedly for the good of the betrayed in which Antoine's parents indulge at least twice, first his father by taking him to the police, and then his mother by brutally rejecting him (exactly why we are never told) once he is in reform school.

All this is conveyed, though – and draws most of its power from the fact – without any hint of preaching, of theorization. Truffaut does not *tell* us anything, he just shows us. He shows us the moments of ecstasy like the visit to the cinema, the final freedom after captivity. He also shows us the blackest times, the moments when disillusion with the adult world either corrupts or sows the seeds of revolt. (The most remarkable of these is the other 'freeze', at the police station, when Antoine, brought in among prostitutes and petty criminals, is suddenly isolated and held in a moment of revelation as the idea of captivity is branded on his soul.) Always Truffaut is master of the expressive metaphor, whether in the amusement-park sequence, when the centrifuge with Antoine in it offers an extraordinary image of dissociation and disorientation, or in the removal of Antoine to the reformatory shot from outside the barred window of the van, with the camera drawing sometimes nearer, sometimes falling back, always emphasizing the complete apartness of Antoine at this moment of time, even to the extent of accompanying the scene with an ironic waltz on the sound-track.

Because of its relative technical conservatism and its 'Words-worthian' side (for despite the considerable divergence of Truffaut's view of childhood from Wordsworth's the film may very reasonably be seen as a cinematic equivalent of *The Prelude*, vividly chronicling the 'growth of a poet's mind'), *Les Quatre Cents Coups* proved one of the most popular of all New Wave films, especially in Britain and America. Its one disadvantage, though, to the cinemagoer not content merely to accept masterpieces wherever they come from, no questions asked, and be duly grateful, was the distinct possibi-lity it held out of being the one film of a one-film director. Para-doxically it was at once the most and the least promising of the early New Wave films: most because its extraordinary qualities seemed in many ways to presage the arrival of a first-rate talent; least, because such a film, being something in the nature of a personal confession, might well prove to exhaust whatever Truffaut might have to say, like so many autobiographical first novels.

In the circumstances his second film was awaited with an eager-ness not altogether unmixed with trepidation. When it appeared it at once discouraged many of the first film's more sentimental admirers and reassured those who wondered if Truffaut had said his say in one film. *Tirez sur le pianiste* (1960) represents a complete change of pace from *Les Quatre Cents Coups*, though one for which *Les Mistons* should not have left us altogether unprepared. Here it is the technical possibilities of the medium which seem above all to fascinate the director; if *Les Quatre Cents Coups* was something of a personal confession, *Tirez sur le pianiste* is a film critic's profession of faith. It is a brilliant *mélange* of devices borrowed from favoured American directors – Hitchcock, Aldrich, even Tashlin – and com-bined in a completely personal whole, half thriller, half parody-thriller, with a lot of wild, iconoclastic humour and occasional attempts (the least successful parts of the film, as it happens) to suggest some sort of deeper significance behind it all. The story, adapted from an American novel, is extremely complicated, but briefly it concerns the attempts of Charlie, a former concert pianist now playing in a bar under an assumed name, to assist two brothers on the run from gangsters they have double-crossed. In the process he gets involved with Lena, a sympathetic waitress, and acciden-tally kills the bar-keeper; meanwhile the gangsters kidnap Charlie's youngest brother Fido, and in a final gun-fight near a snow-covered mountain chalet Fido is saved, but Lena shot. This plot in the event matters very little; it is simply a slight thread of continuity (made stronger than it might otherwise be by a telling performance from Charles Aznavour as the fatalistic Charlie) on which a number of gags, private jokes and cinematic set-pieces are strung.

The film is full of abrupt changes of mood, switching from comic to sinister from one shot to the next, and no joke or reference seems too far out to be dragged in, provided only that it diverts the director. A famous instance is the inserted 'thinks' shot (borrowed from strip cartoon technique) in which a gangster swears 'May my mother drop dead if I'm lying' and we get a quick flash of an old woman collapsing. But there are many more, sometimes used for comic effect, as in the triple-screen presentation of the bar-keeper Plyne which suggests at once *avant-garde* shorts like *La Symphonie Mécanique* and the homelier split screens of *On the Town*, or seriously, as in the bedroom scene between Charlie and Lena which seems deliberately to recall the parallel scene in Godard's *À Bout de Souffle*. Sometimes effects seem to be used entirely because they have taken the director's fancy in themselves, like a vast wide-screen close-up of a finger on a door-bell, or the decorative use of snow in the final sequence; sometimes a joke is made entirely for the benefit of cinema addicts, like Charlie's instruction of a prostitute to pull up the sheet over her breasts as she lies naked in bed because 'that's the way they do it in films'. But always there is a unifying factor to bind together all these diverse elements: the personality of the director who puts in everything he likes for no other reason than that it amuses him to do so. Perhaps the film is, as Truffaut himself has subsequently remarked, 'self-indulgent', but in this lies much of its charm; it irradiates throughout the happy holiday feeling of a film-maker out for once to please nobody but himself and a few friends.

For this reason, too, because the director has considered himself free to put in whatever he fancied – devices from the silent screen, like irising in and out from scenes (that is, darkening the screen so that only a small 'iris' of picture is visible), freezing shots and so on – the film has been influential quite out of proportion to its apparent success – with critics or public – at the time; it is very

13a. *Les Quatre Cents Coups* (Jean-Pierre Léaud, right). Dir: François Truffaut

b. *Jules et Jim* (Henri Serre; Jeanne Moreau; Oscar Werner). Dir: François Truffaut

14a. Jean-Luc Godard directs Anna Karina and Jean-Paul Belmondo in
Une Femme est une Femme
14b. *Vivre sa Vie* (Anna Karina; Brice Parain). Dir: Jean-Luc Godard

much a director's film for other directors, and has been used freely
as a quarry in a number of more recent films from a surprising
variety of sources. But the evidence of films like Tony Richardson's
The Loneliness of the Long Distance Runner and *Tom Jones*, for
instance, suggests very clearly that only Truffaut can fully control
Truffaut's style; with him it is natural, felt, and his extreme eclecticism in his choice of sources does not prevent the result from
achieving the coherence of one man's highly personal taste. When
anyone else tries to achieve the same effect with the same materials
the result is just a ragbag of remembered bits from other men's
work.

Truffaut's following film, *Jules et Jim*, seems for a variety of
reasons less likely to have the same sort of effect on the film world
at large. For one thing it is technically much quieter; more like
Renoir than ever, it shows the film critic in Truffaut only very
occasionally, in the odd reference (to Murnau in the wood-sawing
scene, for example) which can easily escape notice, and in the
inventive handling of the newsreel material with which the story is
intercut. In general, though, Truffaut contents himself with telling
the story fairly straightforwardly, concentrating closely on his
three central characters (this is very much an actor's film) and the
highly evocative, poetically suggestive backgrounds in which they
move. The film, consequently, is nearly always enchanting to look
at, a symphony of greys carried out with spectacular brilliance and
devotion by Truffaut's cameraman Raoul Coutard, and, moreover,
is remarkably well acted by the three members of its central
ménage-à-trois, Oscar Werner (Jules), Henri Serre (Jim), and
Jeanne Moreau (Catherine, the woman they both love). And yet,
for me at any rate, there is something radically wrong with it.

To define what this is we have to come back to elements which
it is unfashionable these days to consider very seriously in film
criticism, plot and characterization. Once critics tended to write as
though the literary side of the film was all-important, now on the
contrary they tend to write as though it does not matter at all.
With many films it does not matter (one would not get very far
with *Tirez sur le pianiste* on literary considerations), but *Jules et
Jim* is a personal drama based on a serious novel by Henri-Pierre
Roche which is really adapted rather than used as a pretext. By
concentrating on character it inevitably invites us to consider the

C.E.–O

characters and what happens to them, and it would be merely perverse not to do so. The film is the story of two friends – one French and one German – who fall in love with the same girl and find that if anything this binds them closer in a relationship without jealousy and incapable of clear resolution other than by death. The main motive force of the plot, then, is Catherine, since it is her decision or lack of it which determines each move in the story; which shall she marry, which shall give her the child she wants, which she chooses to live with, which she chooses to die with. And Catherine, I think, is the main obstacle to the film's complete success.

She is one of those ever-womanly women, inscrutable, changeable, indecisive, a creature of impulse who is yet supposed to be completely enchanting to all that come in contact with her. Which may be all very well in a novel, but creates all sorts of problems in any dramatic form, first because it places a heavy weight on the actress called upon to play the part (it is asking a lot of any solid creature of flesh and blood to be at once so tiresome and so universally delectable) and second because once we appreciate that the woman is never going to make up her mind her choppings and changings are likely to seem mechanical and repetitious. In *Jules et Jim* the second is the primary problem, though it is aggravated by the first. If anyone in the modern cinema can achieve the mythical stature, the divine feminine inscrutability Catherine requires it is Jeanne Moreau, and she gives a powerfully magnetic reading of the part. But temperamentally I feel she is all wrong; she lacks entirely vagueness, the sheer silliness indeed, of Catherine. One feels not that she really is a free soul unable to choose because for her all choice is limitation, but that she is perfectly capable of arranging matters comfortably for all concerned and is just *pretending* to be indecisive. Why? Because the plot demands it. But what is the plot? Merely a series of changes and indecisions on the part of Catherine. So the plot is the character, but because of miscasting the character seems to act as she does only because the plot forces her to do so. It is a vicious circle, and the result is that the film lacks motive force and finally seems only contrived and emptily beautiful.

If I am right about its failure (many critics, I should add, regard *Jules et Jim* as Truffaut's greatest success) and the reasons why it fails, it is obvious that it is impossible to build either hopes or fears very securely upon it; Truffaut remains unpredictable and his latest work, an episode in an international co-production *L'Amour à Vingt Ans*, with a grown-up Jean-Pierre Léaud in the central role, does not make him any less so. Nor does his long-standing project, a film version of Ray Bradbury's science-fiction novel *Fahrenheit 451*, temporarily shelved for a new drama of adultery, *La Peau Douce*. Taking all his works together, though, one thing at least is unmistakable: that even when he makes mistakes he is a born film-maker expressing himself on film as naturally and inevitably as earlier generations did on paper or canvas. And beneath the superficial eclecticism of his style runs, from *Les Mistons* to *L'Amour à Vingt Ans*, a streak of Renoirian romantic warmth and tenderness which gives definition and personality to what might otherwise seem the casual and undisciplined anthologizing of a critic with a good memory but no creative personality of his own. Truffaut's films may vary in quality, but it seems unlikely that Truffaut himself will ever too severely disappoint us; he belongs to that select group of artists whose failures are far more exciting than most other men's successes.

Jean-Luc Godard

Jean-Luc Godard, like Truffaut, is a graduate of *Les Cahiers du Cinéma*, a critic turned creator. They even once co-directed a film, a brief slapstick comedy called *Une Histoire d'Eau* (1958). But there the similarity ends. If Truffaut, beneath his apparent anarchism and stylistic eccentricity, is really a traditionalist, referring back to the lyrical humanism of Renoir seasoned with the classic virtues represented by the long-established Hollywood purveyors of popular entertainment, Godard is a complete original, one of those directors after whom the cinema can never again be exactly the same. Of course, there is nothing new under the sun, and no doubt precedents could be sought out for each feature of his style, but what matters above all is not the detail, but the overall effect of Godard's approach to the cinema. He is, first and foremost, not intimidated by the medium; he takes nothing on trust, does not believe that there is anything one absolutely must or must not do until he has tried it himself. His films are entirely fresh and informal; they are made with great speed and freedom, and have the pleasant air of being made up as he goes along, which to a large extent they often are. It is altogether possible that he is not a 'great' director – though it is rather early yet to decide one way or the other – and it seems likely that here and there he has tended already to take himself too seriously. But as a liberating, invigorating force in the cinema he has already had a considerable effect and, in the long run more importantly, he has made a number of films which are in themselves and for themselves very striking achievements.

Godard was born in Paris in 1930, but his family background is Swiss and most of his early life was spent in Switzerland, in and around that Geneva which is the setting for his second feature film, *Le Petit Soldat*. He was educated in Switzerland (a fact which many French critics have found significant in relation to the vigour of his mental processes), studied ethnology at university, and worked for a while as cameraman and assistant editor with Swiss television in Zurich. His first film was a documentary about dam-building, *Opération Béton*, made in 1954, and shortly afterwards he came to Paris, where he joined the staff of *Les Cahiers du Cinéma* and began a succession of short-story films, mostly comedies, in which little by little he developed his free-and-easy, coolly informal approach to the cinema (*Une Femme Coquette* in 1955, *Tous les Garçons s'appellent Patrick* in 1957, *Charlotte et son Jules* and *Une Histoire d'Eau* in 1958) before embarking on his first feature film, *À Bout de Souffle* (*Breathless*) in 1959. This was made very cheaply, in four weeks, with two relatively insignificant players in the leading roles and the more or less nominal assistance of two already successful confrères from *Cahiers*, Truffaut (on the script) and Chabrol (as supervisor) to secure the finance. It had a tremendous and immediate success, made its principals into important stars, and turned Godard overnight into one of the most talked-about of New Wave directors.

There are many reasons for this, apart from the obvious merits of the film itself. Its principal character is perfectly designed to be a cult-hero of a new generation of filmgoers, who can see in him all their less avowable dreams and desires acted out: he models himself conscientiously on Humphrey Bogart and the American B-feature hero-villain; he is 'anarchic' only in a very limited, *bourgeois* sort of way, in that he has no views about laws, rules, and regulations *per se*, but simply does not regard them as applying to him; he does not want to lead a revolution, but merely to contract out. And, of course, he is successful in most things he does – he gets the girls, he steals the cars, he makes the money, and only finally gets his come-uppance because his girl, for not very clearly defined reasons of her own, betrays him to the police.

The precise nature and intention of this character have caused a lot of ink to be spilt, and a number of violent arguments to arise, mainly between those who think he is meant as a modern anarchist, a Camusian 'outsider' who rejects the current social set-up altogether, and that he succeeds as such, and those who think he is meant to be taken that way but does not for a moment achieve the sort of stature such a reading requires. As to what exactly Godard intended, what his own attitude to his hero is, I can profess no great degree of certainty; it seems to me that there is a very real ambiguity here, but that, in fact, this strengthens rather than weakens the film by enabling it to escape all pat schematizations. The character is just there, presented take-it-or-leave-it, and as a representative of certain perfectly credible attitudes of mind (whatever our opinions of those attitudes) he rings completely true, even if we draw the line at believing in all the melodramatic incidents in which he is insouciantly involved in the course of the film.

For here the keynote is not objective truth at all, but truth to a private fantasy world which yet mirrors a real truth about the dreamer and those willing to share his dream. It is not so much what is said as the tone of voice in which it is said which counts, and here we come back to the central issue of the film, Godard's way with film form. Although undeniably there is an element of deliberate desire to shock in that, too – in the jump-cuts from beginning to end of a familiar process if that process has no inherent significance in the film; in the abrupt changes of locale, lighting and mood; in the whole improvised, unpremeditated air of it – what strikes one above all is the ease and effectiveness of it all, the readiness with which one can accept these ellipses, the ruthless elimination of routine inessentials. Godard's style is essentially fast and witty, and almost abstract in its total effect; it keeps us at a critical distance from his characters and the situations they find themselves in. And for all its seeming inconsequence it proves on examination to be rigidly controlled; however *outré* the devices, the result is always perfectly clear – Godard knows exactly how much he can safely leave out without losing his audience.

The effect of *À Bout de Souffle* depended to a large extent on its perfect timing: it provided the young French cinema with a new hero and, in Jean-Paul Belmondo, a new star to play him; and stylistically it marked a clearer, more decisive break with the academic conventions of film-making than any other new director had at that time dared to attempt. It was, however, an entertainment, a rather self-conscious homage to the American B-feature, and naturally the first question the more solemn sort of filmgoer asked was what would the director do, now that he had made his mark, with a 'serious' subject which would really tax his powers. In his next film, *Le Petit Soldat* (1960), Godard set out, perhaps deliberately, to answer this question, though because the characters were involved – rather inscrutably – in the Algerian crisis the film was banned for nearly three years and finally released only when all the fuss had died down.

Le Petit Soldat is something of a problem picture, the problem being: is it an acute, detached study of silly, pretentious people, or a silly, pretentious film about people its author takes to be intelligent? Not since the heyday of Albert Lewin has there been a film quite so stuffed with culture. The hero cannot accept any experience without seeking a literary or artistic parallel for it; the heroine reminds him when he first sees her of a character from a Giraudoux play; he wants to die like Cocteau's *Thomas l'imposteur*; Aragon, Bernanos, Bach, Mozart, Beethoven, Klee, Velasquez, Renoir, all spatter his conversation like some sort of intellectual rash, and even the film's principal bedroom scene has to begin with a close-up of a hand significantly putting down a copy of *La Condition Humaine*. Is this all fair comment on a character we are supposed to find a little tiresome, even if he is symptomatic, an intellectual incapable of decisive action, a weakling in love with the idea of rebellion, a coward infatuated by courage? Or does Bruno, the muddled counter-terrorist, represent to a considerable extent his creator's own views on life and the modern world, as his lengthy credo near the end ('I love France because I love Joachim du Bellay and Louis Aragon. I love Germany because I love Beethoven . . . I love America because I love American cars . . .') seems strongly to imply?

In many ways, fortunately, such considerations are irrelevant. Whatever one may think of the script, the film still remains a fascinating experience, if only because Godard lives and breathes cinema to such an extent that everything he touches comes at once to life and affects us even in spite of ourselves. The film is patchy; devices which in later films he has completely under control (like the endlessly repeated shots of Anna Karina combing and shaking out her beautiful hair) are here too uncritically indulged in; the famous torture sequence, with its 'quotations' from Dreyer's *La Passion de Jeanne d'Arc* (the Danish heroine is, teasingly, named Dreyer), looks too affected in its attempts at 'detachment' to touch us on any level of imagination or emotion. But even with such reservations the fact remains that there are marvellous things in the film; little touches in the dialogue, sudden, telling moments in the acting, the often dazzling black-and-white camerawork of Raoul Coutard, the occasional Brechtian ruptures of tone which come off perfectly, notably during Bruno's escape from his Arab tormentors, where the hero considers in advance the chances that their flat is on the first floor, takes a chance by jumping out of the window, and casually informs us that he was lucky as we cut immediately to a shot of a towering block of flats at the top of which his girl-friend lives. To a certain extent *Le Petit Soldat* suffered in public estimation from being seen out of sequence in Godard's work; by the time it appeared not only Godard but the whole New Wave had changed a lot, and one had constantly to remember that the film had been made three years earlier. But even when Godard does not consistently succeed in what he sets out to do (which happens here perhaps more frequently than in any of his other films) his work is still spectacularly worth watching; at least, whatever may be wrong with it, it is 100 per cent cinema all the way.

After *Le Petit Soldat* Godard returned to his first cinematic love, comedy, and made *Une Femme est une Femme*, a cinemascope, colour vehicle for the charms of Anna Karina, by now his wife. The excuse for the film is an idea by the actress Geneviève Cluny which Godard originally wrote as a scenario in 1958. It was subsequently taken up by another young director, Philippe de Broca, in his film *Les Jeux de l'Amour* (1959), but de Broca modified it so much that Godard decided he was still free to use it in its original form. And reasonably enough at that, for what in *Les Jeux de l'Amour* became a completely articulated (and truth to tell rather wearisome) plot about a young woman's manœuvres to recapture her lover's complete attention and make him give her a child by carrying on with his best friend, is here left simply as a situation within which the personalities of the three stars (Anna Karina, Jean-Paul Belmondo, and Jean-Claude Brialy) can flourish undisturbed and on to which can be grafted all sorts of odd devices and ideas which take the director's fancy. The result, for me, is the most irresistible of all Godard's films; the style, with its lightness and freedom, lends itself perfectly to this sort of nonsense, and the film retains throughout the gaiety and *joie de vivre* of a private joke in which all can share – the joke being, not least, that the resources of a 'big picture' – colour, cinemascope, important stars – are being used with the greatest casualness for the production of riotously irresponsible home movies. But *Une Femme est une Femme*, for all its ease and freedom, for all its lack of pretension (which distinguish it splendidly from such other plodding French attempts at knockabout surrealist humour as Malle's *Zazie dans le Métro*, Mocky's *Les Snobs* and Baratier's *La Poupée*), is not about nothing; it is really, as a critic in *Les Cahiers du Cinéma* very acutely observed, a documentary about Anna Karina, lightly disguised as a fiction film. Once this is understood most of the film's most superficially puzzling elements fall into perspective. This is why, for instance, Godard so often uses the worst instead of the best takes in any given scene. The takes which come off, in which nothing gets in the way of the plot's requirements, may well tell us most about the character; but the worst takes – those in which the actress forgets a line or unexpectedly trips over something – tell us most about her, and that is what Godard is after. *Le Petit Soldat* already has many elements of a *chant d'amour*; in *Une Femme est une Femme* there is no doubt that what we are greeted with is a hymn of praise of one particular woman, and a woman, moreover, sufficiently fascinating on the cinema screen for virtually all spectators to agree wholeheartedly with her husband's estimate of her charms.

Godard's next feature film, *Vivre sa Vie* (1962), is equally devoted to the same object, though this time the medium is supposedly a crisp, anti-romantic film about prostitution, telling in a series of twelve 'tableaux', each preceded by a title summarizing what happens (a self-consciously Brechtian, endistancing device), how Nana, a Parisian shopgirl short of money, takes up casual and then regular prostitution, falls in love, begins to rethink her life and is accidentally shot when her pimp tries to double-cross the people he is selling her to. But Godard's own summary hints at something different: Nana 'gives her body but keeps her soul while she experiences a series of adventures which bring her knowledge of all possible deep human emotions'. A Romantic enough concept in all conscience, and indeed so much has been made of the Brechtian structure of the film, its 'objective', 'anti-romantic' quality, that it is perhaps time to insist again on the passionate romanticism embodied in the endistancing epic framework. When Godard talks of Anna Karina's qualities as an actress it is the comparison with Garbo which predominates; within the film the author called upon to epitomize the creator's attitude to his work is the arch-Romantic Edgar Allan Poe, whose story of the painter who painted a portrait of his beloved so perfect that she died as it was completed is read to Nana by the young man she loves with the voice of Godard himself (literally, dubbed on the sound-track). And the purpose of the film is not really at all a study of prostitution psychologically or sociologically considered, even though the facts and figures are clinically retailed in Section VIII; for such a purpose Karina's Nana would be a wildly unsuitable centrepiece – this glamorous being who weeps at Falconetti's Joan of Arc and talks philosophy, who chooses prostitution as a conscious existentialist choice and at the same time retains her soul, who is, in short, no more credible as a 'representative' prostitute than Garbo's Camille.

But then that, *pace* the critics, is not the point of the film. What the film seems to say, in its own terms, is that life is a testing; one chooses, perhaps, the ground upon which one is to be tested, as Nana chooses prostitution, but beyond that there is little to be done except *vivre sa vie*; the facts and figures about prostitution provide a background, but the story's continuity is essentially a spiritual odyssey in which the trappings of external realism count for little (Nana might just as well, for instance, contract a loveless marriage with a rich man; the background could then be one of statistics on marriage settlements, divorce rates, alimony, suicide rates and so on, and the theme, though not the film, remain exactly the same).

If this is what the film says within itself, however, it has another significance seen from outside, taking into account the rest of Godard's work and the fact that Anna Karina is his wife. The film is, more systematically than *Une Femme est une Femme*, a portrait of

Anna Karina, disguised as a film narrative. Physically, it is a portrait of her which starts, logically enough, with a series of profiles,
left and right alternating, behind the credits; emotionally the
'adventures' of Nana are so many tests put to Anna Karina, and
from her various reactions to them we only learn more about her.
The Poe story is planted, indeed, to tell us in so many words what
Godard is up to: in that, too, the artist sets out as an act of love to
make permanent the image of his loved one, to transform her into
art, and when the transformation is complete, she has to die; her
soul has been transferred to the likeness. So, it has been said, Nana
has to die in the film, and the end is not arbitrary. But here, surely
the parallel is faulty, which may explain why one may continue
obstinately to feel that the end is arbitrary all the same: strictly
speaking, according to Poe's Romantic postulate, it is not Nana but
Karina who should die at the end of the film (which, naturally,
heaven forbid), and the death of Nana considered in this light
suggests that the painter is cutting up his portrait unfinished as a
sort of life-restoring ritual which has no real relevance to the work
of art in question.

In one respect the film offers an interesting parallel with the
recent works of Godard's cinematic *bête noire* Antonioni; it is as
difficult with Anna Karina as it is with Monica Vitti to know
whether one can legitimately talk of a performance, any more than
one can talk of the 'performance' of the Bibliothèque Nationale in
Toute la Memoire du Monde; is she, after all, merely the object from
which the artist works? The answer to that is the answer to the
paradox of screen acting; if Karina is being used, it is only in the
same way that Garbo or Louise Brooks or Marilyn Monroe was
used; she, like them, has a quality of incandescence which makes
everything she does, however apparently trivial it may be, absorb-
ing to watch. The film has its showpieces, like the fantastic mating
dance she weaves about the unresponsive figure of the young man
in the pool-room, and gradually transforms into something wholly
private and self-satisfying. But mainly the pleasure to be derived
from it is simply that of watching the small gestures, the unconscious movements and inflexions through which, as with the
schoolgirl's hen in the first section, we can take away the outside to
get at the inside, and take away the inside to get at the soul. Only
the very greatest 'screen actors' (to use an unavoidably equivocal

term) have the gift, or the courage, to go thus spiritually naked into the world.

In keeping with the director's voluntary self-abnegation in favour of his star, *Vivre sa Vie* is technically considerably quieter and more conventional than any of Godard's three previous films. It is, and this not perhaps an unalloyed blessing, much more carefully and precisely planned; there is nothing improvisatory or *gratuit* about it. Whether this should be taken to imply that Godard is likely in future to become more conventional in his approach to the cinema it is difficult to decide. There has been little sign of it in his other recent works, which include a number of sequences for episode films, such as the 'Sloth' episode in *Les Sept Péchés Capitaux* (1961), a brief but fetching cinematic joke; 'The New World' in *Rogopag* (1962), a parable about the disturbing results of an atomic explosion on the human mind, and one of the four *Plus Belles Escroqueries du Monde* (1963). In 1962 Godard announced, rather surprisingly, that he was about to film Giraudoux's play *Pour Lucrèce*, very fast and in a very controlled, formal style, but then this was delayed at the last moment and he made instead *Les Carabiniers*, from a script worked on by Roberto Rossellini, one of the long-time idols of Godard's criticism.

Les Carabiniers is a sort of parable set in a deliberately vague, non-committal background. Two peasants live in rough desolate country with their wives, and one day four carabiniers in curiously assorted uniforms arrive. They tell the peasants that a war is on, and expatiate on the advantages of war, which means that men can do legally all the things which are normally forbidden: rape, pillage, kill. Thereupon they turn out the peasants and take over their wives and property. The peasants decide that they will try this war for themselves and go off. Later they arrive back, having in the meantime taken all sorts of loot, including most of the major buildings of Paris, represented for them by a case full of picture-postcards. When peace is declared they try to lay claim to their plunder, but discover that as a condition of peace the king has declared all his soldiers war criminals, and they are promptly shot.

The film, made very quickly in Godard's most casual and arbitrary improvisatory style, is perhaps the extreme expression of his Brechtian impulses in the cinema: alienation is carried to such a pitch that all most critics could see in the film is a complete and all-rejecting misanthropy, making all the characters equally brutish and repellent. Certainly the film has had less success than any other Godard film with the general public, running for less than a week in Paris, though to the sympathetically disposed it offers a uniquely stimulating and unpredictable experience. Certainly with his next film, *Le Mépris*, adapted from a Moravia novel and with an international cast headed by Brigitte Bardot and Jack Palance, Godard has returned to a far more conventional, 'classical' style, though obviously only time will tell whether this is a necessary pause before further experiment or the development of a quieter, less showy but none the less brilliant and imaginative Godard. Certainly by what he has done up to now Godard has shown himself one of the most original and dynamic forces at work in the cinema today, and it is difficult to believe that all his evident talent will not continue to enliven the cinema for many years to come, whatever his incidental setbacks along the way.

Alain Resnais

During the first sixty-odd years of film history the most important single development has been one which the simple passage of time made inevitable; the arrival of a generation for which not only the cinema itself, but specifically the sound cinema was not a new thing, difficult to come to terms with, but something as natural and unquestioned as writing or painting or music. For these it was finally possible to take the film for granted as a means of expression and to think directly in terms of film rather than thinking literarily and then translating literary conceptions laboriously into cinematic terms. Hence, inevitably, the development of the 'auteur', the all-round film-creator who, whatever the source of his materials and whatever collaborators he may take to help him realize his intentions, is essentially responsible himself for the whole film from initial conception to end product. Of course, for all sorts of practical reasons this often remains only an ideal; in America and even in Britain most films still tend to be made by committees, in which the director is only one of a number of technicians. But in the 'art' cinema, so far as this may be tentatively and unsatisfactorily distinguished from the commercial, the film as a one-man creation is almost universally recognized as a practicable ideal towards which everybody strives. Hence the peculiar interest of Alain Resnais, a strange solitary who has set off firmly against this tide of feeling.

Alain Resnais was born at Vannes in 1922, came to Paris in 1940 and took a course in film at IDHEC in 1943-4, but left before the end because he found the instruction too theoretical. For the next two years he worked mainly as an actor, and began making 16 mm. films, among them a short with Gérard Philipe, *Schéma d'une Identification*, and feature-length film called *Ouvert pour cause d'inventaire*, both of which he claims now to have lost. There followed a number of silent 16 mm. film 'visites' to famous painters, and other shorts, one of which, on *Van Gogh*, led to his being commissioned to remake it in 35 mm. The new version was a great success, winning a prize at the Venice Festival and a Hollywood Oscar. Further art films followed, two of them, on Picasso's *Guernica* (co-directed with Robert Hessens) and on the decadence of native art in France's African colonies, *Les Statues Meurent Aussi* (co-directed with Chris Marker), having strong political overtones, so insistent in the latter case that the film was banned and has even now been shown in France only in a heavily cut version.

It was still in the field of short films that Resnais embarked on the experiment which has continued throughout his subsequent career and which makes him of particular interest to us now: the collaboration on equal terms with distinguished figures from the literary world. First, in *Nuit et Brouillard*, his documentary about concentration camps, it was Jean Cayrol. Then for *Le Chant du Styrène*, a commissioned piece about the manufacture of the plastic polystyrene, Raymond Queneau was called on for a characteristic punning verse commentary. In Resnais's first feature, *Hiroshima Mon Amour*, the original screenplay was by the novelist Marguerite Duras; in his second, *L'Année Dernière à Marienbad*, it was the turn of Alain Robbe-Grillet; and for the third, *Muriel, ou le Temps d'un Retour*, he returned to Jean Cayrol. It is an impressive enough list, and its consistency suggests that the succession is more than just chance. When questioned on the point Resnais is evasive, but talks of his interest in 'experiments' in the cinema, in trying out ideas which come to him, and expresses a conviction that the word is undervalued in the cinema today, hence his determined attempts to restore it to its proper place. As for the exact role of the script in the total ensemble, Resnais's remark about *Hiroshima Mon Amour* might stand for all the films: 'I encouraged Marguerite Duras to "faire littéraire" and not worry about it. I wanted to compose a sort of poem in which the images would work only as a counterpoint to the text.'

Which is all very well in theory – there is no reason in theory why anything should be ruled out before it has been tried. The only question is, how does it turn out in practice? My own feeling is that the system works well enough in documentary, if only because with documentary one tends to expect something rather more academic and unexciting than in the feature film; at any rate, one is more willing to accept it. The material of *Nuit et Brouillard* is in any case so highly charged emotionally that the cooling, endistancing effect of a very precise, formal, controlled montage establishing a clear, unequivocal relation between newsreel material of Auschwitz then and coloured film of the site now, between document and evocation, is a positive advantage, and the discreetly literary terms of Jean Cayrol's commentary have something of the same effect. As for *Le Chant du Styrène*, the effect here is largely humorous; against the highly coloured abstract patterns of the plastic as it is pushed backwards and forwards, stamped in presses, trimmed and shunted up and down the conveyor belt, the equally highly coloured patterns of Queneau's verbal fantasy (adequately indicated by the title itself) form an amusing counterpoint and help to dress up divertingly what is, at bottom, simply a very expert example of a rather dreary type of sponsored film.

It is with the features that we really come up against the problems that this sort of writer-director collaboration poses. Resnais's principal weakness as a director, even in his simplest documentaries, has always been an excessively chilling and intellectual approach. In the analytical art films this was quite in keeping, but elsewhere it sometimes showed through rather disturbingly, turning the films into private intellectual games. There is an excellent instance of this in *Toute la Mémoire du Monde*, a short about the Bibliothèque Nationale which Resnais made between *Nuit et Brouillard* and *Le Chant du Styrène*. The film begins with a mysterious shot behind the credits of something eyelike in the dark, which turns out to be some sort of epidiascope. But the composition and lighting of the shot irresistibly recall the microphone at the end of *Citizen Kane* as Orson Welles gives the credits of that film. And from there on there are constant references to *Citizen Kane* in *Toute la Mémoire du Monde*: the camera slowly moving upwards behind meshes which gradually get smaller and smaller; the camera roaming casually over a litter of boxes and cases which recall precisely the same treatments of the packing-cases at Xanadu; the way in which interiors and roofscapes are photographed, even to the precise texture of the photography. This must be deliberate, a sort of private joke, but it is a very academic private joke, strangely remote from the infectious enjoyment of the medium with which Truffaut and Godard introduce their references to other films and film-makers.

The taint of academicism is just as strongly present in Resnais's feature films, and one cannot help thinking (perhaps unfairly; it would be difficult to make out a reasonable case for the thought) that the very idea of the sort of equal collaboration Resnais envisages would not occur to anyone but a born academic; it implies a deliberate withdrawal of self, a deliberate reduction of the film-director's role to that of faithful interpreter and repository of technical expertise which looks like the very opposite of the real creative temperament. And this is just what I at least find most difficult to take in Resnais's feature films. In *Hiroshima Mon Amour* (1959) the trouble is particularly evident because, to state it in the simplest possible terms, the film is a love story, a story of sudden physical passion, and the treatment, formidably intelligent though it is, has not the slightest trace of sensuousness, let alone sensuality. Now though this is a film which has ambitions far beyond the love story at its centre ('I asked Marguerite Duras', Resnais tells us, 'for a love story set in Hiroshima which would not look too absurdly trivial in the context of the atomic bomb'), it does matter, because there is really something between the French film-star heroine and her Japanese lover, and we must believe that there is, or the progress of their affair against the great, past horror of Hiroshima and the less great but in some ways more immediate horror of her wartime experiences at Nevers will not make sense.

Without this vital dimension of real feeling on some level, even if merely the physical, the film loses urgency and finally appears more than a little pretentious. Though meant, apparently, to be a film about both characters almost equally, it very rapidly becomes a film about the Frenchwoman only; on her life vaguely impinges a shadowy Japanese whom she little by little conflates in her mind with her wartime, German, lover and then, after the famous 'gifle' he delivers in the restaurant, rapidly disentangles again, but essentially this is her story. The attitudes and situation of the Japanese remain mysterious, even if we accept that the long 'documentary' introduction about Hiroshima does in some measure provide 'background' for him, even if only intellectual background, since the script makes it clear that he has not personally suffered Hiroshima as she has suffered Nevers.

All this is not to detract from the distinction of Marguerite Duras's screenplay, which is so expressive in itself that it often reads better than it looks on film. In fact, I feel that on the whole the illustration of the words in pictures – for too often it is illustration instead of the promised counterpoint – generally weakens what is already fully expressed in the text, and that only the flashbacks to wartime Nevers and the heroine's disastrous affair with a German soldier really serve the intended purpose of the film; they at least are powerfully evocative of romantic desolation and stay in one's mind when otherwise all one can remember is the words.

With Resnais's next film, *L'Année Dernière à Marienbad* (1961), at least there is no doubt about the efficacy of the pictures. Resnais and his cameraman, Sacha Vierny, seem to have set out deliberately to make the film as beautiful as possible to look at, judged simply as a series of elaborate art photographs, and in this at least they have succeeded: the look of the film is unforgettable. The main question the film has raised in critics' minds, though, is the value of visual beauty just by itself, without any apparent meaning or significance outside itself. For *L'Année Dernière à Marienbad* is in some ways less of a film than an intellectual trap. Certainly it is a trap if the spectator goes at it with the intellect, wanting to know what it means and determined to work out one explanation which will fit all the facts (if they are facts) the film offers, or at least enable him to distinguish the fact from the fiction. Some critics have plunged in straight away with intricate explanations; others have been provoked only to outbursts of outraged puritanism, announcing brusquely that of course the film is only a confidence trick and they, for their part, are not going to be taken in by it. But if a confidence

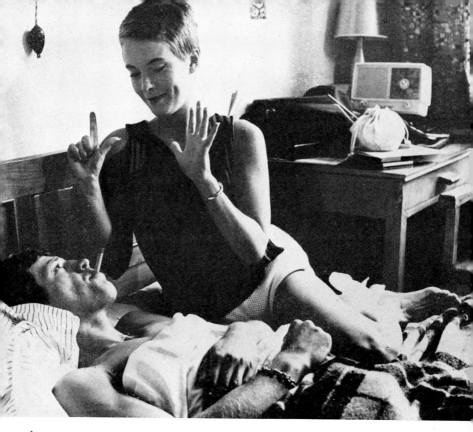

15a. *À Bout de Souffle* (Jean-Paul Belmondo; Jean Seberg). Dir: Jean-Luc Godard
15b. *Hiroshima Mon Amour* (Emmanuelle Riva; Eiji Okada). Dir: Alain Resnais

16a. *L'Année Dernière à Marienbad* (Delphine Seyrig; Giorgio Albertazzi). Dir: Alain Resn

16b. *Muriel* (Delphine Seyrig; Jean-Pierre Kerien). Dir: Alain Resnais

trick is involved at all, it is a trick which the spectator persists, in spite of all warnings to the contrary, in playing on himself: neither the author, Alain Robbe-Grillet, nor the director gives him any reason, either explicitly, in their statements on the film, or implicitly, in the film itself, to suppose that it does all 'mean' anything, and if nevertheless he goes on rationalizing and worrying when he fails to rationalize, he has no one to blame but himself.

Nevertheless, the temptation is too great (it is, after all, part of the film-makers' game) for us not to ask what, if anything, the film is about. Well, it is about a persuasion. A man meets a woman in a large, luxurious, overpoweringly gloomy hotel and puts it to her that they met last year at Marienbad, that they had, or nearly had, an affair there and were on the brink of going away together when (perhaps) something dramatic happened, but in any case she asked for a year's grace before they should meet again. At first she denies everything, then little by little accepts what he says, and finally they leave together (or appear to do so). So much is as certain as anything in the ambiguous world the film conjures up. But from here on we are out on our own. The first question which must strike the would-be explorer is, which of them is right? Did they or did they not meet last year? The film's creators are no help at all here. Robbe-Grillet says that of course they did not: it is the story of a battle of wills and personalities which X (the man) wins, forcing A (the woman) to accept his account. Resnais, perhaps in sheer perversity (there was a similar disagreement between him and Marguerite Duras over what happens at the end of *Hiroshima Mon Amour*), says that he believes they did meet before and that he made the film on this assumption. There is also the third possibility, offered by Resnais in an interview with *Les Cahiers du Cinéma*, that they are both right, and the film shows the working of some semi-Ouspenskian spiral of time.

At this stage various other strands of meaning (or possible meaning) make themselves felt. For instance, is the hotel really an hotel? According to one way of looking at it it might actually be a luxurious mental home. X would be a psychiatrist, amateur or professional, and his job would be to resolve some sort of trauma inflicting A. Or again, the hotel might be Hell (shades of *Huis Clos*) or at least Purgatory. Near the beginning there is a reference, obviously applicable to the immediate surroundings, to 'cet hôtel, lui-même, avec ses salles désormais désertes, ses domestiques immobiles, muets, morts depuis longtemps sans doute, qui montent encore la garde a l'angle des couloirs', and the whole joyless death-in-life of the hotel society suggests some sort of 'city of dreadful night' which no one can escape (in another casual exchange a man says to a young woman, 'C'est un drôle d'endroit', and when she answers 'Vous voulez dire: pour être libre?' he replies, 'Pour être libre, oui, en particulier'). Moreover, the grounds are suggestive (deliberately?) of a graveyard, with no grass or foliage but only stones – something frequently insisted on in the dialogue – and when we see the main walk of the French garden inhabited for once by guests they are all standing immobile, like monumental statuary (an eerie effect deliberately achieved by giving them painted shadows on a dull, otherwise shadowless day). Or again, X could himself be Death, pursuing an unwilling A like some hound of heaven (consider the overtones of his last words to her, as they leave . . . 'vous étiez maintenent déjà en train de vous perdre, pour toujours, dans la nuit tranquille, seule avec moi'). Or the whole thing could be a metaphysical commentary on the last two reels of *Vertigo* and the 'Hitchcock silhouette' on the wall by the lift early in the film could be a deliberate cryptogrammatic pointer. And so on and so on.

So, then, it means many things partly, but means nothing when it is all put together? Yes and no. It all depends – to hedge tiresomely – on what you mean by 'mean'. Noticeably, nearly all the parallels one picks up are from romantic poetry – *The City of Dreadful Night, The Hound of Heaven* and the rest – and clearly the Symbolists could yield many more. And as in Romantic or Symbolist poetry, we are dealing with symbols, properly speaking, not allegories. There is no simple, complete equivalence for anything, and yet meanings hover in a cloud and each object presented to our attention – the hotel, the garden, even the curiously depersonalized characters – gradually accumulates significances which our minds hold simultaneously in suspension. And right down the middle of the film is a conflict which assumes various guises – present against past (real or imagined), freedom against convention, life against death – but remains appreciably the Romantic Agony at its last gasp. And this, finally, is what the film is 'about' (whatever that means): it is a series of variations on a romantic theme disguised as a film for film's sake, depending in the end on its power to enrapture us into suspending intellectual judgement.

Whether we are willing to do so, to capitulate at once to the beauty of the images and ask for nothing more than faint and perhaps rather pretentious hints of meaning, depends obviously very much on the temperament and mood of the individual spectator. There is no doubt that what is being done is being supremely well done, but one comes back always to the square but inescapable question, was it worth doing at all in the first place? In any case the whole thing turns finally on the writer and the script: *L'Année Dernière* is really a Robbe-Grillet film with sumptuous illustrations by Resnais rather than a Resnais film scripted by Robbe-Grillet. As such it is going firmly against the tide of the modern cinema to reach a sort of *ne plus ultra* of 'pure' *mise en scène* instead of fully integrated one-man film-creation.

Whether Resnais comes nearer to achieving this with his third feature film, *Muriel, ou le temps d'un retour*, is a question much debated, with no very decisive result. It is certainly a film which permits no critical half-measures: either you think it is a masterpiece or you cannot stomach it at all. My own feeling, I must confess, is closest to the latter position: the film seems to me essentially false, an elaborate piece of mystification built on, this time, a fairly straightforward story (by Jean Cayrol) which does not demand such oblique treatment and does not gain anything from it. Disentangled, the story runs something like this. Hélène Aughain, a widow living in Boulogne with her stepson, writes on an impulse (she is, as we later discover, a compulsive gambler) to Alphonse, with whom, years before, she had an affair. Obedient to her summons, he arrives, with a girl he introduces as his niece, though in fact she is nothing of the sort. All the characters except Françoise, the supposed niece, are tied up one way or another in the past: to Hélène and Alphonse it represents a sort of escape from the present, even though, or perhaps because, they are no longer sure themselves what really happened between them and what was the true nature of the relationship they are trying to re-create. Bernard, Hélène's stepson, is involved with the past in another way: his memory constantly returns to Muriel, a girl whom a comrade of his tortured and killed in Algeria. This incident recurs constantly, poisoning his relations with his girl-friend, Marie-Do, with Hélène, and with Alphonse and Françoise; and finally he takes action by shooting the comrade responsible and leaving town. Meanwhile it turns out that Alphonse has been telling a pack of lies; that his stories of a prosperous restaurant in Algiers from which he was driven by the revolution are all untrue, and that instead he has been married for some years and running a restaurant in Paris which, now it is bankrupt, he has abandoned along with his wife.

All this is told in a remote and highly precious manner, with tricksy cutting, intricately oblique dialogue, some (apparently deliberately) dowdy and inexpressive colour photography, and a faintly grotesque score by Hans-Werner Henze featuring vocal interludes at climactic moments. Indeed, to me the whole thing approaches far too close to self-parody; it certainly resembles with uncanny accuracy the image of the highbrow cinema most lowbrow cinemagoers love to hate. There are, admittedly, striking moments in it, usually the most simple and direct: the exteriors of the town, the strange little scene in which Bernard goes riding along the clifftops, some of the unexplained glimpses of people on the fringes of the story – the waitress in the café, the girl Hélène meets on a park bench – going about their own separate lives. But I find this very little to compensate for the heaviness and pretention of the ensemble, its chilly, rigidly intellectual application of directorial ideas from here, there and everywhere to a basically quite interesting and original story-idea in such a way as to complicate it without making it more complex. But the film is, perhaps even more decisively than *L'Année Dernière à Marienbad*, one which you have to give in to totally or not at all; and about such films there is really very little point in arguing.

And yet, when all this is said, when all allowance has been made for Resnais's cool, academic side as a film-maker (he seems, unmistakably, more interested in solving intellectual and aesthetic problems than in film-making *per se*) there is still a strange consistency in his films: they are nearly all, even his art films, concerned with memory and the transmuting power of the imagination. Does this consistency of theme make him properly speaking an *auteur*? I doubt it, but perhaps it is still too early to pontificate. Up to now his film-making career has been almost entirely occupied with the conscientious attempt to produce film art with a capital 'A', an aim more often inhibiting than encouraging its actual appearance. Maybe in his next film, the long-planned, often postponed *Les Aventures d'Harry Dickson*, being, it would seem, an altogether less pretentious undertaking, may bring us rather nearer an answer. Or at least demonstrate that the question is irrelevant anyway.

Filmographies : Bibliographies

FEDERICO FELLINI

1939 Gagman on *Lo Vedi Come Sei* (Mario Mattoli).

1940 Gagman on *No Me Lo Dire* (Mario Mattoli). Gagman on *Il Pirato Sono Io* (Mario Mattoli).

1941 Collaborated on script: *Documento Z 3* (Alfredo Guarini).

1942 Collaborated on story and script: *Quarta Pagina* (Nicola Manzari, Domenico Gambino). Collaborated on script: *Avanti c'e Porto* (Mario Bonnard). Collaborated on story and script: *Chi l'ha Visto?* (Goffredo Alessandrini). Collaborated on script: *Campo de Fiori* (Mario Bonnard).

1943 Collaborated on script: *Apparizione* (Jean de Limur). Collaborated on script: *L'Ultima Carrozzella* (Mario Mattoli). Collaborated on script: *Tutta la Citta Canta* (Riccardo Freda).

1945 Collaborated on script, assistant director: *Roma, Citta Aperta* (Roberto Rossellini).

1946 Collaborated on script: *Il Delitto di Giovanni Episcopo* (Alberto Lattuada). Collaborated on story and script (monastery episode), assistant director: *Paisa* (Roberto Rossellini).

1947 Collaborated on story and script: *Senza Pieta* (Alberto Lattuada).

1948 Script (with Tullio Pinelli), assistant director, actor: *Il Miracolo* (Roberto Rossellini). Collaborated on script: *In Nome della Legge* (Pietro Germi).

1949 Collaborated on script: *Il Mulino del Po* (Alberto Lattuada).

1950 Script (with Rossellini): *Francesco, Giullare di Dio* (Roberto Rossellini). Collaborated on story and script: *Il Cammino della Speranza* (Pietro Germi).

LUCI DEL VARIETA

Directed: Fellini and Alberto Lattuada. *Produced:* Fellini, Lattuada. *Script:* Fellini, Ennio Flaiano, Lattuada, Tullio Pinelli, based on a story by Fellini. *Photographed:* Otello

Martelli. *Sets:* Aldo Buzzi. *Edited:* Mario Bonotti. *Music:* Felice Lattuada. *Cast:* Peppino De Filippo, Carla De Poggio, Giulietta Masina, John Kitzmiller, Folco Lulli, Franca Valeri, Carlo Romano, Silvio Bagolini, Dante Maggio, Nando Bruno, Gina Mascetti, Bonucci-Caprioli.

1951 Collaborated on story and script: *La Citta si Difende* (Pietro Germi).
1952 Collaborated on script: *Il Brigante di Tacca del Lupo* (Pietro Germi). Collaborated on script: *Europa 51* (Roberto Rossellini).

LO SCIECCO BIANCO

Produced: Luigi Rovere. *Script:* Fellini, Ennio Flaiano, Tullio Pinelli, based on a story by Michelangelo Antonioni, Fellini and Pinelli. *Photographed:* Arturo Gallea. *Sets:* Fellini. *Edited:* Rolando Benedetti. *Music:* Nino Rota. *Cast:* Brunella Bovo, Leopoldo Trieste, Alberto Sordi, Giulietta Masina, Lilia Landi, Ernesto Almirante, Fanny Marchio, Gina Mascetti, Enzo Maggio, Poldino.

1953 I VITELLONI

Produced: Lorenzo Pegoraro. *Script:* Fellini, Ennio Flaiano, Tullio Pinelli. *Photographed:* Otello Martelli, Luciano Trasatti, Carlo Carlini. *Sets:* Mario Chiari. *Edited:* Rolando Benedetti. *Music:* Nino Rota. *Cast:* Franco Interlenghi, Alberto Sordi, Franco Fabrizi, Leopoldo Trieste, Riccardo Fellini, Eleonora Ruffo, Paola Borboni, Jean Brochard, Claude Farère, Carlo Romano, Enrico Viarisio, Lida Baarova, Arlette Sauvage, Vira Silenti, Maja Nipora, Giovanna Galli, Achile Majeroni, Silvio Bagolini, Franca Gandolfi, Gondrano Trucchi, Guido Marturi.

AMORE IN CITTA: episode UN' AGENZIA MATRIMONIALE

Produced: Cesare Zavattini, Renato Ghione, Marco Ferrere. *Script:* Fellini, Tullio Pinelli. *Photographed:* Gianni Di Venanzo. *Sets:* Gianni Polidori. *Edited:* Eraldo da Roma. *Music:* Mario Nascimbene. *Cast:* Antonio Cifariello and non-actors recreating their real-life roles.

1954 LA STRADA

Produced: Carlo Ponti, Dino De Laurentiis. *Script:* Fellini, Ennio Flaiano, Tullio Pinelli, based on a story by Fellini and Pinelli. *Photographed:* Otello Martelli. *Sets:* Mario Ravasco. *Edited:* Leo Cattozzo. *Music:* Nino Rota. *Cast:* Giulietta Masina, Anthony Quinn, Richard Basehart, Aldo Silvani, Marcella Rovena, Lidia Venturini.

1955 IL BIDONE

Production Manager: Giuseppe Colizzi. *Script:* Fellini, Ennio Flaiano, Tullio Pinelli. *Photographed:* Otello Martelli. *Sets:* Dario Cecchi. *Edited:* Mario Serandrei, Giuseppe Vari. *Music:* Nino Rota. *Cast:* Broderick Crawford, Giulietta Masina, Richard Basehart, Franco Fabrizi, Alberto De Amicis, Xenia Valderi, Maria Zanoli, Irene Cefaro, Lorella De Luca, Sue Ellen Blake, Giacomo Gabrielli, Mario Passante, Lucietta Muratori.

1956 LE NOTTI DI CABIRIA

Produced: Dino De Laurentiis. *Script:* Fellini, Ennio Flaiano, Tullio Pinelli. *Additional dialogue:* Pier Paolo Pasolini. *Photographed:* Aldo Tonti. *Sets:* Piero Gherardi. *Edited:* Leo Cattozzo. *Music:* Nino Rota. *Cast:* Giulietta Masina, François Perier, Franca Marzi, Amedeo Nazzari, Dorian Gray, Aldo Silvani, Mario Passante, Ennio Girolami, Christian Tassou.

1958 Script (with Ennio Flaiano, Tullio Pinelli): *Fortunella* (Eduardo De Filippo), with Giulietta Masina, Paul Douglas, Alberto Sordi, Franca Marzi.

1960 LA DOLCE VITA

Produced: Giuseppe Amato. *Script:* Fellini, Ennio Flaiano, Tullio Pinelli, Brunello Rondi, based on a story by Fellini, Flaiano and Pinelli. *Artistic collaborator:* Brunello Rondi. *Photographed* (Totalscope): Otello Martelli. *Sets:* Piero Gherardi. *Edited:* Leo Cattozzo. *Music:* Nino Rota. *Cast:* Marcello Mastroianni, Yvonne Furneaux, Anouk Aimée, Anita Ekberg, Alain Cuny, Annibale Ninchi, Magali Noël,

Lex Barker, Nadia Gray, Jacques Sernas, Walter Santesso, Valeria Ciangottini, Polidor, Mino Doro, Riccardo Garrone, Harriet White, Alain Dijon, Giulio Girola, Nico Otzak, Audrey McDonald, Renée Longarini, Giulio Paradisi, Enzo Cerusico, Enzo Doria, Carlo Di Maggio, Adriana Moneta, Sandra Lee, Henry Thody, Donatella Della Nora, Maité Morand, Donato Castellaneta, John Francis Lane, Iris Tree, Tito Buzzo, Leo Coleman.

1962 BOCCACIO '70: episode LE TENTAZIONI DEL DOTTOR ANTONIO

Produced: Carlo Ponti, Antonio Cervi. *Script:* Fellini, Ennio Flaiano, Tullio Pinelli. *Photographed* (Colour, widescreen): Otello Martelli. *Sets:* Piero Zuffi. *Edited:* Leo Cattozzo. *Music:* Nino Rota. *Cast:* Peppino De Filippo, Anita Ekberg, Giacomo Furia, Alberto Sorrentino, Mario Passante, Silvio Bagolino.

1963 *8½*

Produced: Angelo Rizzoli. *Script:* Fellini, Ennio Flaiano, Tullio Pinelli, Brunello Rondi, based on a story by Fellini and Ennio Flaiano. *Photographed:* Gianni Di Venanzo. *Sets:* Piero Gherardi. *Edited:* Leo Cattozzo. *Music:* Nino Rota. *Cast:* Marcello Mastroianni, Claudia Cardinale, Anouk Aimée, Sandra Milo, Rossella Falk, Barbara Steele, Guido Alberti, Madeleine Lebeau, Jean Rougeul, Caterina Boratto, Annibale Ninchi, Giuditta Rissone.

1964 GIULIETTA DEGLI SPIRITI

In colour: with Giulietta Masina.

MICHELANGELO ANTONIONI

1942 Collaborated on script and assistant director: *I Due Foscari* (Enrico Fulchignoni). Collaborated on script: *Un Pilota Ritorna* (Roberto Rossellini). Assistant director: *Les Visiteurs du Soir* (Marcel Carné).

1943 GENTE DEL PO

> Short (completed 1947). *Script:* Antonioni. *Photographed:*
> Piero Portalupi. *Music:* Mario Labroca.

1947 Collaborated on script: *Caccia Tragica* (Giuseppe De Santis).

1948 N.U. (NETTEZZA URBANA)

> Short. *Script:* Antonioni. *Photographed:* Giovanni Venti-
> miglia. *Music:* Giovanni Fusco, a prelude by Bach.

1949 L'AMOROSA MENSOGNA

> Short. *Script:* Antonioni. *Photographed:* Renato Del Frate.
> *Music:* Giovanni Fusco.

SUPERSTIZIONE

> Short. *Script:* Antonioni. *Photographed:* Giovanni Venti-
> miglia. *Music:* Giovanni Fusco.

1950 SETTE CANNE, UN VESTITO

> Short. *Script:* Antonioni. *Photographed:* Giovanni Venti-
> miglia. *Music:* from stock.

LA VILLA DEI MOSTRI

> Short. *Script:* Antonioni. *Photographed:* Giovanni De
> Paoli. *Music:* Giovanni Fusco.

LA FUNIVIA DEL FALORIA

> Short. *Script:* Antonioni. *Photographed:* Goffredo Belli-
> sario, Ghedina. *Music:* Teo Usuelli.

1950 CRONACA DI UN AMORE

> *Produced:* Franco Vilani, Stefano Caretti. *Script:* Antoni-
> oni, Daniele d'Anza, Silvio Giovaninetti, Francesco
> Maselli, Piero Tellini, based on a story by Antonioni.
> *Photographed:* Enzo Serafin. *Sets:* Piero Filippone. *Edited:*
> Antonioni (uncredited). *Music:* Giovanni Fusco. *Cast:*

Lucia Bose, Massimo Girotti, Ferdinando Sarmi, Gino Rossi, Marika Rowsky, Rosa Mirafiore, Rubi D'Alma.

1952 Collaborated on script: *Lo Sciecco Bianco* (Federico Fellini).

I VINTI

Production Manager: Paolo Moffa. *Script:* Antonioni, Suso Cecchi D'Amico, Diego Fabbri, Turi Vasile, Roger Nimier, based on stories by Antonioni. *Photographed:* Enzo Serafin. *Sets:* Gianni Polidori. *Edited:* Eraldo Da Roma. *Music:* Giovanni Fusco. *Cast* (Italian episode): Anna Maria Ferrero, Franco Interlenghi, Eduardo Cianelli, Evi Maltagliati, Umberto Spadaro, Gastone Renzelli; (French episode): Jean-Pierre Mocky, Etchika Choureau, Henri Poirier, André Jacques, Annie Noël; (English episode): Peter Reynolds, Fay Compton, Patrick Barr, Eileen Moore.

1953 LA SIGNORA SENZA CAMELIE

Produced: Domenico Forges Davanzati. *Script:* Antonioni, Suso Cecchi D'Amico, Francesco Maselli, P. M. Pasinetti, based on a story by Antonioni. *Photographed:* Enzo Serafin. *Sets:* Gianni Polidori. *Edited:* Antonioni (uncredited). *Music:* Giovanni Fusco. *Cast:* Lucia Bose, Andrea Checchi, Gino Cervi, Ivan Desny, Alain Cuny, Monica Clay, Anna Carena, Enrico Glori, Laura Tiberti, Oscar Andriani, Elio Steiner, Nino Del Fabbro.

AMORE IN CITTA: episode TENTATO SUICIDIO

Produced: Cesare Zavattini, Renato Ghione, Marco Ferreri, *Script:* Antonioni. *Photographed:* Gianni De Venanzo. *Edited:* Eraldo Da Roma. *Music:* Mario Nascimbene. *Cast:* Non-actors recreating their real-life roles.

1955 Produced short: *Uomini in Piu* (Nicolo Ferrari).

LE AMICHE

Production Manager: Pietro Notarianni. *Script:* Antonioni, Suso Cecchi D'Amico, Alba De Cespedes, based on

Antonioni's free adaptation of *Tra Donne Sole*, by Cesare Pavese. *Photographed:* Gianni Di Venanzo. *Sets:* Gianni Polidori. *Edited:* Eraldo Da Roma. *Music:* Giovanni Fusco. *Cast:* Eleonora Rossi Drago, Valentina Cortese, Gabriele Ferzetti, Franco Fabrizi, Ettore Manni, Madeleine Fischer, Yvonne Furneaux, Anna Maria Pancani, Maria Ganbarelli.

1957 IL GRIDO

Produced: Franco Cancellierei. *Script:* Antonioni, Elio Bartolini, Ennio De Concini, based on a story by Antonioni. *Photographed:* Gianni Di Venanzo. *Sets:* Franco Fontana. *Edited:* Eraldo Da Roma. *Music:* Giovanni Fusco. *Cast:* Steve Cochran, Alida Valli, Dorian Gray (dubbed by Monica Vitti), Betsy Blair, Lyn Shaw, Mirna Girardi, Gaetano Matteucci, Guerrino Campanilli, Pina Boldrini, Pietro Corvelatti.

Technical supervision (nominal only) of *Questro Nostro Mondo* (Ugo Lazzari, Eros Macchi, Angelo Negri). *Edited:* Erando Da Roma.

1958 LA TEMPESTA (TEMPEST)

Antonioni collaborated (uncredited) with Alberto Lattuada on the direction. *Produced:* Dino De Laurentiis. *Script:* Louis Peterson, Ivo Perilli, Lattuada, Irwin Shaw (after Pushkin's *The Revolt of Pugachev* and *The Captain's Daughter*). *Photographed* (colour, Technirama): Aldo Tonti. *Sets:* Mario Chiari. *Edited:* Otello Colangeli. *Music:* Piero Piccioni. *Cast:* Silvana Mangano, Van Heflin, Viveca Lindfors, Geoffrey Horne, Vittorio Gassman, Oscar Homolka, Agnes Moorehead, Robert Keith, Helmut Dantine, Finlay Currie, Laurence Naismith, Claudio Gora.

NEL SEGNO DI ROMA (SIGN OF THE GLADIATOR)

Antonioni directed (uncredited) all the interiors and some of the exteriors; the major exteriors were directed by Riccardo Freda; the credited director, Guido Brignone, was taken ill before shooting and had no hand in the finished film. *Produced:* Enzo Merolle. *Script:* Antonio

Thellung, Francesco De Feo, Roberti Sergio Leone, Giuseppe Mangione. *Photographed* (Dyaliscope, colour): Luciano Trasatti. *Sets:* Ottavio Scotti. *Edited:* Giovanni Baragli. *Music:* Angelo-Francesco Lavagnino. *Cast:* Anita Ekberg, Georges Marchal, Jacques Sernas, Lorella De Luca, Chelo Alonso, Gino Cervi.

1959 L'AVVENTURA
Produced: Cino Del Duca. *Script:* Antonioni, Elio Bartolini, Tonino Guerra, based on a story by Antonioni. *Photographed:* Aldo Scavarda. *Sets:* Pietro Poletto. *Edited:* Eraldo Da Roma. *Music:* Giovanni Fusco. *Cast:* Monica Vitti, Gabriele Ferzetti, Lea Massari, Dominique Blanchar, Renzo Ricci, James Addams, Dorothy Di Poliolo, Lelio Luttazzi, Giovanni Petrucci, Esmeralda Ruspoli, Enrico Bologna, Franco Cimino, Giovanni Danesi.

1960 LA NOTTE
Produced: Emmanuel Cassuto. *Script:* Antonioni, Ennio Flaiano, Tonino Guerra. *Photographed:* Gianni Di Venanzo. *Sets:* Piero Zuffi. *Edited:* Eraldo Da Roma. *Music:* Giorgio Gaslini. *Cast:* Jeanne Moreau, Marcello Mastroianni, Monica Vitti, Bernhard Wicki, Rosy Mazzacurati, Maria Pia Luzi, Guido A. Marsan.

1962 L'ECLISSE
Produced: Robert and Raymond Hakim. *Script:* Antonioni, Tonino Guerra, with the assistance of Elio Bartolini, Ottiero Ottieri. *Photographed:* Gianni Di Venanzo. *Sets:* Piero Poletto. *Edited:* Eraldo Da Roma. *Music:* Giovanni Fusco. *Cast:* Alain Delon, Monica Vitti, Francisco Rabal, Lilla Brignone, Rossana Rory, Mirella Ricciardi, Louis Seignier, Cyrus Elias.

1964 DESERTO ROSSO
In colour: with Monica Vitti and Richard Harris.

LUIS BUÑUEL
In France
1926 Assistant director: *Mauprat* (Jean Epstein).

1927 Assistant director: *La Sirène des Tropiques* (Mario Nalpas and Étiévant).

1928 Assistant director: *La Chute de la Maison Usher* (Jean Epstein).

UN CHIEN ANDALOU

Produced: Luis Buñuel, Pierre Braunberger. *Script:* Buñuel and Salvador Dali. *Photographed:* Albert Dubergen (Duverger). *Edited:* Buñuel. *Sets:* Schilzneck. *Music* (soundtrack added in 1960): from Wagner's *Tristan und Isolde*, and an Argentinian tango. *Cast:* Simone Mareuil, Pierre Batcheff, Jaime Miravilles, Salvador Dali, Luis Buñuel.

1930 L'AGE D'OR

Produced: Vicomte de Noailles, Pierre Braunberger. *Script:* Buñuel (and, nominally, Salvador Dali). *Photographed:* Albert Dubergen. *Edited:* Buñuel. *Sets:* Schilzneck. *Music:* Georges Van Parys, with extracts from Wagner, Beethoven, Mendelssohn and Debussy. *Cast:* Gaston Modot, Lya Lys, Max Ernst, Pierre Prévert, Jose Artigas, Cardidal de Lamberdesque.

In Spain

1932 LAS HURDES (TIERRA SINPAN) (English title *Land without Bread*)

Produced: Ramon Acin. *Script:* Buñuel. *Assistant directors:* Pierre Unik, Sanchez Ventura. *Commentary:* Pierre Unik. *Photographed:* Eli Lotar. *Edited:* Buñuel. *Music:* extracts from Brahms and Mendelssohn.

1935 Executive producer: *Don Quentin el Amargao* (Luis Marquina). Executive producer: *La Hija de Juan Simon* (Jose Luis Saenz de Heredia).

1936 Executive producer: *Quien me quiere a mi?* (Jose Luis Saenz de Heredia). Executive producer: *Centinela! Alerta!* (Jean Grémillon, completed by Buñuel).

1937 Collaborated on documentary *España leal en armas* (the section *Madrid 36*).
Supervised *Espagne 39* (Jean-Paul le Chanois).

In the U.S.A.

1939-42 Propaganda films.

1946 Worked on script of *The Beast with Five Fingers* (eventually directed by Robert Florey).

In Mexico

1947 GRAN CASINO (EN EL VIEJO TAMPICO)

Produced: Oscar Dancigers. *Story:* Michael Weber. *Adaptation:* Mauricio Magdaleno. *Dialogue:* Javier Mateos. *Photographed:* Jack Draper. *Sets:* Javier Torres Torija. *Edited:* Gloria Schoeman. *Music:* Manuel Esperon. *Cast:* Libertad Lamarque, Jorge Negrete, Mercedes Barba, Augustin Isunza, Julio Villaréol, Charles Rooner.

1949 EL GRAN CALAVERA

Produced: Oscar Dancigers. *Script:* Raquel Rojas, Luis Alcoriza, after a comedy by Adolfo Torrado. *Photographed:* Ezequiel Carrasco. *Sets:* Luis Moya and Dario Cabanas. *Edited:* Carlos Savage. *Music:* Manuel Esperon. *Cast:* Fernando Soler, Rosario Granados, Ruben Rojo, Andres Soler, Maruja Grifell, Gustavo Rojo, Luis Alcoriza.

1950 LOS OLVIDADOS (English title *The Young and the Damned*)

Produced: Oscar Dancigers. *Script:* Luis Buñuel and Luis Alcoriza. *Photographed:* Gabriel Figueroa. *Sets:* Edward Fitzgerald. *Edited:* Carlos Savage. *Music:* Rodolfo Halffter, on themes of Gustavo Pittaluga. *Cast:* Estela Inda, Miguel Inclan, Roberto Cobo, Alfonso Mejia, Hector Lopez Portillo, Salvador Quiros, Victor Manuel Mendoza, Alma Delia Fuentes.

SUSANA (DEMONIO Y CARNE)

Produced: Oscar Dancigers. *Script:* Jaime Salvador, after a novel by Manuel Reachi. *Photographed:* Jose Ortiz Ramos. *Sets:* Gunter Gerzso. *Edited:* Jorge Bustos. *Music:* Raul Lavista. *Cast:* Rosita Quintana, Fernando Soler, Victor Manuel Mendoza, Matilde Palau.

1951 LA HIJA DEL ENGAÑO (DON QUINTIN EL AMARGAO)
Produced: Oscar Dancigers. *Script:* Raquel Rojas, Luis Alcoriza, after the play *Don Quintin el Amargao* by Carlos Arniches. *Photographed:* Jose Ortiz Ramos. *Sets:* Edward Fitzgerald. *Edited:* Carlos Savage. *Music:* Manuel Esperon. *Cast:* Fernando Soler, Alicia Caro, Ruben Rojo, Nacho Contra, Fernando Soto, Lily Aclemar.

UNA MUJER SIN AMOR
Produced: Oscar Dancigers. *Script:* Jaime Salvador (after Guy de Maupassant's novel *Pierre et Jean*). *Photographed:* Raul Martinez Solares. *Sets:* Gunter Gerszo. *Edited:* Jorge Bustos. *Music:* Raul Larista. *Cast:* Rosario Granados, Julio Villareal, Tito Junco, Joaquin Cordero.

SUBIDA AL CIELO
Produced: Manuel Altolaguirre. *Script:* Manuel Altolaguirre, Juan la Cabado, Buñuel, after a story by Manuel Altolaguirre. *Dialogue:* Juan de la Cabada. *Photographed:* Alex Philips. *Sets:* Edward Fitzgerald, Jose Rodriguez Granada. *Edited:* Rafael Portillo. *Music:* Gustavo Pitaluga. *Cast:* Lilia Prado, Carmelita Gonzales, Esteban Marquez, Manuel Donde, Roberto Cobo, Acevez Castenada.

1952 EL BRUTO
Produced: Oscar Dancigers. *Script:* Buñuel, Luis Alcoriza. *Photographed:* Augustin Jimenez. *Sets:* Gunter Gerzso. *Edited:* Jorge Bustos. *Music:* Raul Lavista. *Cast:* Pedro Armendariz, Katy Jurado, Rosita Arenas, Andres Soler, Roberto Meyer.

THE ADVENTURES OF ROBINSON CRUSOE
Produced: Oscar Dancigers, Henry F. Ehrlich. *Script:* Buñuel, Philip Roll (after the novel by Daniel Defoe). *Photographed* (colour): Alex Philips. *Sets:* Edward Fitzgerald. *Edited:* Carlos Savage, Alberto Valenzuela. *Music:* Anthony Collins. *Cast:* Dan O'Herlihy, Jaime Fernandez, Felipe de Alba, Chel Lopez, Jose Chaves, Emilio Garibay.

EL
Produced: Oscar Dancigers. *Script:* Buñuel, Luis Alcoriza (after *Pensamientos*, by Mercedes Pinto). *Photographed:*

Gabriel Figueroa. *Sets:* Edward Fitzgerald. *Edited:* Carlos Savage. *Music:* Luis Hernandes Breton. *Cast:* Arturo de Cordova, Delia Garces, Luis Beristain, Aurora Walker, Manuel Donde, Martinez Baena.

1953 CUMBRES BORRASCOSAS (ABISMOS DE PASION)

Produced: Oscar Dancigers. *Script:* Buñuel, Arduino Maiuri and Julio Alejandro (after *Wuthering Heights*, by Emily Brontë). *Photographed:* Agustin Jimenez. *Sets:* Edward Fitzgerald. *Edited:* Carlos Savage. *Music:* Raul Lavista, excerpts from Wagner. *Cast:* Irasema Dilian, Jorge Mistral, Lilia Prado, Ernesto Alonso, Luis Aceves Castenada, Francisco Requeira.

LA ILUSION VIAJA EN TRANVIA

Produced: Armando Orive Alba. *Script:* Mauricio de la Serna, Jose Revueltas, based on a story by Mauricio de la Serna. *Photographed:* Raul Martinez Solares. *Sets:* Edward Fitzgerald. *Edited:* Jorge Bustos. *Music:* Luis Hernandes Breton. *Cast:* Lilia Prado, Carlos Navarro, Domingo Soler, Fernando Soto, Augustin Isunza, Miguel Manzano, Javier de la Parra, Guillermo Bravo Soso, Felipe Montojo.

1954 EL RIO Y LA MUERTE

Produced: Armando Orive Alba. *Script:* Buñuel, Luis Alcoriza (after the novel *Muro Blanco en Roca Negra*, by Miguel Alvarez Acosta). *Photographed:* Raul Martinez Solares. *Sets:* Edward Fitzgerald, Gunter Gerzso. *Edited:* Jorge Bustos. *Music:* Raul Lavista. *Cast:* Columba Dominguez, Miguel Torruco, Joaquin Cordero, Jaime Fernandez, Victor Alcover.

1955 LA VIDA CRIMINAL DE ARCHIBALDO DE LA CRUZ (ENSAYO DE UN CRIMEN)

Produced: Alfonso Patino Gomez. *Script:* Buñuel, Eduardo Ugarte (after the novel *Ensayo de un Crimen*, by Rodolfo

C.E.–Q

Usigli). *Photographed:* Augustin Jimenez. *Sets:* Jesus Bracho. *Edited:* Pablo Gomez. *Music:* Jorge Perez Herrera. *Cast:* Ernesto Alonso, Miroslava Stern, Rita Macedo, Adriana Welter, Rodolfo Landra, Andrea Palma, Carlos Riquelme, J. Maria Linares Rivas, Leonor Llansas.

In France

CELA S'APPELLE L'AURORE

Produced: André Cultet. *Script:* Buñuel, Jean Ferry (after the novel by Emmanuel Roblès). *Dialogue:* Jean Ferry. *Photographed:* Robert le Febvre. *Sets:* Max Douy. *Edited:* Marguerite Renoir. *Music:* Joseph Kosma. *Cast:* Georges Marchal, Lucia Bose, Giani Esposito, Julien Bertheau, Nelly Borgeaud, Jean-Jacques Delbo, Robert Le Fort, Brigitte Elloy, Henri Nassiet, Gaston Modot.

In Mexico

1956 LA MORT EN CE JARDIN (English title *Evil Eden*)

Produced: Oscar Dancigers. *Script:* Buñuel, Luis Alcoriza, Raymond Queneau (after the novel by José-André Lacour). *Dialogue:* Raymond Queneau, Gabriel Arout. *Photographed* (colour): Jorge Stahl Jr. *Sets:* Edward Fitzgerald. *Edited:* Marguerite Renoir. *Music:* Paul Misraki. *Cast:* Georges Marchal, Simone Signoret, Michel Piccoli, Michèle Girardon, Charles Vanel, Tito Junco.

1958 NAZARIN

Produced: Manuel Barbachano Ponce. *Script:* Buñuel, Julio Alejandro (after the novel by Benito Perez Galdos). *Photographed:* Gabriel Figueroa. *Sets:* Edward Fitzgerald. *Edited:* Carlos Savage. *Cast:* Francisco Rabal, Marga Lopez, Rita Macedo, Jesus Fernandez, Ignacio Lopez-Tarso, Ofelia Guilmain, Noe Muragama, Luis Aceves Castenada.

1959 LA FIÈVRE MONTE À EL PAO (English title *Republic of Sin*)

Produced: Raymond Borderie. *Script:* Lus Alcoriza, Buñuel, Charles Dorat, Louis Sapin (after the novel by

Henry Castillou). *Dialogue:* Louis Sapin. *Photographed:* Gabriel Figueroa. *Sets:* Jorge Fernandez. *Edited:* James Guénet. *Music:* Paul Misraki. *Cast:* Gérard Philipe, Maria Felix, Jean Servais, M-A. Ferres, Raoul Dantes, Domingo Soler, Victor Junco, Roberto Canedo.

1960 THE YOUNG ONE (ISLAND OF SHAME)

Produced: George P. Werker. *Script:* Buñuel, H. B. Addis (after the novel *Travelin' Man,* by Peter Matthiessen). *Photographed:* Gabriel Figueroa. *Sets:* Jesus Bracho. *Edited:* Carlos Savage. *Music:* Jesus Zarzosa, Leon Bibb. *Cast:* Kay Meersman, Bernie Hamilton, Zachary Scott, Claudio Brook, Graham Denton.

In Spain

1961 VIRIDIANA

Produced: Gustavo Alatriste. *Script:* Buñuel, Jorge Alejandro. *Photographed:* Jose F. Aguayo. *Sets:* Francisco Canet. *Edited:* Pedro del Rey. *Music:* Alleluia Chorus from Handel's *Messiah.* *Cast:* Francisco Rabal, Silvia Pinal, Fernando Rey, Margarita Lozano, Victoria Zinny, Teresa Rabal, Jose Calvo, Joaquin Roa, Luis Heredia, Jose Manuel Martin, Dolores Gaos, Juan Garcia Tienda, Maruja Isbert, Joaquin Mayol, Palmira Guerra, Servio Mendizabal, Milagros Tomas, Alicia J. Barriga.

1962 EL ANGEL EXTERMINADOR

Produced: Gustavo Alatriste. *Script:* Buñuel, after a screenplay by Buñuel and Luis Alcoriza, *Les Naufragés de la Rue de la Providence* (based on the play *Los Naufragos,* by Jose Benjamin). *Photographed:* Gabriel Figueroa. *Sets:* Jesus Bracho. *Edited:* Carlos Savage. *Music:* excerpts from Scarlatti, and a sonata by Paradisi. *Cast:* Silvia Pinal, Enrique Rembal, Jacqueline Andere, Jose Baviera, Augusto Benedico, Luis Beristain, Antonio Bravo, Claudio Brook, Cesar del Campo, Rosa Elena Durgel, Lucy Gallardo, Enrique Garcia Alvarez, Ofelia Guilmain, Nadia

Haro Oliva, Tito Junco, Xavier Loya, Xavier Masse, Angel Merino, Ofelia Montesco, Patricia Moran, Patricia de Morelos, Bertha Moss.

In France

1964 LE JOURNAL D'UNE FEMME DE CHAMBRE
Produced: Serge Silberman and Michel Safra. *Script:* Buñuel, Jean-Claude Carrière (after the novel by Octave Mirbeau). *Photographed* (Franscope): Roger Fellous. *Sets:* Georges Wakhévitch. *Edited:* Louisette Hautecoeur. *Cast:* Jeanne Moreau, Michel Piccoli, Georges Geret, Françoise Lugagne, Jean Ozenne, Daniel Ivernel, Marguerite Dubourg.

ROBERT BRESSON

1934 LES AFFAIRES PUBLIQUES
Satirical short with the clown Babys; no copy seems to survive.

1936 Script collaborator on *Les Jumeaux de Brighton* (Claude Heymann).

1937 Script collaborator on *Courrier Sud* (Pierre Billon).

1940 Assistant director on *L'Air Pure* (René Clair, unfinished).

1943 LES ANGES DU PÉCHÉ (BÉTHANIE)
Produced: Roland Tual. *Script:* Bresson, Father Bruckenberger, Jean Giraudoux. *Dialogue:* Jean Giraudoux. *Photographed:* Philippe Agostini. *Sets:* René Renoux. *Edited:* Yvonne Martin. *Cast:* Renée Faure, Jany Holt, Sylvie, Marie-Hélène Dasté, Paula Dehelly, Silvia Monfort, Mila Parély, Yolande Laffon, Louis Seigner.

1944 LES DAMES DU BOIS DE BOULOGNE
Produced: Raoul Ploquin. *Script:* Bresson (after a section of Diderot's *Jacques le Fataliste*). *Dialogue:* Jean Cocteau. *Photographed:* Philippe Agostini. *Sets:* Max Douy. *Edited:* Jean Feyte. *Music:* Jean-Jacques Grünenwald. *Cast:* Maria Casarès, Elina Labourdette, Lucienne Bogaert, Paul Bernard, Jean Marchat.

1950 LE JOURNAL D'UN CURÉ DE CAMPAGNE

Produced: Léon Carre. *Script:* Bresson (after the novel by Georges Bernanos). *Photographed:* Léonce-Henry Burel. *Sets:* Pierre Charbonnier. *Edited:* Paulette Robert. *Music:* Jean-Jacques Grünenwald. *Cast:* Claude Laydu, Armand Guibert, Marie-Monique Arkell, Nicole Ladmiral, Jean Riveyre, Nicole Maurey, Jean Danet, Antoine Balpêtré, Martine Lemaire.

1956 UN CONDAMNÉ À MORT S'EST ÉCHAPPÉ (LE VENT SOUFFLE OÙ IL VEUT)

Produced: Robert Sussfeld. *Script:* Bresson (after the autobiographical narrative of André Devigny). *Photographed:* L-H. Burel. *Sets:* Pierre Charbonnier. *Edited:* Raymond Lamy. *Music:* from Mozart's Mass in C Minor. *Cast:* François Leterrier, Charles Le Clainche, Maurice Beerblock, Roland Monod, Jacques Ertaud, Roger Tréherne.

1959 PICKPOCKET

Produced: Agnès Delahaie. *Script:* Bresson. *Photographed:* L-H. Burel. *Sets:* Pierre Charbonnier. *Edited:* Raymond Lamy. *Music:* from Lully. *Cast:* Martin Lassalle, Marika Green, Pierre Leymarie, Jean Pelegri, Kassagi, Pierre Étaix, Mme. Scal.

1962 PROCÈS DE JEANNE D'ARC

Produced: Agnès Delahaie. *Script:* Bresson, from the original records. *Photographed:* L-H. Burel. *Sets:* Pierre Charbonnier. *Edited:* Germaine Artus. *Music* (drumbeats): Francis Seyrig. *Cast:* Florence Carrez, Jean-Claude Fourneau, Roger Honorat, Marc Jacquier, Richard Pratt, André Brunet, Philippe Dreux, Gérard Zing, Paul-Robert Nimet, Marcel Darbaud, Jean Gillibert, Michel Herubel, André Regnier, André Maurice.

INGMAR BERGMAN

1944 Original story and script of *Hets* (Alf Sjöberg). (English title: *Frenzy:* U.S. title: *Torment.*)

1945 KRIS

> *Produced:* Carl Anders Dymling. *Script:* Bergman (after a play by Leck Fischer). *Photographed:* Gosta Roosling. *Sets:* Arne Akermak. *Edited:* Oscar Rosander. *Music:* Erland von Koch. *Cast:* Inga Landgre, Marianne Löfgren, Dagny Lind, Stig Olin.

1946 DET REGNAR PÅ VÅR KÄRLEK

> *Produced:* Lorens Malmstedt. *Script:* Bergman, Herbert Grevenius (after Oskar Braathen's play *Bra Mennesker*). *Photographed:* Hilding Bladh, Göran Strindberg. *Sets:* P. A. Lundgren. *Edited:* Tage Holmberg. *Music:* Erland von Koch. *Cast:* Birger Malmsten, Barbro Kollberg, Gösta Cederlund, Ludde Gentzel, Gunnar Björnstrand, Ake Fridell, Bengt-Ake Bengtsson, Sif Ruud, Ulf Johansson, Hjördis Pettersson, Douglas Håge.

1947 SKEPP TILL INDIALAND

> *Produced:* Lorens Malmstedt. *Script:* Bergman (after the play by Martin Söderhjelm). *Photographed:* Göran Strindberg. *Sets:* P. A. Lundgren. *Edited:* Tage Holmberg. *Music:* Erland von Koch. *Cast:* Birger Malmsten, Anna Lindahl, Holger Löwenadler, Gertrud Fridh, Ake Fridell, Jan Molander, Erik Hell, Naemi Briese, Hjördis Pettersson, Peter Lindgren.
>
> Original story and script of *Kvinna Utan Ansikte* (Gustaf Molander).

MUSIK I MÖRKER (English Title: *Night is my Future*)

> *Produced:* Lorens Malmstedt. *Script:* Dagmar Edquist. *Photographed:* Goran Strindberg. *Sets:* P. A. Lundgren. *Edited:* Lennart Wallén. *Music:* Erland von Koch. *Cast:*

Mai Zetterling, Birger Malmsten, Bengt Eklund, Olof Winnerstrand, Naima Wifstrand, Bibi Skoglund, Hilda Borgström, Douglas Håge, Gunnar Björnstrand, Ake Claesson, John Elfström, Bengt Logardt.

1948 HAMNSTAD (English title: *Port of Call*)

Produced: Allan Ekelund. *Script:* Bergman (after a story by Olle Länsberg). *Photographed:* Gunnar Fischer. *Sets:* Nils Svenwall. *Edited:* Oscar Rosander. *Music:* Erland von Koch. *Cast:* Nine-Christine Jönsson, Bengt Eklund, Mimi Nelson, Bertha Hall, Birgitta Valberg, Erik Hell, Nils Dahlgren, Stig Olin, Sif Ruud, Hans Straat.

FÄNGELSE (English title: *The Devil's Wanton*)

Produced: Lorens Marmstedt. *Script:* Bergman. *Photographed:* Göran Strindberg. *Sets:* P. A. Lundgren. *Edited:* Lennart Wallén. *Music:* Erland von Koch. *Cast:* Doris Svedlund, Birger Malmsten, Eva Henning, Hasse Ekman, Stig Olin, Irma Christensson, Anders Henriksson, Marianne Lofgren, Carl-Henrik Fant, Inger Juel, Curt Masrelicz, Ake Fridell, Bibi Lindquist, Arne Ragneborn.

Original story and script (with Gustav Molander) of *Eva* (Molander).

1949 TÖRST (U.S. title *Three Strange Loves*)

Produced: Carl Anders Dymling. *Script:* Herbert Grevenius (after the story by Birgit Tengroth). *Photographed:* Gunnar Fischer. *Sets:* Nils Svenwall. *Edited:* Oscar Rosander. *Music:* Erik Nordgren. *Choreography:* Ellen Bergman. *Cast:* Eva Henning, Birger Malmsten, Birgit Tengroth, Mimi Nelson, Hasse Ekman, Bengt Eklund, Gaby Stenberg, Naima Wifstrand, Sven-Eric Gamble, Gunnar Nielsen, Astrid Hesse, Else-Merete Heiberg, Helge Hagerman, Calle Flygare.

TILL GLÄDJE

Produced: Carl Anders Dymling. *Script:* Bergman. *Photographed:* Gunnar Fischer. *Sets:* Nils Svenwall. *Edited:*

Oscar Rosander. *Music:* Mozart, Mendelssohn, Smetana, Beethoven. *Cast:* Maj-Britt Nilsson, Stig Olin, Victor Sjöström, Birger Malmsten, John Ekman, Margit Carlquist, Sif Ruud, Rune Stylander, Erland Josephsson, Georg Skarstedt, Berit Holmström, Björn Montin, Carin Svenson, Svea Holm.

Original story of *Medan Staden Sover* (Lars-Erik Kjellgren).

1950 SOMMARLEK (English title *Summer Interlude*, U.S. title *Illicit Interlude*).

Produced: Allan Ekelund. *Script:* Bergman, Herbert Grevenius, from a story by Bergman. *Photographed:* Gunnar Fischer, Bengt Järnmark. *Sets:* Nils Svenwall. *Edited:* Oscar Rosander. *Music:* Erik Nordgren, excerpts from Tchaikowsky's *Swan Lake. Cast:* Maj-Britt Nilsson, Birger Malmsten, Alf Kjellin, Georg Funquist, Renee Bjorling, Mimi Pollak, Annalisa Ericsson, Stig Olin, Gunnar Olsson, John Botvid, Douglas Håge, Julia Caesar, Carl Ström.

SÅNT HÄNDER INTE HÄR (English title *High Tension*)

Produced: Helge Hagerman. *Script:* Herbert Grevenius. *Photographed:* Gunnar Fischer. *Sets:* Nils Svenwall. *Edited:* Lennart Wallén. *Music:* Erik Nordgren. *Cast:* Signe Hasso, Alf Kjellin, Ulf Palme, Gösta Cederlund, Ingve Nordwall, Stig Olin, Ragnar Klange, Hanno Kompus, Sylvia Tael, Els Vaarman, Edmar Kuus, Rudolf Lipp.

Original story of *Franskild* (Gustaf Molander).

1951 BRIS

Nine short advertising films for the manufacturers of the Swedish soap Bris.

1952 KVINNORS VANTAN (English title *Waiting Women*, U.S. title *Secrets of Women*)

Produced: Allan Ekeland. *Script:* Bergman. *Photographed:* Gunnar Fischer. *Sets:* Nils Svenwall. *Edited:* Oscar Rosander. *Cast:* Anita Bjork, Maj-Britt Nilsson, Eva Dahlbeck, Gunnar Björnstrand, Birger Malmsten, Jarl

Kulle, Karl-Arne Holmsten, Gerd Andersson, Björn Bjelvenstam, Aino Taube, Hakan Westergren, Naima Wifstrand.

SOMMAREN MED MONIKA (English title *Summer with Monika*, U.S. title *Monika*)

Produced: Allan Ekeland. *Script:* Bergman, Per-Anders Fogelström, after a story by Per-Anders Fogelström. *Photographed:* Gunnar Fischer. *Sets:* P. A. Lundgren, Nils Svenwall. *Edited:* Tage Holmberg, Gösta Lewin. *Music:* Erik Nordgren. *Cast:* Harriet Andersson, Lars Ekborg, John Harryson, Georg Skarstedt, Dagmar Ebbesen, Ake Fridell, Naemi Briese, Ake Gronberg, Gösta Eriksson, Bengt Eklund, Renée Björling.

1953 GYCKLARNAS AFTON (English title *Sawdust and Tinsel*, U.S. title *The Naked Light*)

Produced: Rune Waldekranz. *Script:* Bergman. *Photographed:* Sven Nykvist, Hilding Bladh. *Sets:* Bibi Lindström. *Edited:* Carl-Olof Skeppstedt. *Music:* Karl-Birger Blomdahl. *Cast:* Ake Grönberg, Harriet Andersson, Hasse Ekman, Anders Ek, Gudrun Brost, Annika Tretow, Gunnar Björnstrand, Erik Strandmark, Curt Löwgren, Kiki.

1954 EN LEKTION I KÄRLEK (English title *A Lesson in Love*)

Produced: Carl-Anders Dymling. *Script:* Bergman. *Photographed:* Martin Bodin, Bengt Nordwall. *Sets:* P. A. Lundgren. *Edited:* Oscar Rosander. *Music:* Dag Wirén. *Cast:* Eva Dahlbeck, Gunnar Björnstrand, Yvonne Lombard, Harriet Andersson, Ake Grönberg, Olof Winnerstrand, Birgitte Relmer, Renée Björling, John Elfstrom, Dagmar Ebbesen, Helge Hagerman.

1955 KVINNODRÖM (English title *Journey into Autumn*, U.S. title *Dreams*)

Produced: Rune Waldekranz. *Script:* Bergman. *Photographed:* Hilding Bladh. *Sets:* Gittan Gustafsson. *Edited:* Carl-Olof Skeppsted. *Cast:* Eva Dahlbeck, Harriet

Andersson, Gunnar Björnstrand, Ulf Palme, Inga Land-gré, Sven Lindberg, Naima Wifstrand, Benk-Ake Benkts-son, Kerstin Hedeby, Ludde Gentzel, Axel Düberg.

SOMMARNATTENS LEENDE (English title *Smiles of a Summer Night*)

Produced: Allan Ekelund. *Script:* Bergman. *Photographed:* Gunnar Fischer, Ake Nilsson. *Sets:* P. A. Lundgren. *Edited:* Oscar Rosander. *Music:* Erik Nordgren. *Cast:* Gunnar Björnstrand, Ulla Jacobsson, Björn Bjelvenstam, Eva Dahlbeck, Anders Wulff, Jarl Kulle, Margit Carlquist, Harriet Andersson, Jullan Kindahl, Gull Natorp, Gunnar Nielsen, Ake Fridell, Birgitta Valberg, Bibi Andersson, Naima Wifstrand.

1956 Original story and screenplay (with Alf Sjöberg) of *Sista Paret Ut* (Sjöberg).

DET SJUNDE INSEGLET (English title *The Seventh Seal*)

Produced: Allan Ekelund. *Script:* Bergman, after his own play *Trämalning. Photographed:* Gunnar Fischer, Ake Nilsson. *Sets:* P. A. Lundgren. *Edited:* Lennart Wallén. *Music:* Erik Nordgren. *Choreography:* Else Fischer. *Cast:* Max von Sydow, Gunnar Björnstrand, Nils Poppe, Bibi Andersson, Bengt Ekerot, Ake Fridell, Inga Gill, Erik Strandmark, Bertil Anderberg, Gunnel Lindblom, Inga Landgré, Anders Ek, Maud Hanson, Gunnar Olson, Lars Lind, Benkt-Ake Benktsson, Gudrun Brost, Ulf Johansson.

1957 SMULTRONSTÄLLET (English title *Wild Strawberries*)

Produced: Allen Ekelund. *Script:* Bergman. *Photographed:* Gunnar Fischer, Björn Thermenius. *Sets:* Gittan Gustafsson. *Edited:* Oscar Rosander. *Music:* Erik Nordgren. *Cast:* Victor Sjöström, Bibi Andersson, Ingrid Thulin, Gunnar Björnstrand, Folke Sundquist, Björn Bjelvenstam, Naima Wifstrand, Jullan Kindahl, Gunnar Sjöberg, Gunnel Broström, Gertrud Fridh, Ake Fridell, Max von Sydow, Sif Ruud, Yngve Nordwall, Per Sjöstrand, Gio Petré,

Gunnel Lindblom, Maud Hansson, Lena Bergman, Monica Ehrling, Göran Lundquist, Eva Norée, Gunnar Olson, Josef Norman, Anne-Marie Wiman, Wulff Lund.

NÄRA LIVET (English title *So Close to Life*, U.S. title *Brink of Life*)

Produced: Gösta Hammarbäck. *Script:* Bergman, Ulla Isaksson (after Ulla Isaksson's story *Det Vänliga, Värdiga*). *Photographed:* Max Willen. *Sets:* Bibi Lindström. *Edited:* Carl-Olof Skeppstedt. *Cast:* Eva Dahlbeck, Ingrid Thulin, Bibi Andersson, Barbro Hiort af Ornäs, Erland Josephsson, Max von Sydow, Gunnar Sjöberg, Ann-Marie Gyllenspetz, Inga Landgré, Margareta Krook, Lard Lind, Sissi Kaiser, Monika Ekberg, Gun Jönsson, Inga Gill.

1958 ANSIKTET (English title *The Face*, U.S. title *The Magician*)

Produced: Allan Ekeland. *Script:* Bergman. *Photographed:* Gunnar Fischer, Rolf Halmquist. *Sets:* P. A. Lundgren. *Edited:* Oscar Rosander. *Music:* Erik Nordgren. *Cast:* Max von Sydow, Ingrid Thulin, Gunnar Björnstrand, Naima Wifstrand, Bengt Ekerot, Bibi Andersson, Gertrud Fridh, Lars Ekborg, Toivo Pawlo, Erland Josephsson, Ake Fridell, Sif Ruud, Oscar Ljung, Ulla Sjöblom, Axel Düberg, Birgitta Petersson.

1959 JUNGFRUKÄLLAN (English title *The Virgin Spring*)

Produced: Allan Ekelund. *Script:* Ulla Isaksson. *Photographed:* Sven Nykvist, Rolf Halmquist. *Sets:* P. A. Lundgren. *Edited:* Oscar Rosander. *Music:* Erik Nordgren. *Cast:* Max von Sydow, Birgitta Valberg, Birgitta Petersson, Gunnel Lindblom, Axel Düberg, Tor Isedal, Ove Porath, Allan Edwall, Axel Slangus, Gudrun Brost, Oscar Ljung, Tor Borong, Leif Forstenberg.

1960 DJÄVULENS ÖGA (English title *The Devil's Eye*)

Produced: Allan Ekelund. *Script:* Bergman. *Photographed:* Gunnar Fischer, Rolf Halmquist. *Sets:* P. A. Lundgren. *Edited:* Oscar Rosander. *Music:* from Domenico Scarlatti.

Cast: Jarl Kulle, Bibi Andersson, Stig Järrel, Nils Poppe, Gertrud Fridh, Sture Lagerwall, Georg Funquist, Gunnar Sjöberg, Axel Düberg, Allan Edwall, Gunnar Björnstrand, Inga Gill, Borje Lund.

1961 SÅSOM I EN SPEGEL (English title *Through a Glass Darkly*)

Produced: Allan Ekelund. *Script:* Bergman. *Photographed:* Sven Nykvist. *Sets:* P. A. Lundgren. *Edited:* Ulla Ryghe. *Music:* Bach's Suite No. 2 in D Minor for cello. *Cast:* Harriet Andersson, Gunnar Björnstrand, Max von Sydow, Lars Passgård.

1962 NATTVARDSGÄSTERNA (English title *Winter Light*)

Produced: Allan Ekelund. *Script:* Bergman. *Photographed:* Sven Nykvist. *Sets:* P. A. Lundgren. *Edited:* Ulla Ryghe. *Cast:* Ingrid Thulin, Gunnar Björnstrand, Max von Sydow, Gunnel Lindblom, Allan Edwall, Kolbjörn Knudsen, Olof Thunberg.

1963 TRYSTNADEN (English title *The Silence*)

Produced: Allan Ekelund. *Script:* Bergman. *Photographed:* Sven Nykvist. *Sets:* P. A. Lundgren. *Edited:* Ulla Ryghe. *Music:* Bach, Bo Nilsson. *Cast:* Ingrid Thulin, Gunnel Lindblom, Jörgen Lindström, Birger Malmsten, Håkan Jahnberg.

1964 FÖR ATT INTE TALA OM ALLA DESSA KVINNOR (English title *Not to Mention All These Women*)

Produced: Allan Ekelund. *Script:* Bergman, Erland Josephsson. *Photographed:* (Eastmancolour): Sven Nykvist. *Sets:* P. A. Lundgren. *Edited:* Ulla Ryghe. *Cast:* Jarl Kulle, Eva Dahlbeck, Barbro Hiort af Ornäs, Mona Malm, Bibi Andersson, Gertrud Fridh, Karin Kavli, Harriet Andersson, Georg Funquist, Allan Edwall.

ALFRED HITCHCOCK

1921–2 Wrote and designed titles for *Call of Youth* (Hugh Ford), *The Great Day* (Hugh Ford), *The Princess of New York* (Donald Crisp), *Tell Your Children* (Donald Crisp), *Three Live Ghosts* (George Fitzmaurice), etc.

1921 NUMBER THIRTEEN

Unfinished. *Produced:* Hitchcock. *Photographed:* Rosenthal. *Cast:* Clare Greet, Ernest Thesiger.

1922 ALWAYS TELL YOUR WIFE

Hitchcock completed this film in collaboration with the star, Seymour Hicks, when the director was taken ill. Designer, assistant director and collaborator on script of *Woman to Woman* (Graham Cutts).

1923 Designer, assistant director and collaborator on script of *The White Shadow* (Graham Cutts).
1924 Designer, assistant director and script-writer of *The Passionate Adventure* (Graham Cutts).
1925 Designer, assistant director and script-writer (after a novel by Raymond Paton) of *The Blackguard* (Graham Cutts). Designer, assistant director and script-writer of *The Prude's Fall* (Graham Cutts).

THE PLEASURE GARDEN

Produced: Michael Balcon. *Script:* Eliot Stannard (after a novel by Oliver Sandys). *Photographed:* Baron Ventimiglia. *Cast:* Virginia Valli, Carmelita Geraghty, Miles Mander, John Stuart, Nita Naldi, Frederick Martini, Florence Helminger.

1926 THE MOUNTAIN EAGLE (U.S. title *Fear o' God*)

Produced: Michael Balcon. *Script:* Eliot Stannard. *Photographed:* Baron Ventimiglia. *Cast:* Bernard Goetzke, Nita Naldi, Malcolm Keen, John Hamilton.

THE LODGER

Produced: Michael Balcon. *Script:* Hitchcock, Eliot Stannard (after the novel by Mrs. Belloc-Lowndes). *Photographed:* Hal Young. *Sets:* C. Wilfred Arnold, Bertram Evans. *Edited:* Ivor Montagu. *Cast:* Ivor Novello, June, Malcolm Keen, Arthur Chesney, Marie Ault.

1927 DOWNHILL (U.S. title *When Boys Leave Home*)

Produced: Michael Balcon. *Script:* Eliot Stannard (after a story by Ivor Novello and Constance Collier, under the pseudonym of David Lestrange). *Photographed:* Claude McDonnell. *Edited:* Ivor Montagu. *Cast:* Ivor Novello, Ben Webster, Robin Irvine, Sybil Rhoda, Lillian Braithwaite, Violet Farebrother, Isabel Jeans, Hannah Jones, Norman McKinnell, Jerrold Robertshaw, Ian Hunter, Annette Benson, Barbara Gott, Alf Goddard, J. Nelson.

EASY VIRTUE

Produced: Michael Balcon. *Script:* Eliot Stannard (after the play by Noel Coward). *Photographed:* Claude McDonnell. *Edited:* Ivor Montagu. *Cast:* Isabel Jeans, Franklyn Dyall, Bransby Williams, Ian Hunter, Robin Irvine, Violet Farebrother, Frank Elliott, Dacia Deane, Dorothy Boyd, Enid Stamp-Taylor.

THE RING

Produced: John Maxwell. *Script:* Hitchcock. *Adaptation:* Alma Reville. *Photographed:* Jack Cox. *Cast:* Carl Brisson, Lillian Hall-Davies, Ian Hunter, Harry Terry, Gordon Harker, Forrester Harvey, Billy Wells.

1928 THE FARMER'S WIFE

Produced: John Maxwell. *Script:* Hitchcock (after the play by Eden Philpotts). *Photographed:* Jack Cox. *Edited:* Alfred Booth. *Cast:* Jameson Thomas, Lillian Hall-Davies, Gordon Harker, Maud Gill, Louise Pounds, Olga Slade, Antonia Brough.

CHAMPAGNE

Produced: John Maxwell. *Script:* Eliot Stannard. *Photographed:* Jack Cox. *Cast:* Betty Balfour, Gordon Harker, Jack Trevor, Ferdinand von Alten, Marcel Vibert, Jean Bradin.

1929 THE MANXMAN

Produced: John Maxwell. *Script:* Eliot Stannard (after the novel by Hall Caine). *Photographed:* Jack Cox. *Cast:* Carl Brisson, Malcolm Keen, Anny Ondra, Randle Ayrton, Clare Greet.

BLACKMAIL

Produced: John Maxwell. *Script:* Hitchcock, Benn W. Levy, Charles Bennett (after a play by Charles Bennett). *Photographed:* Jack Cox. *Sets:* Norman Arnold, Wilfred Arnold. *Edited:* Emile de Ruelle. *Music:* Hubert Bath, Henry Stafford. *Cast:* Anny Ondra, John Longden, Sara Allgood, Charles Paton, Donald Calthrop, Cyril Ritchard, Hannah Jones, Harvey Braban, Phyllis Monkman.

1930 ELSTREE CALLING

Hitchcock directed sketches starring Gordon Harker in a composite revue-film supervised by Adrian Brunel.

JUNO AND THE PAYCOCK

Produced: John Maxwell. *Script:* Hitchcock, Alma Reville (after the play by Sean O'Casey). *Photographed:* Jack Cox. *Sets:* Norman Arnold. *Edited:* Emile de Ruelle. *Cast:* Barry Fitzgerald, Sara Allgood, Edward Chapman, Marie O'Neill, Sidney Morgan, John Laurie, Dennis Wyndham, John Longden, Kathleen O'Regan, Dave Morris, Fred Schwartz.

MURDER

Produced: John Maxwell. *Script:* Alma Reville (after story *Enter Sir John,* by Clemence Dane and Helen Simpson). *Photographed:* Jack Cox. *Sets:* John Mead. *Edited:* Emile de Ruelle, René Harrison. *Cast:* Herbert Marshall, Norah Baring, Phyllis Konstam, Edward Chapman, Miles Mander, Esme Chaplin, A. Brandon Thomas, Joynson Powell, Esme Percy, Donald Calthrop, Marie Wright, Hannah Jones, S. J. Warmington, R. E. Jeffrey, Clare Greet, William Fazan.

1931 THE SKIN GAME

Produced: John Maxwell. *Script:* Alma Reville, Hitchcock (after the play by John Galsworthy). *Photographed:* Jack Cox. *Edited:* René Harrison, A. Gobbett. *Cast:* Edmund Gwenn, Jill Esmond, John Longden, C. V. France, Helen Haye, Phyllis Konstam, Frank Lawton, Herbert Ross, Dora Gregory, Edward Chapman, Ronald Frankau, R. E. Jeffrey, George Blanchof.

1932 RICH AND STRANGE (U.S. title *East of Shanghai*)

Produced: John Maxwell. *Script:* Alma Reville, Val Valentine (after a story by Dale Collins). *Photographed:* Jack Cox, Charles Martin. *Edited:* René Harrison, Winifred Cooper. *Cast:* Henry Kendall, Joan Barry, Betty Amann, Percy Marmont, Elsie Randolph.

NUMBER SEVENTEEN

Produced: John Maxwell. *Script:* Hitchcock, Alma Reville, Rodney Ackland (after a play by Jefferson Farjeon). *Photographed:* Jack Cox, Bryan Langley. *Sets:* Wilfrid Arnold. *Edited:* A. C. Hammond. *Cast:* Leon M. Lion, Anne Grey, John Stuart, Donald Calthrop, Barry Jones, Garry Marsh, Henry Caine.
Produced *Lord Camber's Ladies* (Benn W. Levy).

1933 WALTZES FROM VIENNA (U.S. title *Strauss' Great Waltz*)

Produced: Tom Arnold. *Script:* Alma Reville, Guy Bolton (after the musical *Great Waltz*, by Heinz Reichert, A. M. Willner, Ernst Marischka). *Photographed:* Glen McWilliams. *Sets:* Alfred Junge, Peter Bond. *Music:* Johann Strauss, Sr and Jr, adapted by Hubert Bath. *Cast:* Jessie

Matthews, Esmond Knight, Frank Vosper, Edmund Gwenn, Fay Compton, Robert Hale, Hindle Edgar, Marcus Barron, Charles Heslop, Sybil Grove, Bill Shine, B. M. Lewis, Cyril Smith, Betty Huntley Wright, Bertram Dench.

1934 THE MAN WHO KNEW TOO MUCH

Produced: Michael Balcon and Ivor Montagu. *Script:* A. R. Rawlinson, Edwin Greenwood, based on an original story by Charles Bennett and D. B. Wyndham-Lewis. *Additional dialogue:* Emlyn Williams. *Photographed:* Curt Courant. *Sets:* Alfred Junge, Peter Proud. *Edited:* H. St. C. Stewart. *Music:* Arthur Benjamin and Louis Levy. *Cast:* Leslie Banks, Peter Lorre, Edna Best, Nova Pilbeam, Hugh Wakefield, Pierre Fresnay, Frank Vosper, George Carson, Willy Oates, D. A. Clarke-Smith.

1935 THE THIRTY-NINE STEPS

Produced: Michael Balcon and Ivor Montagu. *Script:* Charles Bennett, Ian Hay (after the novel by John Buchan). *Adaptation:* Alma Reville. *Photographed:* Bernard Knowles. *Sets:* Otto Werndorff, Albert Jullion. *Edited:* Derek Twist. *Music:* Louis Levy. *Cast:* Robert Donat, Madeleine Carroll, Lucy Mannheim, Godfrey Tearle, John Laurie, Peggy Ashcroft, Helen Haye, Frank Cellier, Wylie Watson, Peggy Simpson, Gus McNaughton, Jerry Verno.

1936 THE SECRET AGENT

Produced: Michael Balcon, Ivor Montagu. *Script:* Charles Bennett (after a play by Campbell Dixon, based on *Ashenden*, by Somerset Maugham). *Adaptation:* Alma Reville. *Additional dialogue:* Ian Hay, Jesse Lasky, Jr. *Photographed:* Bernard Knowles. *Sets:* Otto Werndorff, Albert Jullion. *Edited:* Charles Frend. *Music:* Louis Levy. *Cast:* Madeleine Carroll, John Gielgud, Peter Lorre, Robert Young, Percy Marmont, Florence Kahn, Lilli Palmer, Charles Carson.

C.E.–R

SABOTAGE (U.S. title *A Woman Alone*)

Produced: Michael Balcon, Ivor Montagu. *Script:* Charles Bennett (after the novel *The Secret Agent*, by Joseph Conrad). *Adaptation:* Alma Reville. *Additional dialogue:* Ian Hay, E. V. H. Emmett, Helen Simpson. *Photographed:* Bernard Knowles. *Sets:* Otto Werndorff, Albert Jullion. *Edited:* Charles Frend. *Music:* Louis Levy. *Cast:* Sylvia Sidney, Oscar Homolka, Desmond Tester, John Loder, Joyce Barbour, Matthew Bolton, S. J. Warmington, William Dewhurst, Peter Bull, Torin Thatcher, Austin Trevor, Clare Greet, Sam Wiskinson, Sara Allgood, Martita Hunt, Pamela Bevan.

1937 YOUNG AND INNOCENT (U.S. title *The Girl was Young*)

Produced: Edward Black. *Script:* Charles Bennett (after the novel *A Shilling for Candles*, by Josephine Tey). *Adaptation:* Alma Reville. *Photographed:* Bernard Knowles. *Sets:* Alfred Junge. *Edited:* Charles Frend. *Music:* Louis Levy. *Cast:* Derrick de Marney, Nova Pilbeam, Percy Marmont, Edward Rigby, Mary Clare, John Longden, George Curzon, Basil Radford, Pamela Carne, George Merritt, J. H. Roberts, Jerry Verno, H. F. Maltby, John Miller, Torin Thatcher, Peggy Simpson, Anna Konstam.

1938 THE LADY VANISHES

Produced: Edward Black. *Script:* Sidney Gilliatt, Frank Launder (after the novel *The Wheel Spins*, by Ethel Lina White). *Adaptation:* Alma Reville. *Photographed:* Jack Cox. *Sets:* Alec Vetchinsky, Maurice Carter, Albert Jullion. *Edited:* R. E. Dearing. *Music:* Louis Levy. *Cast:* Michael Redgrave, Margaret Lockwood, Paul Lukas, Dame May Whitty, Googie Withers, Cecil Parker, Linden Travers, Mary Clare, Naunton Wayne, Basil Radford, Emile Boreo, Sally Stewart, Philippe Leaver, Zelma Vas Dias, Catherine Lacey, Josephine Wilson, Charles Oliver, Kathleen Tremaine.

1939 JAMAICA INN

Produced: Erich Pommer, Charles Laughton. *Script:* Sidney Gilliatt and Joan Harrison (after the novel by Daphne du Maurier). *Additional dialogue:* J. B. Priestley. *Photographed:* Harry Stradling, Bernard Knowles. *Sets:* Tom Morahan. *Edited:* Robert Hamer. *Music:* Eric Fenby. *Cast:* Charles Laughton, Maureen O'Hara, Robert Newton, Emlyn Williams, Leslie Banks, Horace Hodges, Hay Petrie, Frederick Piper, Marie Ney, Wylie Watson, Morland Graham, Edwin Greenwood, Mervyn Johns, Stephen Haggard, Herbert Lomas, Clare Greet, William Devlin, Basil Radford, Jeanne de Casalis, George Curzon, Mabel Terry Lewis, A. Bromley Davenport.

In U.S.A.

1940 REBECCA

Produced: David O. Selznick. *Script:* Robert E. Sherwood, Joan Harrison (after the novel by Daphne du Maurier). *Adaptation:* Philip MacDonald, Michael Hogan. *Photographed:* George Barnes. *Sets:* Lyle Wheeler. *Edited:* Hal C. Kern. *Music:* Franz Waxman. *Cast:* Laurence Olivier, Joan Fontaine, George Sanders, Judith Anderson, Nigel Bruce, Reginald Denny, C. Aubrey Smith, Gladys Cooper, Florence Bates, Melville Cooper, Leo G. Carroll, Leonard Carey, Lumsden Hare, Edward Fielding, Philip Winter, Forrester Harvey.

FOREIGN CORRESPONDENT

Produced: Walter Wanger. *Script:* Charles Bennett, Joan Harrison. *Additional dialogue:* James Hilton, Robert Benchley. *Photographed:* Rudolph Maté. *Sets:* William Camerson Menzies, Alexander Golitzen. *Edited:* Otto Lovering, Dorothy Spencer. *Music:* Alfred Newman. *Cast:* Joel McCrea, Laraine Day, Herbert Marshall, George Sanders, Albert Basserman, Robert Benchley, Edmund Gwenn, Harry Davenport, Eduardo Ciannelli, Martin Kosleck, Barbara Pepper, Eddie Conrad, Cranford

Kent, Gertrude W. Hoffman, Jane Novak, Joan Brodel, Louis Borrell, Eily Malyon, E. E. Clive.

1941 MR AND MRS SMITH (R.K.O.)

Produced: Harry Edlington. *Script:* Norman Krasna. *Photographed:* Harry Stradling. *Sets:* Van Nest Polglase. *Edited:* William Hamilton. *Music:* Roy Webb. *Cast:* Carole Lombard, Robert Montgomery, Gene Raymond, Jack Carson, Philip Merivale, Lucile Watson, William Tracy, Charles Halton, Esther Dale, Emma Dunn, Betty Compson, Patricia Farr, William Edmunds, Adele Pearce.

SUSPICION (R.K.O.)

Produced: uncredited. *Script:* Samson Raphaelson, Joan Harrison, Alma Reville (after the novel *Before the Fact*, by Francis Iles). *Photographed:* Harry Stradling. *Sets:* Van Nest Polglase, Darrell Silvera. *Edited:* William Hamilton. *Music:* Franz Waxman. *Cast:* Cary Grant, Joan Fontaine, Cedric Hardwicke, Nigel Bruce, Dame May Whitty, Isabel Jeans, Heather Angel, Auriol Lee, Reginald Sheffield, Leo G. Carroll.

1942 SABOTEUR (Universal)

Produced: Frank Lloyd, Jack H. Skirball. *Script:* Peter Viertel, Joan Harrison, Dorothy Parker, based on an original story by Hitchcock. *Photographed:* Joseph Valentine. *Sets:* Jack Otterson. *Edited:* Otto Ludwig. *Music:* Charles Previn. *Cast:* Robert Cummings, Priscilla Lane, Otto Kruger, Norman Lloyd, Alan Baxter, Clem Bevans, Alma Kruger, Vaughn Glaazer, Dorothy Peterson, Murray Alper, Ian Wolfe, Frances Carson, Kathryn Adams, Pedro de Cordoba, Billy Curtis, Anita Le Deaux, Anita Bolster, Jeanne and Lynn Romer.

1943 SHADOW OF A DOUBT (Universal)

Produced: Jack H. Skirball. *Script:* Thornton Wilder, Alma Reville, Sally Benson, based on an original story by

Gordon McDonnell. *Photographed:* Joseph Valentine. *Sets:* John B. Goodman, R. A. Gansman. *Edited:* Milton Carruth. *Music:* Dimitri Tiomkin. *Cast:* Joseph Cotten, Teresa Wright, MacDonald Carey, Henry Travers, Patricia Collinge, Hume Cronyn, Wallace Ford, Charles Bates, Edna May Wonacott, Irving Bacon, Clarence Muse, Janet Shaw, Estelle Jewell.

1944 LIFEBOAT (Fox)

Produced: Kenneth Macgowan. *Script:* Jo Swerling, based on an original story by John Steinbeck. *Photographed:* Glen MacWilliams. *Sets:* James Basevi, Maurice Ransford. *Edited:* Dorothy Spencer. *Music:* Hugo Friedhofer. *Cast:* Tallulah Bankhead, William Bendix, Walter Slezak, Mary Anderson, John Hodiak, Henry Hull, Heather Angel, Hume Cronyn, Canada Lee.

BON VOYAGE

Produced: Ministry of Information. *Script:* J. O. C. Orton, Angus McPhail, based on an original story by Arthur Calder-Marshall. *Photographed:* Gunther Krampf. *Sets:* Charles Gilbert. *Cast:* John Blythe, The Molière Players.

AVENTURE MALGACHE

Produced: Ministry of Information. *Script:* J. O. C. Orton, Angus McPhail. *Photographed:* Gunther Krampf. *Sets:* Charles Gilbert. *Cast:* The Molière Players.

1945 SPELLBOUND (Selznick International)

Produced: David O. Selznick. *Script:* Ben Hecht (after the novel *The House of Dr Edwardes*, by Francis Beeding). *Adaptation:* Angus McPhail. *Photographed:* George Barnes. *Sets:* James Basevi, John Ewing. *Dream sequence:* Salvador Dali. *Edited:* William Ziegler. *Music:* Miklos Rozsa. *Cast:* Ingrid Bergman, Gregory Peck, Michael Chekhov, Jean Acker, Donald Curtis, Rhonda Fleming, John Emery, Leo G. Carroll, Norman Lloyd, Steven

Geray, Paul Harvey, Erskine Sanford, Janet Scott, Victor Kilian, Wallace Ford, Bill Goodwin, Dave Willcock, George Meader, Matt Moore, Harry Brown, Art Baker, Regis Toomey, Clarence Straight, Joel Davis, Teddy Infuhr, Addison Richards, Richard Bartell, Edward Fielding.

1946 NOTORIOUS (R.K.O.)

Produced: Hitchcock. *Script:* Ben Hecht, based on an original story by Hitchcock. *Photographed:* Ted Tetzlaff. *Sets:* Albert S. D'Agostino, Carroll Clark, Darrell Silvera. *Edited:* Theron Warth. *Music:* Roy Webb. *Cast:* Cary Grant, Ingrid Bergman, Claude Rains, Madame Konstantin, Reinhold Schuntzel, Moroni Olsen, Ivan Triesault, Alex Minotis, Wally Brown, Sir Charles Mendl, Eberhardt Krumschmidt, Fay Baker, Peter Von Zernack, Lenore Ulric, Ramon Nomar, Ricardo Costa.

1947 THE PARADINE CAST (Selznick International)

Produced: David O. Selznick. *Script:* Selznick (after the novel by Robert Hitchins). *Adaptation:* Alma Reville. *Photographed:* Lee Garmes. *Sets:* Thomas Morahan, J. MacMillan Johnson. *Edited:* Hal C. Kern, John Faure. *Music:* Franz Waxman. *Cast:* Gregory Peck, Charles Laughton, Ann Todd, Charles Coburn, Ethel Barrymore, Louis Jourdan, Alida Valli, Leo G. Carroll, Joan Tetzel, John Goldsworthy, Lester Matthews, Pat Aherne, Colin Hunter, Isobel Elsom, John Williams.

1948 ROPE (Warner, then M.G.M.)

Produced: Hitchcock, Sidney Bernstein. *Script:* Arthur Laurents (after the play by Patrick Hamilton). *Adaptation:* Hume Cronyn. *Photographed* (colour): Joseph Valentine, William V. Skell. *Sets:* Perry Ferguson. *Edited:* William A. Ziegler. *Music:* Leo F. Forbstein, based on a theme of Poulenc. *Cast:* James Stewart, John Dall, Farley Granger, Joan Chandler, Sir Cedric Hardwicke, Constance Collier, Douglas Dick, Edith Evanston, Dick Hogan.

1949 UNDER CAPRICORN (Warner)

> *Produced:* Hitchcock, Sidney Bernstein. *Script:* James Bridie (after the novel by Helen Simpson). *Adaptation:* Hume Cronyn. *Photographed* (colour): Jack Cardiff. *Sets:* Thomas Morahan. *Edited:* A. S. Bates. *Music:* Richard Addinsell. *Cast:* Ingrid Bergman, Joseph Cotten, Michael Wilding, Margaret Leighton, Cecil Parker, Denis O'Dea, Jack Watling, Harcourt Williams, John Ruddock, Bill Shine, Victor Lucas, Ronald Adam, Francis de Wolff, G. H. Mulcaster, Olive Sloane, Maureen Delaney, Julia Lang, Betty McDermott, Roderick Lovell.

1950 STAGE FRIGHT (Warner)

> *Produced:* Hitchcock, Fred Ahern. *Script:* Whitfield Cook (after stories *Man Running* and *Outrun the Constable*, by Selwyn Jepson). *Adaptation:* Alma Reville. *Additional dialogue:* James Bridie. *Photographed:* Wilkie Cooper. *Sets:* Terence Verity. *Edited:* Edward Jarvis. *Music:* Leighton Lucas. *Cast:* Marlene Dietrich, Jane Wyman, Michael Wilding, Richard Todd, Alastair Sim, Sybil Thorndike, Kay Walsh, Miles Malleson, Hector Mac-Gregor, Joyce Grenfell, André Morell, Patricia Hitchcock.

1951 STRANGERS ON A TRAIN (Warner)

> *Produced:* Hitchcock. *Script:* Raymond Chandler, Czenzi Ormonde (after the novel by Patricia Highsmith). *Adaptation:* Whitfield Cook. *Photographed:* Robert Burks. *Sets:* Ted Haworth, George-James Hopkins. *Edited:* William H. Ziegler. *Music:* Dimitri Tiomkin. *Cast:* Robert Walker, Farley Granger, Ruth Roman, Leo G. Carroll, Patricia Hitchcock, Laura Elliott, Marion Lorne, Jonathan Hale, Howard St. John, John Brown, Norma Varden, Robert Gist, John Doucette.

1953 I CONFESS (Warner)

> *Produced:* Hitchcock. *Script:* George Tabori, William Archibald (after the play *Our Two Consciences*, by Paul

Anthelme). *Photographed:* Robert Burks. *Sets:* Edward S. Haworth, George-James Hopkins. *Edited:* Rudi Fehr. *Music:* Dimitri Tiomkin. *Cast:* Montgomery Clift, Anne Baxter, Karl Malden, Brian Aherne, O. E. Hasse, Roger Dann, Dolly Haas, Charles André, Judson Pratt, Oulia Legare, Gilles Pelletier.

1954 DIAL M FOR MURDER (Warner)

Produced: Hitchcock. *Script:* Frederick Knott, based on his own play. *Photographed* (colour, 3-D): Robert Burks. *Sets:* Edward Carrere, George-James Hopkins. *Edited:* Rudi Fehr. *Music:* Dimitri Tiomkin. *Cast:* Ray Milland, Grace Kelly, Robert Cummings, John Williams, Anthony Dawson, Leo Britt, Patrick Allen, George Leigh, George Alderson, Robin Hughes.

REAR WINDOW (Paramount)

Produced: Hitchcock. *Script:* John Michael Hayes (after a short story by Cornell Woolrich). *Photographed* (colour): Robert Burks. *Sets:* Hal Pereira, Sam Comer, Ray Meyer. *Edited:* George Tomasini. *Music:* Franz Waxman. *Cast:* James Stewart, Grace Kelly, Wendell Cory, Thelma Ritter, Raymond Burr, Judith Evelyn, Ross Bagdasarian, Georgine Darcy, Sara Berner, Frank Cady, Jesslyn Fax, Rand Harper, Irene Winston.

1955 TO CATCH A THIEF (Paramount)

Produced: Hitchcock. *Script:* John Michael Hayes (after the novel by David Dodge). *Photographed* (colour, Vistavision): Robert Burks. *Sets:* Sam Comer, Hal Pereira, Arthur Crams, Joseph MacMillan Johnson. *Edited:* George Tomasini. *Music:* Lynn Murray. *Cast:* Cary Grant, Grace Kelly, Jessie Royce Landis, John Williams, Charles Vanel, Brigitte Auber, Jean Martinelli, Georgette Anys, Roland Lasaffre, Gérard Buhr, Jean Hebey, René Blancard.

*REVENGE

Script: A. J. Bezzerides, Francis Cockrell, from a story by Samuel Blas. *Photographed:* John L. Russell. *Cast:* Ralph Meeker, Vera Miles.

*BREAKDOWN

Script: Francis Cockrell, Louis Pollack. *Photographed:* John L. Russell. *Cast:* Joseph Cotten

*THE CASE OF MR PELHAM

Script: Francis Cockrell, from a story by Anthony Armstrong. *Photographed:* John L. Russell. *Cast:* Tom Ewell.

1956 THE TROUBLE WITH HARRY (Paramount)

Produced: Hitchcock. *Script:* John Michael Hayes (after the novel by Jack Trevor Story). *Photographed* (colour, Vistavision): Robert Burks. *Sets:* Hal Pereira, John Goodman, Sam Comer, Emile Kuri. *Credits:* Saul Steinberg. *Edited:* Alma Macrorie. *Music:* Bernard Herrmann. *Cast:* Edmund Gwenn, John Forsythe, Shirley MacLaine, Mildred Natwick, Mildred Dunnock, Jerry Mathers, Royal Dano, Parker Fennelly, Barry Macollum, Dwight Manfield, Leslie Wolff, Philip Truex, Ernest Curt Bach.

*BACK FOR CHRISTMAS

Script: Francis Cockrell, from a story by John Collier. *Photographed:* John L. Russell. *Cast:* John Williams, Isabel Elsom.

THE MAN WHO KNEW TOO MUCH (Paramount)

Produced: Hitchcock. *Script:* John Michael Hayes, Angus McPhail, based on an original story by Charles Bennett and D. B. Wyndham-Lewis. *Photographed* (colour, Vistavision): Robert Burks. *Sets:* Hal Pereira, Henry Bumstead, Sam Comer, Arthur Krams. *Edited:* George Tomasini. *Music:* Bernard Herrmann. *Cast:* James Stewart, Doris Day, Brenda de Banzie, Bernard Miles, Ralph Truman,

Daniel Gélin, Mogens Wieth, Alan Mowbray, Christopher Olsen, Hillary Brooke, Reggie Nalder, Richard Wattis, Noel Willman, Alix Talton, Carolyn Jones, Ives Brainville, Abdelhaq Chraibi, Betty Baskcomb, Leo Gordon, Patrick Aherne, Louis Mercier, Anthony Warde, Lewis Martin.

*WET SATURDAY

Script: Marian Cockrell, from a story by John Collier. *Photographed:* John L. Russell. *Cast:* Sir Cedric Hardwicke, John Williams, Tita Purdom.

*MR. BLANCHARD'S SECRET

Script: Sarett Rudley, from a story by Emily Neff. *Photographed:* John L. Russell. *Cast:* Mary Scott, Robert Horton, Dayton Lummis, Meg Mundy.

1957 THE WRONG MAN (Warners)

Produced: Hitchcock. *Script:* Maxwell Anderson, Angus McPhail, based on the true story of Christopher Emmanuel Balestrero. *Photographed:* Robert Burks. *Sets:* Paul Sylbert, William L. Kaehl. *Edited:* George Tomasini. *Music:* Bernard Herrmann. *Cast:* Henry Fonda, Vera Miles, Anthony Quayle, Harold J. Stone, Charles Cooper, John Heldabrand, Esther Minciotti, Doreen Lang, Laurinda Barrett, Norma Connolly, Nehemiah Persoff, Lola D'Annunzio, Kippy Campbell, Robert Essen, Richard Robbins, Dayton Lummis, Frances Reid, Peggy Webber.

*ONE MORE MILE TO GO

Script: James P. Cavanagh, from a story by F. J. Smith. *Photographed:* John L. Russell. *Cast:* David Wayne, Steve Brodie.

*FOUR O'CLOCK

Script: Francis Cockrell, from a story by Cornell Woolrich. *Photographed:* John L. Russell. *Cast:* E. G. Marshall, Nancy Kelly, Richard Long.

*THE PERFECT CRIME

Script: Stirling Silliphant, from a story by Ben Ray Redman. *Photographed:* John L. Russell. *Cast:* Vincent Price, James Gregory.

1958 *LAMB TO THE SLAUGHTER

Script: Roald Dahl, from his own short story. *Photographed:* John L. Russell. *Cast:* Barbara Bel Geddes, Allan Lane, Harold J. Stone.

VERTIGO (Paramount)

Produced: Hitchcock. *Script:* Alec Coppel, Samuel Taylor (after the novel *D'Entre les Morts*, by Pierre Boileau and Thomas Narcejac). *Photographed* (colour, Vistavision): Robert Burks. *Sets:* Hal Pereira, Henry Bumstead, Sam Comer, Frank McKelvey. *Credits:* Saul Bass. *Edited:* George Tomasini. *Music:* Bernard Herrmann. *Cast:* James Stewart, Kim Novak, Barbara Bel Geddes, Tom Helmore, Henry Jones, Raymond Bailey, Ellen Corby, Lee Patrick, Konstantin Shayne.

*DIP IN THE POOL

Script: Francis Cockrell, from a story by Roald Dahl. *Photographed:* John L. Russell. *Cast:* Keenan Wynn, Louise Platt, Philip Bournef, Fay Wray, Doreen Lang.

1959 *BANQUO'S CHAIR

Script: Francis Cockrell, from a story by Rupert Croft-Cooke. *Photographed:* John L. Russell. *Cast:* John Williams, Kenneth Haigh, Reginald Gardiner, Max Adrian.

NORTH BY NORTHWEST (M.G.M.)

Produced: Hitchcock. *Script:* Ernest Lehman. *Photographed* (colour, Vistavision): Robert Burks. *Sets:* Robert Boyle, William A. Horning, Merrill Pye, Henry Grace, Frank McKelvey. *Credits:* Saul Bass. *Edited:* George Tomasini. *Music:* Bernard Herrmann. *Cast:* Cary Grant, Eva Marie Saint, James Mason, Jessie Royce Landis, Leo G. Carroll, Philip Ober, Josephine Hutchinson, Martin

Landau, Adam Williams, Edward Platt, Robert Ellenstein, Les Tremayne, Philip Coolidge, Patrick McVey, Edward Binns, Ken Lynch.

*ARTHUR

Script: James P. Cavanagh, from a story by Arthur Williams. *Photographed:* John L. Russell. *Cast:* Laurence Harvey, Hazel Court.

*THE CRYSTAL TOUCH

Script: Stirling Silliphant, from a story by A. E. W. Mason. *Photographed:* John F. Warren. *Cast:* James Donald, Patricia Owens.

1960 *INCIDENT AT A CORNER

Script: Charlotte Armstrong, from her own story. *Photographed* (colour): John L. Russell. *Cast:* Vera Miles, Paul Hartman, George Peppard.

PSYCHO (Paramount)

Produced: Hitchcock. *Script:* Joseph Stefano (after the novel by Robert Bloch). *Photographed:* John L. Russell. *Sets:* Joseph Harley, Robert Clatworthy, George Milo. *Credits:* Saul Bass. *Edited:* George Tomasini. *Music:* Bernard Herrmann. *Cast:* Anthony Perkins, Janet Leigh, Vera Miles, John Gavin, Martin Balsom, John McIntire, Simon Oakland, Frank Albertson, Patricia Hitchcock, Vaughn Taylor, Lurene Tuttle, John Anderson, Mort Mills.

*MRS BIXBY AND THE COLONEL'S COAT

Script: Halsted Welles, from a story by Roald Dahl. *Photographed:* John L. Russell. *Cast:* Audrey Meadows, Les Tremayne.

1961 *THE HORSEPLAYER

Script: Henry Slesar. *Photographed:* John L. Russell. *Cast:* Claude Rains, Ed Gardner.

*BANG! YOU'RE DEAD

Script: Harold Swanton, from a story by Margery Vosper. *Photographed:* John L. Russell. *Cast:* Biff Elliott, Lucy Prentiss, Billy Muny, Steve Dunne.

1962 *I SAW THE WHOLE THING

Script: Henry Cecil, Henry Slesar. *Photographed:* John L. Russell. *Cast:* John Forsythe, Kent Smith, Evan Evans, Philip Ober, John Fiedler, Claire Griswold.

1963 THE BIRDS (Universal-International)

Produced: Hitchcock. *Script:* Evan Hunter (after the short story by Daphne du Maurier). *Photographed* (colour): Robert Burks. *Sets:* Robert Boyle. *Edited:* George Tomasini. *Sound consultant:* Bernard Herrmann. *Cast:* Rod Taylor, Tippi Hedren, Jessica Tandy, Suzanne Pleshette, Veronica Cartwright, Ethel Griffes, Charles McGraw, Doreen Lang, Rath McDevitt, Joe Mantell, Malcolm Atterbury, Karl Swenson, Elizabeth Wilson, Lonny Chapman, Doodles Weaver, John McGovern, Richard Deacon, Bill Quinn.

1964 MARNIE (Universal-International)

Produced: Hitchcock. *Script:* Mrs. J. Presson Allen (after the novel by Winston Graham). *Photographed* (colour): Robert Burks. *Sets:* Robert Boyle. *Edited:* George Tomasini. *Music:* Bernard Herrmann. *Cast:* Tippi Hedren, Sean Connery, Diane Baker, Louise Latham, Alan Napier, Martin Gabel, Mariette Hartley, S. John Launer.

Items marked * are television films.

THE NEW WAVE

FRANÇOIS TRUFFAUT

1954 UNE VISITE (16 mm.)

1957 LES MISTONS

> *Produced:* Robert Lachenay. *Script:* Truffaut (after a story by Maurice Pons). *Photographed:* Jean Malige. *Edited:* Cecile Decugis. *Music:* Maurice le Roux. *Cast:* Gérard Blain, Bernadette Lafont and the 'mistons'. *Commentary spoken by* Michel François.

1958 UNE HISTOIRE D'EAU

> *Produced:* Pierre Braunberger. *Shot by:* Truffaut. *Script and editing:* Jean-Luc Godard. *Photographed:* Michel Latouche. *Cast:* Jean-Claude Brialy, Caroline Dim.

1958–60 Produced *Paris Nous Appartient* (Jacques Rivette)

1959 LES QUATRE CENTS COUPS

> *Production Superviser:* Georges Charlot. *Script:* Truffaut, Marcel Moussy, from an original story by Truffaut. *Dialogue:* Marcel Moussy. *Photographed* (Franscope): Henri Decae. *Sets:* Bernard Evein. *Edited:* Marie-Joseph Yoyotte. *Music:* Jean Constantin. *Cast:* Jean-Pierre Léaud, Claude Maurier, Albert Remy, Patrick Auffay, Robert Beauvais, Bouchon, Christian Brocard, Yvonne Claudie, Guy Decomble, Georges Flamant, Marius Laurey, Claude Mansard, Luc Andrieux, Jacques Monod, Pierre Repp, Henri Virlogeux (Jeanne Moreau, Jean-Claude Brialy uncredited).

1959 Original story of *À Bout de Souffle* (Jean-Luc Godard).
1960 Produced *Le Testament d'Orphée* (Jean Cocteau).

1960 TIREZ SUR LE PIANISTE

Produced: Pierre Braunberger. *Script:* Truffaut, Marcel Moussy (after the novel *Down There*, by David Goodis). *Dialogue:* Truffaut. *Photographed:* Raoul Coutard. *Edited:* Claudine Bouché, Cécile Decugis. *Music:* Georges Delerue, with songs by Félix Leclerc, Boby Lapointe. *Cast:* Charles Aznavour, Marie Dubois, Nicole Berger, Michèle Mercier, Jean-Jacques Aslanian, Daniel Boulanger, Serge Davri, Claude Heymann, Alex Joffé, Richard Kanayan, Catherine Lutz, Claude Mansard, Albert Remy.

1961 Produced, collaborated on script and supervised direction of *Tire au Flanc* (Claude de Givray).

JULES ET JIM

Production Manager: Marcel Berbert. *Script:* Truffaut, Jean Gruault (after the novel by Henri-Pierre Roche). *Photographed* (Franscope): Raoul Coutard. *Edited:* Claudine Bouché. *Music:* Georges Delerue, with a song by Bassiak. *Cast:* Jeanne Moreau, Oscar Werner, Henri Serre, Vanna Urbino, Boris Bassiak, Sabine Haudepin, Marie Dubois, Jean-Louis Richard, Michel Varesano, Pierre Fabre, Danielle Bassiak, Bernard Largemains, Elen Bober, the voice of Michel Subor.

1962 Collaborated on script of *Une Grosse Tête* (Claude de Givray).

1962 L'AMOUR À VINGT ANS: Episode ANTOINE ET COLETTE

Produced: Pierre Roustang. *Script:* Truffaut. *Dialogue:* Yvon Samuel. *Photographed:* Raoul Coutard. *Edited:* Claudine Bouché. *Music:* Georges Delerue. *Cast:* Jean-Pierre Léaud, Marie-France Pisier.

1964 LA PEAU DOUCE

Production Manager: Marcel Berbert. *Script:* Truffaut, Jean-Louis Richard. *Dialogue:* Truffaut. *Photographed:* Raoul Coutard. *Edited:* Claudine Bouché. *Music:* Georges Delerue. *Cast:* Jean Desailly, Françoise Dorléac, Nelly Benedetti, Laurence Bady.

JEAN-LUC GODARD

1954 OPÉRATION BÉTON

Script, edited: Godard. *Photographed:* Adrien Porchet.

1955 UNE FEMME COQUETTE

Produced: Godard. *Script:* 'Hans Lucas' (Godard, after Maupassant). *Photographed:* 'Hans Lucas'. *Cast:* Maria Lysandre, Roland Tolma.

1957 TOUS LES GARÇONS S'APPELLENT PATRICK

Produced: Pierre Braunberger. *Script:* Eric Rohmer. *Photographed:* Michel Latouche. *Edited:* Cécile Decugis. *Cast:* Nicole Berger, Jean-Claude Brialy, Anne-Colette.

1958 CHARLOTTE ET SON JULES

Produced: Pierre Braunberger. *Script:* Godard. *Photographed:* Michel Latouche. *Music:* R. Monsigny. *Cast:* Jean-Paul Belmondo, Anne-Colette, Gérard Blain.

UNE HISTOIRE D'EAU

Produced: Pierre Braunberger. *Shot by:* François Truffaut. *Script and editing:* Godard. *Photographed:* Michel Latouche. *Cast:* Jean-Claude Brialy, Caroline Dim.

1959 À BOUT DE SOUFFLE

Produced: Georges de Beauregard. *Script:* Godard, from an original story by François Truffaut. *Photographed:* Raoul Coutard. *Edited:* Cécile Decugis, Lila Herman. *Music:* Martial Solal. *Cast:* Jean-Paul Belmondo, Jean

Seberg, Henri-Jacques Huet, Liliane David, Claude Mansard, Van Daude, Daniel Boulanger, Jean-Luc Godard,
Jean Domarchi, Jean-Pierre Melville.

1960 LE PETIT SOLDAT

Produced: Georges de Beauregard. *Script:* Godard. *Photo-
graphed:* Raoul Coutard. *Edited:* Agnès Guillemot, Nadine
Marquand. *Music:* Maurice Leroux. *Cast:* Michel Subor,
Anna Karina, Henri-Jacques Huet, Paul Beauvais, Laszlo
Szabo.

1961 UNE FEMME EST UNE FEMME

Produced: Georges de Beauregard. *Script:* Godard. *Photographed* (colour, Franscope): Raoul Coutard. *Sets:* Bernard Evein. *Edited:* Agnès Guillemot. *Music:* Michel
Legrand. *Cast:* Anna Karina, Jean Paul Belmondo, Jean-
Claude Brialy, Nicole Paquin, Marie Dubois.

LES SEPT PECHÉS CAPITAUX: Episode LA PARESSE

Produced: J. Bercholz, Tonio Suné. *Script:* Godard.
Photographed: Henri Decae. *Edited:* Jacques Gaillard.
Music: Michel Legrand. *Cast:* Eddie Constantine, Nicole
Mirel.

1962 VIVRE SA VIE

Produced: Pierre Braunberger. *Script:* Godard. *Photo-
graphed:* Raoul Coutard. *Edited:* Agnès Guillemot. *Music:*
Michel Legrand, with a song by Jean Ferrat. *Cast:* Anna
Karina, Sady Rebbot, André S. Labarthe, Guylaine
Schlumberger, Gérard Hoffman, Monique Messine, Paul
Pavel, Dimitri Dineff, Peter Kassowitz, Eric Schlum-
berger, Brice Parain, Henri Atel, Gilles Queant, Odile
Geoffroy, Marcel Charton, Jacques Florency.

ROGOPAG: Episode IL NUOVO MONDO

Produced: Alfredo Bini. *Script:* Godard. *Photographed:*

C.E.–S

Jean Rabier. *Edited:* Agnes Guillemot. *Music:* A Beethoven quartet. *Cast:* Jean-Marc Bory, Alexandra Stewart.

1963 LES CARABINIERS

Produced: Georges de Beauregard. *Script:* Roberto Rossellini, Jean Gruault, Godard (after a play by Benjamino Joppolo). *Photographed:* Raoul Coutard. *Sets:* Jacques Fabre. *Edited:* Agnès Guillemot. *Music:* Philippe Arthuys. *Cast:* Marino Mase, Albert Juross, Geneviève Galéa, Catherine Ribero, Jean Brassat, Gérard Poirot.

LES PLUS BELLES ESCROQUERIES DU MONDE: Episode LE GRAND ESCROC

Produced: Pierre Roustang. *Script:* Godard. *Photographed:* Raoul Coutard. *Edited:* Agnès Guillemot. *Music:* Michel Legrand. *Cast:* Jean Seberg, Charles Denner, Lazslo Szabo.

LE MÉPRIS (A GHOST AT NOON)

Produced: Carlo Ponti, Joseph Levine, Georges de Beauregard. *Script:* Godard, after Alberto Moravia's novel *Il Disprezzo*. *Photographed* (Franscope Technicolor): Raoul Coutard. *Edited:* Agnès Guillemot. *Music:* Georges Delerue. *'Odyssey' sequences directed by:* Fritz Lang. *Cast:* Brigitte Bardot, Jack Palance, Fritz Lang, Michel Piccoli, Giorgia Moll.

ALAIN RESNAIS

1945 SCHÉMA D'UNE IDENTIFICATION (16 mm.)

Surrealistic comedy with Gérard Philipe and François Chaumette; no copy now in existence.

1946 OUVERT POUR CAUSE D'INVENTAIRE (16 mm.)

Feautre-length film with Danièle Delorme, Nadine Alari, Pierre Trabaud and (briefly) Gérard Philipe; no copy now in existence.

1946–7 VISITE À LUCIEN COUTAUD, VISITE À FÉLIX LABISSE,
VISITE À HANS HARTUNG, VISITE À CÉSAR DOMELA,
VISITE À OSCAR DOMINGUEZ (16 mm.)
A series of short, silent films of visits to artists.

PORTRAIT D'HENRI GOETZ (16 mm.)
LA BAGUE, mime-drama with Marcel Marceau (16 mm.)
JOURNÉE NATURELLE, film on Max Ernst (16 mm., colour)

1947–8 Assistant director and editor on *Paris 1900* (Nicole Vedrès)

1948 VAN GOGH (16 mm.)

VAN GOGH (remake in 35 mm.)
Produced: Pierre Braunberger. *Script:* Robert Hessens,
Gaston Diehl. *Commentary:* Gaston Diehl (spoken by
Claude Dauphin). *Photographed:* Henri Ferrand. *Edited:*
Resnais. *Music:* Jacques Besse.

MALFRAY (16 mm.)
Script: Robert Hessens, Gaston Diehl. *Music:* Pierre
Barbaud.

1950 GAUGUIN
Produced: Pierre Braunberger. *Script:* Gaston Diehl.
Commentary: from Gauguin's writings (spoken by Jean
Servais). *Photographed:* Henri Ferrand. *Edited:* Resnais.
Music: Darius Milhaud.

L'ALCOOL TUE (16 mm.)
Unfinished fantasy. *Produced:* Paul Renty. *Script:* Rémo
Forlani, from an idea by Paul Renty. *Text, photographed,
edited:* Resnais. *Cast:* Grégoire, Forlani, Mendigal.

GUERNICA
Produced: Pierre Braunberger. *Directed:* Resnais, Robert
Hessens. *Script:* Robert Hessens. *Commentary:* Paul

Éluard (spoken by Maria Casarès). *Photographed:* Henri Ferrand, Dumaître. *Edited:* Resnais. *Music:* Guy Bernard.

1951 LES STATUES MEURENT AUSSI

Directed, script: Resnais, Chris Marker (commentary spoken by Jean Negroni). *Photographed:* Ghislain Cloquet. *Edited:* Resnais. *Music:* Guy Bernard.

1952 Edited *Saint-Tropez, Devoirs de Vacances* (Paul Paviot).
1955 Edited *La Pointe Courte* (Agnès Varda).

NUIT ET BROUILLARD

Text: Jean Cayrol (spoken by Michel Bouquet). *Historical advisers:* André Michel, Olga Wormser. *Photographed* (black-and-white, Eastmancolour): Ghislain Cloquet. *Edited:* Henri Colpi, Jasmine Chasney. *Music:* Hans Eisler.

1956 Edited *Aux Frontières de l'Homme* (Nicole Vedrès).

TOUTE LA MÉMOIRE DU MONDE

Produced: Pierre Braunberger. *Script:* Remo Forlani (text spoken by Jacques Demesnil). *Photographed:* Ghislain Cloquet. *Edited:* Resnais. *Music:* Maurice Jarre.

1957 Edited *L'Oeil du Maître* (Jacques Doniol-Valcroze).
Collaborated on *Le Mystere de l'Atelier Quinze*, with André Heinrich, Chris Marker, Yves Peneau, Jean Brugot, Anne Sarraute, Fernand Marzelle, Claude Joudieux, André Schlotter, Alex Reval.

1958 LE CHANT DU STYRÈNE

Produced: Pierre Braunberger. *Text:* Raymond Queneau (spoken by Pierre Dux). *Photographed* (Cinemascope, Eastmancolour): Sacha Vierny. *Edited:* Resnais. *Music:* Pierre Barbaud.

1959 Edited *Paris à l'Automne* (François Reichenbach).

HIROSHIMA MON AMOUR

Produced: Sacha Kamenka, Samy Halfon. *Script:* Marguerite Duras. *Photographed:* Sacha Vierny (France), Michio Takahaschi (Japan). *Sets:* Esaka, Mayo, Petri. *Edited:* Henri Colpi, Jasmine Chasney. *Music:* Giovanni Fusco, Georges Delerue. *Cast:* Emmanuelle Riva, Eiji Okada, Bernard Fresson, Stella Dallas, Pierre Barbaud.

1960 Supervised *Une Aussi Longue Absense* (Henri Colpi).

1961 L'ANNÉE DERNIÈRE À MARIENBAD

Produced: Pierre Coureau, Raymond Froment. *Script:* Alain Robbe-Grillet. *Photographed:* Sacha Vierny. *Sets:* Jacques Saulnier. *Edited:* Henri Colpi, Jasmine Chasney. *Music:* Francis Seyrig. *Cast:* Delphine Seyrig, Giorgio Albertazzi, Sacha Pitoëff, Françoise Bertin, Luce Garcia-Ville, Héléna Kornel, Françoise Spira, Karin Toeche-Mittler, Pierre Barbaud, Wilhelm Von Deek, Jean Lanier, Gerard Lorin, Davide Montemuri, Gille Queant, Gabriel Werner.

1962 Supervised *L'Immortelle* (Alain Robbe-Grillet).

1963 MURIEL, OU LE TEMPS D'UN RETOUR

Produced: Anatol Dauman. *Script:* Jean Cayrol. *Photographed* (Eastmancolour): Sacha Vierny. *Sets:* Jacques Saulnier. *Edited:* Claudine Merlin, Kenout Peltier. *Music:* Hans-Werner Henze. *Credits:* Jan Lenica. *Cast:* Delphine Seyrig, Jean-Pierre Kerien, Jean-Baptiste Thierrée, Nita Klein, Claude Sainval, Laurence Badie, Jean Champion, Jean Dasté, Martine Vatel. (*Singer:* Rita Streich.)

Bibliography

There are so many books, booklets, pamphlets and magazines on the cinema, especially in France, that it is difficult to keep track of them all, and even more difficult to run to earth back numbers and out-of-print items. I have therefore not attempted here to list articles in periodicals, however excellent, though I should mention that even the most cursory inspection of the files of *Sight and Sound* and *Cahiers du Cinéma* can hardly fail to bring to light all sorts of material vitally relevant to the film-makers discussed in this book. I have tried to list all their published scripts, and have otherwise selected only those books and pamphlets which I have myself found useful.

INTRODUCTION

Few of the warranted classics of writing on the film come sufficiently up to date for our purposes. The best general introduction to the cinema scene today is *The Contemporary Cinema*, by Penelope Houston (Penguin Books, 1963). The following general books on various national schools are informative and generally reliable.

Jay Leyda: *Kino* – A History of the Russian and Soviet Film. Allen and Unwin. 1960.

Joseph L. Anderson and Donald Richie: *The Japanese Film* – Art and Industry. Charles E. Tuttle. 1959.

Donald Richie: *Japanese Movies*. Japan Travel Bureau. 1961.

Jean Béranger: *La Grande Aventure du Cinéma Suédois*. Le Terrain Vague. 1960.

Erik Barnouw and S. Krishnaswamy: *Indian Film*. Columbia University Press. 1963.

Georges Sadoul: *Histoire du Cinéma Français*, 1890–1962. Club des Éditeurs 1963.

Henri Agel and others: *Sept Ans de Cinéma Français* (1945–52). Éditions du Cerf: 7e. Art 1953.

Patrice G. Hovald: *Le Néo-Réalisme Italien et ses Créateurs*. Éditions du Cerf: 7e. Art. 1959.

Brunello Rondi: *Il neo-realismo italiana*. Edizioni Guanda. 1956.
Raymond Borde and André Bouissy: *Nouveau Cinéma Italien*.
Premier Plan No. 30. 1963.
Philippe Haudiquet: *Nouveaux Cinéastes Polonais*. Premier Plan
No. 27. 1963.

FEDERICO FELLINI

SCRIPTS

La Strada. Bianco e Nero. September–October 1954.
Il Bidone (in French). Flammarion. 1956.
Le Notti di Cabiria. Capelli: Dal Soggeto al Film No. 5. 1957.
La Dolce Vita. Capelli: Dal Soggeto al Film No. 13. 1960. In
French: Julliard. 1961. In English: Ballantine Books. 1961.
Le Tentazioni del Dottor Antonio. In *Boccaccio '70*. Capelli: Dal
Soggetto al Film No. 22. 1962.
8½. Capelli: Dal Soggetto al Film No. 27. 1963. In French:
Julliard, 1963.

CRITICAL AND BIOGRAPHICAL

Geneviève Agel: *Les Chemins de Fellini* (suivi du *Journal d'un
bidoniste*, par Dominique Delouche). Éditions du Cerf: 7e.
Art. 1956.
Renzo Renzi: *Federico Fellini*. Premier Plan No. 12. 1960.
Angelo Solmi: *Storia di Federico Fellini*. Rizzoli. 1962.
Fellini. Cahiers de la R.T.B. 1962.
Gilbert Salachas: *Federico Fellini*. Éditions Seghers: Cinéma
d'Aujourd'hui. 1963.

MICHELANGELO ANTONIONI

SCRIPTS

Screenplays. Orion Press. 1963. Contains *Il Grido, L'Avventura,
La Notte* and *L'Eclisse* (in English).
Il Grido. Capelli: Dal Soggetto al Film No. 8. 1957.
L'Avventura. Capelli: Dal Soggetto al Film No. 15. 1960. In
French: Buchet-Chastel. 1960.
La Notte (in French). Buchet-Chastel. 1961.
L'Eclisse. Capelli: Dal Soggetto al Film No. 23. 1962.

CRITICAL AND BIOGRAPHICAL

Paul-Louis Thirard: *Michelangelo Antonioni*. Premier Plan No.
15. 1960.
Pierre Leprohon: *Michelangelo Antonioni*. Éditions Seghers:
Cinéma d'Aujourd'hui 1961. In English: Simon and Schuster.
1963.
Ian Cameron: *Michelangelo Antonioni*. Movie. 1963.
Philip Strick: *Antonioni*. Motion. 1963.
Roger Tailleur and P. L. Thirard: *Antonioni*. Éditions Univer-
sitaires: Aussignes du Cinéma. 1963.

LUIS BUÑUEL
SCRIPTS

Un Chien Andalou, L'Age d'Or and *El Angel Exterminador*,
L'Avant-Scène du Cinéma, No. 27–28. July 1963.
Viridiana. Domaine Cinéma No. 2. 1962.

CRITICAL AND BIOGRAPHICAL

Freddy Buache: *Luis Buñuel*. Premier Plan No. 13. 1960.
Luis Buñuel. Positif No. 42. 1961.
Ado Kyrou: *Luis Buñuel*. Éditions Seghers: Cinéma d'
Aujourd'hui. 1962. In English: Simon and Schuster. 1963.
Eduardo Lizalde: *Luis Buñuel*. Cuadernos de Cine No. 2.
1962.
Luis Buñuel. Études Cinématographiques Nos. 20–21, 22–23.
1963.

ROBERT BRESSON
SCRIPTS

Béthanie (Les Anges du Péché): Jean Giraudoux. Gallimard.
1944.
Les Dames du Bois de Boulogne: Jean Cocteau. Cahiers du
Cinéma Nos. 75–77. 1957.
Le Journal d'un Curé de Campagne. Edizioni Filmcritica. 1953
(in Italian).
Procès de Jeanne d'Arc. Julliard. 1962.

CRITICAL AND BIOGRAPHICAL

Paul Guth: *Autour des Dames du Bois de Boulogne*. Julliard. 1945.
René Briot: *Robert Bresson*. Éditions du Cerf: 7e. Art. 1957.

Jean Semolué: *Bresson.* Éditions Universitaires: Classiques du
Cinéma. 1959.
Michel Estève: *Robert Bresson.* Éditions Seghers: Cinéma
Aujourd'hui. 1962.

INGMAR BERGMAN

SCRIPTS

Ingmar Bergman: Oeuvres. Robert Laffont. 1962. Contains
*Summer Interlude, Sawdust and Tinsel, Smiles of a Summer
Night, The Seventh Seal, Wild Strawberries, The Face* (in
French).
Four Screenplays of Ingmar Bergman. Secker and Warburg–
Simon and Schuster. 1960. Contains *Smiles of a Summer
Night, The Seventh Seal, Wild Strawberries, The Magician*
(*The Face*) (in English).
The Virgin Spring: Ulla Isaksson. Ballantine Books. 1960 (in
English).
En Filmtrilogi: Norstedts. 1963. Contains *Through a Glass
Darkly, Winter Light* and *The Silence.*

CRITICAL AND BIOGRAPHICAL

François D. Guyon: *Ingmar Bergman.* Premier Plan No. 3. 1959.
Jean Béranger: *Ingmar Bergman et Ses Films.* Le Terrain Vague.
1959 (revised).
Jacques Siclier: *Ingmar Bergman.* Éditions Universitaires:
Classiques du Cinéma. 1960 (revised).
Jörn Donner: *Djävulens Ansikte.* Aldus–Bonniers. 1962. In
English, revised: Indiana University Press. 1964.
Peter Cowie: *Ingmar Bergman.* Motion. 1961 (revised 1962).
Marianne Hook: *Ingmar Bergman.* Wahlström and Widstrand.
1962.

ALFRED HITCHCOCK

CRITICAL AND BIOGRAPHICAL

Alfred Hitchcock. Cahiers du Cinéma No. 39. 1954.
Eric Rohmer and Claude Chabrol: *Hitchcock.* Éditions Universitaires: Classiques du Cinéma. 1957.

Alfred Hitchcock. Premier Plan No. 7. 1960.
H. P. Manz: *Alfred Hitchcock.* Sanssouci Verlag. 1962.
François Truffaut: *Entretiens avec Alfred Hitchcock.* Robert
Laffont. 1964. In English: Simon and Schuster. 1964.

NEW WAVE

GENERAL STUDIES

Jacques Siclier: *Nouvelle Vague?* Éditions du Cerf: 7e. Art.
1961.
Raymond Borde, Freddy Buache, Jean Curtelin: *Nouvelle
Vague.* Serdoc. 1962.
Nouvelle Vague. Cahiers du Cinéma No. 138. 1962.

FRANÇOIS TRUFFAUT
SCRIPTS: *Les Mistons.* L'Avant-Scène du Cinéma No. 4. 1961.
Une Histoire d'Eau (with Godard). L'Avant-Scène du Cinéma
No. 7. 1961.
Jules et Jim. L'Avant-Scène du Cinéma No. 16. 1962.

JEAN-LUC GODARD
SCRIPTS: *Une Histoire d'Eau* (see Truffaut).
Charlotte et son Jules. L'Avant-Scène du Cinéma No. 5. 1961.
Une Femme est une Femme (treatment). Cahiers du Cinéma No.
98. 1959.
Le Petit Soldat. Cahiers du Cinéma Nos. 119–20. 1961.
Vivre sa Vie. L'Avant-Scène du Cinéma No. 19. 1962.
CRITICAL AND BIOGRAPHICAL: Jean Collet: *Jean-Luc
Godard.* Editions Seghers: Cinéma d'Aujourd'hui. 1963.

ALAIN RESNAIS
SCRIPTS: *Nuit et Brouillard* (Jean Cayrol) and *Le Chant du
Styrène* (Raymond Queneau). L'Avant-Scène du Cinéma
No. 1. 1961.
Les Statues Meurent Aussi (with Chris Marker). In Chris
Marker: *Commentaires.* Éditions du Seuil. 1961.
Hiroshima mon Amour (Marguerite Duras). Gallimard. 1960. In
English: John Calder. 1964.
L'Année Dernière à Marienbad (Alain Robbe-Grillet). Éditions
de Minuit. 1961. In English: John Calder. 1962.
Muriel (Jean Cayrol). Editions du Seuil. 1963.

CRITICAL AND BIOGRAPHICAL: Michel Delahaye, Henri Colpi: *Alain Resnais*. Premier Plan No. 3. 1959.

Bernard Pingaud, etc.: *Alain Resnais*. Premier Plan No. 18. 1961.

Gaston Bounoure: *Alain Resnais*. Éditions Seghers: Cinéma d'Aujourd'hui. 1962.

Raymond Ravar (ed): *Tu n'as rien vu à Hiroshima*. Université Libre de Bruxelles. 1962.

SCRIPTS OF FILMS BY OTHER DIRECTORS MENTIONED

Roger Vadim: *Et Dieu Créa la Femme*. L'Avant-Scène du Cinéma No. 20. 1962. *Les Liaisons Dangereuses* (with Roger Vailland). Julliard. 1960.

Agnès Varda: *Du Côté de la Côte*. In *La Côte d'Azur*. Éditions du Temps. 1961. *Cléo de 5 a 7*. Gallimard. 1962.

Jacques Demy: *Lola*. L'Avant-Scène du Cinéma No. 4. 1961.

Jean Rouch, Edgar Morin: *Chronique d'un Eté*. Domaine Cinéma No. 1. 1961–2.

INDEX

C.E.,–T